Invitation to Philosophy
Issues and Options

Confucius Buddha Pre-Socratics	Socrates Plato	Aristotle	Epicurus Lucretius		Augustine
550–400	400–350	350–300	300–50		400–450

B.C.E.[1]   C.E.

1300–1350
William of Ockam

1600–1650
Francis Bacon

1650–1700
Hobbes

1700–1750
Locke
Newton

1750–1800
Berkeley
Hume

1800–1850
J. Bentham
J. S. Mill
T. Huxley

1900–1950
F. H. Bradley
F. S. C. Schiller
S. Alexander
A. N. Whitehead

1950–2000
A. J. Ayer
G. E. Moore
B. Russell

1850–1900
Kierkegaard

1500–1550
Erasmus

1650–1700
Spinoza

1300–1350
Meister Eckhart

1700–1750
Leibniz

1750–1800
Holbach

1800–1850
Herder
Kant
Fichte
Hegel
Herbart

1850–1900
Schelling
Schopenhauer
Feuerbach
Marx
Fechner
Engels

1900–1950
Nietzsche
Husserl
Scheler

1950–2000
Heidegger
Jaspers
Wittgenstein
Martin Buber

1100–1150
Abelard

1650–1700
Descartes
Pascal

1750–1800
Voltaire
Rousseau

1850–1900
Saint-Simon
Comte

1900–1950
Poincaré
Bergson

1950–2000
Merleau-Ponty
G. Marcel
J. P. Sartre
M. Foucault
J. Derrida
S. de Beauvoir
J. Lyotard

1900–1950
M. Schlick
Freud

100–50 B.C.E.
Lucretius

150–200
Marcus Aurelius

500–550
Boethius

1100–1150
St. Anselm

550–500 B.C.E.
Thales
Anaximander

500–450 B.C.E.
Parmenides
Pythagoras
Heraclitus

1250–1300
Aquinas

1500–1550
Machiavelli

1600–1650
G. Bruno

1900–1950
G. Gentile

1950–2000
B. Croce

450–400 B.C.E.
Zeno of Elea
Empedocies
Anaxagoras
Protagoras

400–350 B.C.E.
Socrates
Gorgias
Democritus
Aristippus
Plato

350–300 B.C.E.
Aristotle

300–250 B.C.E.
Epicurus

100–150 C.E.
Epictetus

1150–1200
Averroes

1200–1250
Maimonides

1900–1950
Unamuno y Jugo

1950–2000
Santayana
Ortega y Gasset

400–450
St. Augustine

---

[1]The contemporary designations B.C.E ("before the common era") and C.E. ("of the common era") are used here in place of the more traditional but sectarian B.C. and A.D.

Aquinas		Bacon	Spinoza Pascal Descartes Hobbes	Locke Newton	Rousseau Voltaire Berkeley Hume Edwards	Kant Mill Jefferson	Feuerbach Marx Thoreau Emerson Kierkegaard	Gandhi Nietzsche Lenin Husserl James Whitehead	Dewey Heidegger Wittgenstein Sartre Russell Moore Derrida
1250–1300		1600–1650	1650–1700	1700–1750	1750–1800	1800–1850	1850–1900	1900–1950	1950–2000

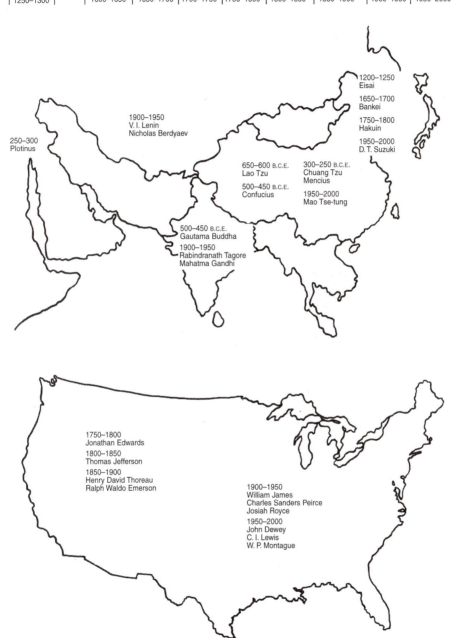

250–300
Plotinus

1900–1950
V. I. Lenin
Nicholas Berdyaev

1200–1250
Eisai

1650–1700
Bankei

1750–1800
Hakuin

1950–2000
D. T. Suzuki

650–600 B.C.E.
Lao Tzu

500–450 B.C.E.
Confucius

300–250 B.C.E.
Chuang Tzu
Mencius

1950–2000
Mao Tse-tung

500–450 B.C.E.
Gautama Buddha

1900–1950
Rabindranath Tagore
Mahatma Gandhi

1750–1800
Jonathan Edwards

1800–1850
Thomas Jefferson

1850–1900
Henry David Thoreau
Ralph Waldo Emerson

1900–1950
William James
Charles Sanders Peirce
Josiah Royce

1950–2000
John Dewey
C. I. Lewis
W. P. Montague

Invitation to Philosophy
Issues and Options

Eighth Edition

Stanley M. Honer
Mt. San Antonio College, Emeritus

Thomas C. Hunt
Mt. San Antonio College, Emeritus

Dennis L. Okholm
Wheaton College

Wadsworth Publishing Company
I(T)P® An International Thomson Publishing Company

Belmont, CA • Albany, NY • Boston • Cincinnati • Johannesburg • London • Madrid • Melbourne
Mexico City • New York • Pacific Grove, CA • Scottsdale, AZ • Singapore • Tokyo • Toronto

Philosophy Editor: Peter Adams
Assistant Editor: Kerri Abdinoor
Editorial Assistant: Kelly Bush
Marketing Manager:Dave Garrison
Print Buyer: Stacey Weinberger
Production: Ruth Cottrell

Compositor: Ruth Cottrell Books
Permissions Editor: Bob Kauser
Copy Editor: Lura Harrison
Cover Design: Bill Stanton
Cover Image: Photo from Digital Stock
Printer: Transcontinental Printing, Inc.

Printed in Canada
    3 4 5 6 7 8 9 10

For more information, contact Wadsworth Publishing Company, 10 Davis Drive, Belmont, CA
94002, or electronically at http://www.wadsworth.com

International Thomson Publishing Europe
Berkshire House
168-173 High Holborn
London, WC1V 7AA, United Kingdom

International Thomson Editores
Seneca, 53
Colonia Polanco
11560 México D.F. México

Nelson ITP, Australia
102 Dodds Street
South Melbourne
Victoria 3205 Australia

International Thomson Publishing Asia
60 Albert Street
#15-01 Albert Complex
Singapore 189969

Nelson Canada
1120 Birchmount Road
Scarborough, Ontario
Canada M1K 5G4

International Thomson Publishing Japan
Hirakawa-cho Kyowa Building, 3F
2-2-1 Hirakawa-cho, Chiyoda-ku
Tokyo 102 Japan

International Thomson Publishing Southern Africa
Building 18, Constantia Square
138 Sixteenth Road, P.O. Box 2459
Halfway House, 1685 South Africa

Library of Congress Cataloging-in-Publication Data

Honer, Stanley M.
    Invitation to philosophy : issues and options / Stanley M. Honer,
  Thomas C. Hunt, Dennis L. Okholm — 8th ed.
        p.   cm.
    Includes bibliographical references and index.
    ISBN 0-534-53393-0
    1. Philosophy—Introduction. I. Hunt, Thomas C. II. Okholm,
  Dennis L. III. Title.
BD21.H645   1998
100—dc21   98-25294

 This book is printed on acid-free recycled paper.

Contents

Preface

Invitation to Philosophy is an introductory book designed to be current, concise, and challenging to either the beginning student or the general reader. The format attempts to solve some of the problems inherent in presenting an introductory college course that can satisfy a general education requirement for a number of students and at the same time establish an adequate foundation for those who plan to study philosophy at a more advanced level.

The book is relatively short and condensed for several reasons: First, the book is intended as a guide and overview from which further and more extensive exploration can proceed. Second, the book can be employed as a handbook or ready resource for fixing philosophical reference points. The glossary of terms at the back of the book should be especially helpful for this purpose. (Terms that are defined in the glossary are identified when they first appear in the text by bold-faced type.) Third, the volume is designed to permit an early transition to selected readings where direct exposure to particular philosophers and their arguments can become an integral part of the beginner's experience. The book can be used equally well with a standard collection of readings or with a series of paperbacks that present contrasting points of view on crucial philosophical issues. In any case, because of the condensed, yet comprehensive, nature of this book, it can become a kind of handbook for future reference in a student's permanent library.

As in previous editions, case studies and discussion questions have been included at the end of each chapter. These are meant to push students to think more deeply about some of the issues and positions to which the reader has been exposed. In addition, these scenarios and questions often help students to see the relevance of the theoretical in their everyday lives. For example, Chapter 9, which examines esthetics, ends with a case study asking the student to apply what she has learned to recent cases involving National Endowment for the Arts funding. The ambitious student who wants to explore further the contents of a chapter will also find a list of suggested readings after the discussion questions.

As with the seventh edition, an instructor's handbook is available for use with this text. The manual offers suggestions for supplementary readings in primary sources, exercises that go beyond the end-of-chapter materials, and test questions. For additional help, instructors can consult the philosophy resource center web site at the address http://philosophy.wadsworth.com.

While retaining from the previous edition discussions of postmodern thought and accompanying emphases on deconstruction and narrative, this eighth edition includes a separate section on feminist epistemologies (in Chapter 4) and a separate section on religious language (in Chapter 7). In addition, some brief materials have been added along the way, such as a list of questions a student should ask when reading philosophical writings (in Chapter 1), an introduction to the classic definition of knowledge as justified belief (in Chapter 4), and an indication of the direction feminist moral philosophy is headed. These are some of the most significant changes in content, while minor changes have been made throughout the book.

We have tried to keep the student current, but we have not compromised the material on classical philosophical positions and issues, and we have resisted the temptation to be faddish. But, again, care has been taken to help students relate classical philosophical discussions to contemporary concerns.

Acknowledgments for long-standing debts include many whose assistance and support have been invaluable at different stages of revisions in eight editions. For their assistance in preparing the manuscript and index and offering suggestions on structure and content special recognition is due Elizabeth Honer, Trudie Hunt, and Trevecca Okholm.

We also acknowledge the encouragement, cooperation, and suggestions of teaching colleagues at various points: Roger Johnson, James D. Thomas, Harold Loy, Jose Jacinto, Ralph Spaulding, Robert O'Connor, and Arthur Holmes. Students at Mt. San Antonio College endured classroom experimentation with the materials that eventually became part of the text, and students at Western Kentucky University and Wheaton College have made valuable observations and suggestions along they way as they have used the text; we owe them our gratitude.

We also thank the following reviewers for many helpful insights and recommendations that assisted in the revisions for this edition: Michael Eldridge, University of North Carolina, Charlotte; Clevis Headley, Florida Atlantic University; Richard Mester, Pennsylvania State University at Erie-Behrend College; and John L. Safford, University of South Carolina at Sumter.

Our thanks also go to Wadsworth Publishing Company, editor Peter Adams, assistant editor Kerri Abdinoor, and an excellent staff. These professionals combine years of publishing knowledge and expertise, support and encouragement, and empathetic patience.

Finally, we recognize our profound indebtedness to the many philosophers and teachers whose ideas have been incorporated in our book, and whose comments here and there have made this a better book.

Any errors and shortcoming of the eighth edition are chargeable to the authors alone.

S.M.H.
T.C.H.
D.L.O.

PROLOGUE

Everybody's Business

Long ago the famous Greek philosopher Aristotle asserted that human beings *must* philosophize. He believed that for most human beings philosophy was an inescapable activity. In our time the American philosopher Mortimer Adler echoed Aristotle's judgment when he proclaimed: "Philosophy is everybody's business." These two declarations, one from the Golden Age of Greece and the other from the twentieth century, set the tone and the direction for what will be explored in this introductory book.

Each person sees the world from a particular perspective; each person exhibits a more or less organized orientation toward life. As thinking human beings, we guide our actions and mold our attitudes in the light of certain beliefs or principles. When we present arguments to support the claim that something is true or real, we philosophize. When we agonize over and defend a moral judgment, we engage in philosophical work. When we give reasons to favor one political candidate over another, we practice philosophy. The professional philosopher would say that we are operating from a relatively limited number of basic assumptions—whether or not those assumptions are clearly recognized or fully examined. The distinction between the ordinary person and the philosopher, then, is merely one of *degree*. Ordinary people usually express their philosophical postures in simple, ordinary language; professional philosophers typically use more abstract and technical language that must be learned. The philosophical positions of ordinary people are expressed largely by implication, by acts and attitudes; professional philosophers make their thought processes explicit through the careful structuring of arguments. Further, the philosophical expressions of ordinary people are often capricious and fragmentary; professionals take pains to organize their positions and make them consistent—to be systematic.

Children ask philosophical questions:

Why is it wrong to tell a lie?

Where do people go when they die?

How can you tell when something is really true?

If I live in a free country, why can't I do whatever I want to?

But at some point in our lives many of us stop asking some of these profound questions. Part of the reason may lie in the fact that we find them so overwhelming or we are too easily comforted by partial or **dogmatic** answers. Philosophy reawakens our interest in basic questions by restoring the childhood spirit of wonder about bigger and deeper issues. Since most of us have engaged to a greater or lesser degree in the very human act of philosophizing, the formal study of philosophy merely encourages us to do it in a more systematic way. That means we are challenged to think intentionally, seriously, rigorously, and thoroughly. It is an invitation to become more completely human. Thus, philosophers' questions often turn out to be more precise and sophisticated versions of the questions many of us asked when we were very young:

Are some things clearly good and right, or do values differ from time to time and place to place?

Is there some ultimate meaning in life?

Who or what am I? Is the universe friendly or indifferent to human beings and their purposes? How can one best proceed to find the truth?

What, if anything, can I firmly believe?

Am I free to shape my future, or is my behavior determined by my past?

Do people have an obligation to their fellow human beings?

So, philosophy starts with questions. In fact, some people argue that philosophy's most important function is to ascertain and then clearly propose meaningful questions. More than 2,000 years ago, Socrates insisted that the unexamined life is not worth living. Socrates took the stand that it is not the responsibility of philosophy to answer our questions; its responsibility is, rather, to question our answers. The position taken in this introductory book is that a systematic review of the major questions is an overture to the study of philosophy.

Why Study Philosophy?

There are many reasons for studying and practicing philosophy. First, philosophy sharpens the mind of the student who is studying disciplines within the academic community. When a person pursues a college degree she is learning to master one or more disciplines, such as biology, theology, art, mathematics, history, education, music, or business. In the pursuit of such mastery the student will eventually run headlong into philosophical problems. This is because each academic field of knowledge (as well as the professor who teaches it) makes assumptions about reality, espouses certain values, and insists on appropriate methods for studying and advancing the particular discipline. Philosophy provides us with training and tools to recognize such presuppositions and **value judgments**. The capacity and the willingness to cut beneath what others simply take for granted are the marks of a truly educated person. One becomes more than just a technician who knows "how"; one becomes a scholar who asks "why." For example, in relation to business the philosophical person is not satisfied with knowing only how to turn a profit but is concerned with understanding the relative values of money, products, and human beings in a society. By so opening up the world of ideas, philosophy can train a person to think more thoroughly and deeply than she would ordinarily, help the student develop intellectual muscles to survive in the heady atmosphere of higher education, and provide critical tools to help master an academic discipline.

Second, philosophy helps us to clarify issues, discriminate among options, and make better decisions. Philosophers embrace the principle that knowledge is preferable to ignorance, that awareness is of greater value than innocence. One professional philosopher expressed this with a bumper sticker on his car that read: "If you think education is expensive, try ignorance." Indeed, what we do not know, or will not face, can hurt us in the long run. We need to have a clear idea of the difference between truth and falsity, between what is real and what is unreal. We also must be able to distinguish what is important and what is trivial. The philosopher insists that it is not enough to know all of the answers in a game of Trivial Pursuit. In an age of information overload, we need to be able to sort out *which* facts are important in order to confront problems and respond adequately. So, philosophy protects us from affirming what is false and contenting ourselves with what is trivial. This protection comes not from blind acceptance of fixed answers or unquestioning conformity to majority opinion but from persistent and systematic inquiry into the assumptions, methods, and criteria by which critical distinctions are made. Philosophy enhances our understanding of the everyday world of human affairs and helps us make rational decisions about significant issues in our lives, such as our vocational goals, ethical dilemmas, and religious commitments.

Third, the activity of philosophy enhances our personal lives. One way that it does this is by enlarging our world beyond our private interests. As Bertrand Russell put it, it makes us "citizens of the universe." We feel new depths, experience new dimensions, and open new vistas. Even though new ideas are often unfamiliar and threatening, the courage to open ourselves up to see a bigger universe sharpens our self-awareness and keeps alive our sense of wonder and our quest for new questions and answers. Philosophy also enhances our lives by strengthening the foundation on which a personally satisfying philosophy of life can be built. It helps us to integrate thought, feeling, and action into a meaningful synthesis that is reasonable and consistent. For instance, one must philosophize carefully to integrate one's views about abortion, war, and euthanasia. We all have certain "feelings" about these issues, and many of us have acted out one or more of them. However, until we study philosophy we may not realize that we must somehow consistently relate all three views to our definition of "human life" nor may we understand in what circumstances—if any—it is permissible to take a life so defined. Any one person's integration of these issues may differ markedly from another's; the point is that one's views should be well reasoned and consistent.

Fourth, and related to all that has been said above, philosophy assists us in penetrating to the roots of our commitments by helping us to investigate and substantiate (or replace) our personal convictions (which all of us have). It frees us from the tyranny of prejudices and habitual beliefs of a generation or a nation and from unexamined convictions. After philosophical investigation we may, indeed, retain such convictions or beliefs, but we will then recognize them as assumptions, and, while we cannot completely demonstrate or prove them, they will at least be reasonable to hold. If, however, our inquiry reveals such beliefs to be unreasonable, our philosophical activity will suggest other possibilities and more satisfying options.

Whether this introduction to philosophy marks the beginning of an academic pursuit of philosophy or simply helps the student to grow personally, all of the reasons for studying and practicing philosophy have to do with its effects on the lives of those who engage in it. Studying philosophy may not result in a "better job" after college, but it will result in a better life. Philosophy, unlike some other disciplines one studies in college, does not usually lead to a lucrative career in terms of money, but it is not for that reason impractical. Philosophy is primarily about ideas, and one need not look far to discover the impact that ideas have had on our world. One has only to recall the political and social effects of the philosophies of Jesus, Karl Marx, Adam Smith, John Locke, Mohandas Gandhi, Martin Luther King, Jr., or Simone de Beauvoir. Some of these lived in poverty, and some even lost their lives because of their ideas. But, as Socrates said, the most important thing is not life, but the good life.

Given what has been said about the value of philosophy, this introductory textbook assumes that it is both the privilege and the obligation of those engaged in philosophical study to make a continual critical evaluation of the frame of reference in which their learning takes place. There is the ever-present danger of being captivated by a certain point of view simply because it is represented by a particular author or a particular teacher. Students whose only concern is with ready-made "answers" may be easily bulldozed by dramatic appeals or poorly reasoned arguments. The trick is to remain open-minded and perceptive and critical—all at the same time.

Toward a Philosophical Attitude

If the human activity called philosophy is based on the assumption that it is important to think clearly about things that are of great concern, what intellectual orientation is appropriate to the learner? What expectations and attitudes are helpful to those who seek wisdom in the company of others? How can the beginner contribute to an atmosphere of learning that will enrich a formal instruction program? A few recommendations can be made.

To be significant to each person in the joint enterprise, philosophical discussion calls for a community of tolerance. In the interest of a broadening intellectual perspective, one must remain open to a wide spectrum of ideas. A typical group of students affords a stimulating range of convictions, prejudices, opinions, and backgrounds. Such a variety is a distinct advantage, for it means that each person can learn from the others. Assumptions and statements can be compared in order to discern their implications, to detect their inadequacies, or to reveal their inconsistencies. The group provides a practice ring in which fledgling ideas can be presented and tested before they are launched into a larger and more violent public arena. The working assumption is that everyone agrees to respect everyone else as a person whose ideas are worth expressing. The object is to promote an environment in which all may freely speak, react, and explore. Of course, this does not mean we are obligated to accept uncritically everyone's opinion. Personal tolerance is expected; intellectual agreement is not. All who wish to enrich and intensify the study of philosophy might consider this covenant: to agree to disagree in an atmosphere of mutual respect. This is not as easy as it sounds; one must have a critical mind without being closed-minded.

The depth and range of philosophical discourse also depend on the accuracy and clarity of communication between all participants. There must be a sustained effort to say what is meant. But an even greater effort is required to understand what is said. Language can be used to distort meaning, and words can be set up as barriers to communication. These difficulties are not easily resolved, but they may prove less formidable if the process of communication is viewed as a **dialogue** rather than as a debate. A debate is a stylized language game played according to formal and arbitrary rules. A debate is won or lost. A dialogue, on the other hand, is a form of conversation in which the communicants strive for reciprocal understanding. A dialogue is not a contest but a mutual search for meaning. This search is what philosophers have in mind when they speak of engaging in the "great conversation"—a conversation that includes not just one's contemporaries but all the philosophers who have gone before us.

One of the earliest difficulties faced by those who would join in philosophical discourse is learning the conventional language used by philosophers. Students must pay particular attention to terminology. The capacity to understand and use correctly the principal philosophical concepts is of primary importance to those who wish to comprehend what the wise, the erudite, or the passionate have had to say about the nature of humankind, meaning, and reality. Demonstrable knowledge of concepts and terms becomes an important criterion of students' academic achievement. Of course, intellectual criteria are not the only meaningful criteria. People who "just feel" about things cannot be dismissed simply by labeling their responses "wrong," "childish," or "absurd." Nevertheless, educational standards of achievement must be more precise (not necessarily "better"). The test of students' comprehension becomes the extent to which they can express thoughts or feelings in a logical and intelligible manner; doing so requires an adequate command of language and closely reasoned thinking. Students should recognize that special restrictions are introduced when philosophy is tailored to fit an academic program. Classroom structures, formal assignments, grading systems, time limitations—all these seriously constrict the environment in which the study of philosophy takes place. Philosophy is not something one simply learns; it is also something one lives. Philosophical explorations far exceed the boundaries of a classroom or a course of study. It was Mark Twain who said: "I have never let my schooling interfere with my education."

The Adventure and the Risk

The eminent philosopher Alfred North Whitehead has described philosophy as "adventures of ideas." So it is. But any adventure involves risks, and the philosophical venture is no exception. It seems only fair to point out some of the hazards that might beset those newly embarked on the adventure of philosophy. It is said that a little knowledge is a dangerous thing. But to attain greater knowledge, one must start, at least, with a small amount. And greater knowledge itself does not eliminate danger. Modern concern over the destructive power of nuclear energy suggests that the mighty effort to penetrate the secrets of the atom may have magnified rather than diminished the dangers people perceive. The realization that increased knowledge can introduce new difficulties is not just a modern discovery. If we examine some of Western civilization's earliest accounts of how knowledge began and what impact it had, we see that knowledge was regarded as a mixed blessing.

1. According to Greek mythology, the god Prometheus stole fire, or knowledge, from the heavenly realm and brought it down to earth for the human race. But Prometheus and humanity came to suffer for it. Seeking revenge, the outraged gods conspired. They created Pandora, endowed her with exceptional beauty and other attractive virtues, and sent her to earth to tempt Prometheus. Pandora was entrusted with a box concerning which she was given explicit instructions. She was at liberty to enjoy the pleasures of earthly existence, but she was forbidden to open the mysterious box. For a time things went smoothly, but, as the gods had contrived, Pandora's curiosity got the better of her. She peeked into the box. As soon as the lid was raised, all manner of evils—death, disease, famine, war, and a host of others—poured forth and escaped into the world. Evil was the price exacted for the gift of knowledge.

2. Some interpret the biblical story of the beginning of humanity in a similar way. Adam and Eve lived naked and unashamed in the Garden of Eden. Their every need was amply supplied. They could wander safely through the garden and be untroubled by anxiety, guilt, or suffering. God imposed but one simple restriction. They were not to eat the fruit of a certain tree,

the tree of the knowledge of good and evil. But Adam and Eve disobeyed God's command, and from that moment their eyes were opened and they saw that they were naked. The knowledge of good and evil defiled their innocence and shut the gates of paradise against them. Unproductive work, fear, pain, and death became the worldly legacy for them and their heirs even unto the last generation.

3. An analogous theme is found in Plato's famous **allegory** of the cave. If men are confined to a cave where they can see only the shadows of things cast on the wall by a flickering fire, they will be content with these distorted appearances. But the man who climbs from the cave into the sunlight, the man who makes the ascent from below and discovers the brilliant world of truth, will not be satisfied to live in the half-light of deception and bondage. Should he return to the cave, his attempts to bring enlightenment will arouse distrust, and he will be persecuted by those whose only realities are the shadows of ignorance.

Any life truly lived is a risky business, and if one puts too many fences against the risks one ends by shutting out life itself.
                              —*Kenneth S. Davis in a biography*
                                        of Dwight D. Eisenhower

God offers to every mind its choice between truth and repose; take which you please—you can never have both.
                              —*Ralph Waldo Emerson*

One of the great risks that all college students presumably share is the risk of higher education. When students go to college, they ask, in effect, to be challenged intellectually. They sign on for an adventure of the mind. They expect new standards of excellence to be projected for them. Even though they may not be fully aware of what is in store, they nevertheless voluntarily accept a certain amount of personal risk: the risk of failure, the risk of more direct self-awareness, the risk of disturbing earlier patterns of thought and action. There is also the subtle but profound risk that comes with all learning. Doors once opened are very hard to close again. Many people are threatened or discouraged when they move into a bigger room, a wider life space. But a significant number respond to the vital challenge, embrace the risk, and set about sharpening their intellectual tools for the exciting work ahead.

The adventure of philosophy is frequently perceived as beginning on a small raft adrift on a turbulent and limitless sea of confusion. This oceanic experience is not uncommon. Some of the philosophical castaways come to a deeper appreciation of the raft and its immediate environment of wave and weather. Others come to an understanding of the drift of the current or the direction of the prevailing wind. Some glimpse the islands of truth and steer toward the harbors of faith. Others become utterly lost in the vast and hopeless middle. The raft and its passengers are not insured. There are no guarantees—but the raft is afloat, and those already aboard will make room for one more.

Popular Philosophy: An Exercise

One way to begin the journey of philosophical discovery is to consider and compare some of the widely differing stands that ordinary people might take on matters of deep concern to them. An array of ten different personal statements will be proposed. The alternative postures are not presented in the language that professional philosophers typically use. Rather, these life perspectives are expressed in more popular terms—the way they might be worded by thoughtful friends trying to explain their outlooks on life and the world to one another.

I

I find the meaning in life by devoting myself to those things that are of great and lasting significance—being dedicated to a goal or ideal that exists outside of myself. It might mean choosing the way of Christ, or believing in the perfectability of humankind, or accepting some other grand model as a guide for belief and behavior. I am convinced that human life takes on meaning only when one is fully committed to a higher power, a bigger truth, an eternal reality.

My relationships with other human beings are dictated by established and universal principles. I judge my behavior not by what is convenient, pleasant, or practical, but by how well it conformed to what is ultimately and eternally right and good. I believe that the future of humanity depends on its recognition of the overall purpose in things. I believe that the survival of society and the salvation of all people begins with humility.

My life is guided by faith, disciplined by loyalty, inspired by hope, and sanctified by worship. I stake my life on an existence that goes beyond my earthly days, beyond my physical body. I believe that what we now see through a glass darkly will someday be clear. I find sense and comfort in these words:

> We look not to the things that are seen but to the things
> that are unseen; for the things that are seen are transient,
> but the things that are unseen are eternal.
> —2 Corinthians 4:18 RSV

II

I believe that there are two sides to reality. There are the facts and objects and events that we call nature. I can't ignore this side of life—that which I know with my five senses and around which I must plan my everyday life. I am a creature who lives and relates in an environment that challenges me to study and serve the needs of an earthly existence—both my own and that of others.

But there is also a spiritual reality that lies beyond and above the matter and motion of daily connections and informs and justifies not only my existence as a creature but also my obligation toward my fellow humans and toward my transcendent possibilities. I live under the eye of the Eternal and I find purpose and meaning in the realm of the spirit.

God as the original reality, and nature as a separately created reality, are both of immediate concern to me. I am soul. I am flesh. I will devote myself to the practical problems of a healthy and rationally ordered society, but I will do this with the knowledge and understanding that I must rigorously apply moral laws that, with the help of the accumulated wisdom of the ages, I have come to know are supreme and just. I will in this way desire and strive to be transformed.

> *Then he said to them, Render therefore to Caesar the things*
> *that are Caesar's; and to God the things that are God's.*
> *   —Matthew 22:21 RSV*

III

I subscribe to the life of reason. To me, being human means being rational. Our humanness is most clearly expressed in our capacity to discover the complexity and regularity in the nature of things and to impose order on ourselves. It is my faith that there are principles in the universe and in human affairs that are accessible to disciplined methods of inquiry.

I believe that perfection of the intellect is the activity that sets us apart from other creatures and at the same time gives us power and wisdom. I am persuaded that human progress is the result of increasingly refined and extended human thought. I defend my case by pointing to the beautifully integrated and logically harmonious model of mathematics. Without this tool human beings would be little more than beasts. I appreciate those who concern themselves with the logic of language, the analysis of symbols, because it is only by laying down the ground rules for communication that human beings can hope to associate meaningfully or construct an intelligible, common social life.

The hope and glory of humanity lies in finding the necessary and consistent patterns of relationship between things. I am convinced that our relations to one another must be guided by clear and orderly principles. When reason takes precedence over emotion and impulse, human beings have the potential for happiness and security.

The true life is one based on order and clarity. Without definable structure, life is chaos. Only with systematic and coherent thought can there be meaning.

> *Nature and nature's laws lay hid in night:*
> *God said, Let Newton be! and all was light.*
> *   —Alexander Pope*

IV

I see life as a test, a challenge. It is my conviction that to live fully and truly is to shape life according to human purpose and desire. It is our destiny to carve a place for ourselves. I find joy and meaning in subduing the forces of nature, in imposing form on inert matter, in creating significant events. I know that my most meaningful and vital moments are those in which head and heart and muscle are intensely integrated in disciplined action. Human beings are competitive by nature, and ordered competition is the crucible in which character is formed.

The best representative of what life is all about is the builder, the explorer, the statesman, the scientist, or the person who stands unmoved against all opposition and adversity. I believe it is better to fight for a lost cause than to stand aside because of indecision or neutrality. Fate is what life does to people; history is what people do to life. If I am not a power, I am a pawn. I intend that the future will be different because I have lived.

In my relations with others I am guided by the principles of integrity, consistency, and courage. Strength of character is a necessary and noble achievement. I speak my mind, act on my convictions, and expect others to do the same. I am a sword to those I trust and a shield to those I love.

In the fell clutch of circumstance
I have not winced or cried aloud.
Under the bludgeonings of chance
My head is bloody, but unbowed.
It matters not how strait the gate,
How charged with punishments the scroll,
I am the master of my fate:
I am the captain of my soul.
                                        —*William E. Henley*

V

I am a practical, down-to-earth sort of person. I am one of the many ordinary natural creatures who live in an impartial cause-and-effect universe. My senses and my experiences tell me what is good to pursue and what is wise to avoid. Because people are neither gods nor inert lumps of matter, they must adapt continually to the middleness of human existence.

The Good consists of helping ordinary human beings make their lives on earth safer, longer, and freer from unanticipated circumstances. I choose courses of action that give the greatest promise of promoting my immediate and tangible goals. I am ready to take another confident step when it is clear that my last step has placed me on firm ground. I judge my own ideas and actions and those of my fellows by their results. The good society is one that promotes the mutually advantageous growth and welfare of its members. Knowledge is a means, not an end.

I am suspicious of those who propose eternal truths, those who build great systems, and those who speculate beyond the reach of everyday proof. The only true visionaries are those who can point to the practical application of their ideas. The slow emergence of humankind from barbarism has been due to the fact that human solutions to the problems of life have met the test of experience.

I believe in getting along with those whose lives are intimately bound up with my own. Life and human welfare—*my* life and *my* welfare—depend to a great extent on mutual give and take. Compromise and adjustment are not signs of weakness; they are the mark of an intelligent and reasonable human being. I often find discretion to be the better part of valor. I say live and let live and let common sense prevail.

> *Man is but a castaway*
>   *On this planet's shore.*
> *He survives from day to day.*
>   *Can he ask for more?*
> *Vast and intricate the store*
>   *Of his printed words.*
> *Short and simple is the lore*
>   *Of the beasts and birds.*[1]
>
> —*Clarence Day*

VI

I believe that people *should* and in fact *do* seek pleasure and avoid pain. Pleasure can take many forms, but in each case it is a combination of approach and avoidance that satisfies the built-in criteria for human well-being. In this sense the body displays a *natural* wisdom, an inherent capacity to make value judgments about our experiences. Temporary pain is tolerated only because of a greater pleasure momentarily anticipated.

It is my conviction that all living things are by nature selfish. Among human organisms, enlightened selfishness is the basis of progress and order. By acknowledging my own inner nature and by acquiring a knowledge of the outside world, I am better able to discern that course of action most productive of my personal well-being. I believe each person has needs and drives that must be met. Societies come into being to adjust and arbitrate the claims

---

[1]From Clarence Shepard Day, "Man Is But a Castaway," *Scenes from the Mesozoic* (New Haven, CT: Yale University Press, 1935). Reprinted by permission.

of its members. Any society that fails to satisfy the needs of its members cannot long endure. As an individual, I can interact and cooperate with others when each of us understands and admits that mutual advantages can result.

Sacrifice with no likelihood of accompanying pleasure is pathological and absurd. My philosophy relates to the world I can feel now. Eternity is irrelevant. When I worry about tomorrow, I lose today.

The good life produces tangible and immediate satisfactions. To ask more is visionary and unrealistic.

> *Come, fill the Cup, and in the fire of Spring*
> *Your Winter-garment of Repentance fling;*
> *The Bird of Time has but a little way*
> *To flutter—and the Bird is on the Wing.*
> *—Rubaiyat of Omar Khayyam*

VII

I cannot speak of what I am because the pronoun "I" is a deceptive restriction that destroys the total relatedness and inclusiveness of Being. Reality is Being—total, inclusive, and concrete. Immersion and complete acceptance— the oneness with everything and nothing—this is the meaning and the non-meaning of Being. Life or Being is not expressible in conventional terms. It can only be hinted at, if it can be understood at all.

I am not going anywhere; I am not trying to be anything. Direction and strife are techniques of denial. What is, simply is; just as what is not, also is. Every time is now, and now is forever. There is nothing to find because nothing has been lost.

If knowing means classifying, or discriminating, or giving names to things, then knowledge builds a dense and impenetrable wall against the truth of Being. Formal knowing is a barrier to Being. Abstractions are the building blocks of blindness. Words are abstractions; they slice and separate and destroy. All words are false because they parcel out total "isness" into opposites like black and white, high and low, lost and found, good and bad. There are no opposites. All is one and one is all.

Life free of classifications and separateness and abstractions is natural, concrete, and serene. It denies nothing, hopes for nothing, regrets nothing, seeks nothing, demands nothing, kills nothing. It is in this sense that "sitting quietly, doing nothing" has profound meaning.

> *Sitting quietly, doing nothing;*
> *Spring comes, and the grass*
> *Grows by itself.*
> *—Zenrin Kushu*

Simply trust:
Do not the petals flutter down,
Just like that?[2]

                                  —Anonymous

VIII

For me, to live life meaningfully is to experience it fully. Any preselected lifestyle sets limits and becomes static. I must keep myself open to the great variety of experiences that life offers. Love and work and art and sorrow and food and danger are on life's menu, and I am hungry and thirsty. I am a wonderer and a seeker. My mind and my body crave change and new horizons. I weave my own being out of the sights and sounds and smells and encounters of the world. I must be aware and sensitive so that the self I become is capable of continued growth and extension.

I am exposed to and infected by the joy and pain, the hope and despair, the courage and sorrow, the groping, desperate humanness of people. In this physical, social, emotional, natural setting I create my life; I create myself. Growth, in the sense of increasing openness to experience, is the underlying principle of life. I intend to reach out and spend myself to realize what it is I can be. In this way I show reverence for life and I embrace the possibilities life holds for my own unique way of putting it all together.

All people are my brothers and sisters. They are my concern, because together, by sharing our individual experiences, by experiencing each other, each of us can grow in a new dynamic way.

I am suspicious of definitions. I intend to plunge in, to immerse myself in the ongoingness of existence. I propose to think critically, to feel deeply, to care. The meaning of life is wide open. My living will be *my* definition of what it is to be human. I will be those possibilities that I have helped bring into being.

May my mind stroll about hungry
and fearless and thirsty and supple
and even if it's sunday may i be wrong
for whenever men are right they are not young.[3]

                                  —e. e. cummings

---

[2]The two poems are from Nancy Wilson Ross (ed.), *The World of Zen* (New York: Random House, 1960).

[3]From "may my heart always be open to little." Copyright © 1926 by Horace Liveright; copyright 1954 by e. e. cummings. Reprinted from his volume *Poems 1923–1954* by permission of Harcourt Brace Jovanovich, Inc., and Granada Publishing Ltd.

Mine is no callous shell,
I have instant conductors all over me whether I
    pass or stop,
They seize every object and lead it harmlessly
    through me.
Is this then a touch? quivering me to a new
    identity. . . .
I am an acme of things accomplish'd and I am an
    encloser of things to be.

—Walt Whitman

IX

I find the meaning of life summed up in the age-old saying "know thyself." The challenge and the focus of life is to search out the unique and particular style or pattern that is somehow the core of me.

I may be a dropout or a saint, a celebrity or a garden-variety human being. I may feel like going along with the crowd, or I may be a minority of one— either way, it doesn't matter as long as I am true to the deepest and most fundamental sense of myself. My unique existence and my own subjective perception of it are what matter. I must discover who I am and then express myself vibrantly, passionately, without apology or compromise.

My awareness of myself and my rootedness in myself will serve as the center of all meaning, all reality. Anything imposed from outside, whether it be scientific knowledge, religious revelation, social norms, or logical proof, must meet the test of my personal willingness to affirm it. Beyond what I am lies a world of meaningless things.

At the heart of everything is the unquestionable actuality of my own raw existence in all of its arbitrariness and with all the uncertainty that attends the possibility that it may end or that I may end it.

I am what I am. I am what I do. To others I may appear improbable, irrational, absurd. Nevertheless, I am I—hopelessly alone and uncomforted. And the I that I am is what I must be and express—all else notwithstanding.

King Christ this world is all aleak;
and lifepreservers there are none:
and waves which only He may walk
Who dares to call Himself a man.[4]
—e. e. cummings

---

[4]From "Jehova buried, Satan dead." Copyright 1935 by e. e. cummings; renewed 1963 by Marion Morehouse Cummings. Reprinted from his volume *Poems 1923–1954* by permission of Harcourt Brace Jovanovich, Inc., and Granada Publishing Ltd.

X

Life is a mistake, a random accident without purpose, plan, meaning, integration, or order.

> *Enter left: (screaming)*
> *There is no audience*
> *no stage*
> *no theater*
> *no drama*
> *no role*
> *nothing*
> *Exit right: (laughing)*

I enter the world crying. I die laughing at the cruel joke that has made me think the world might mean something. Every time I turn around, I destroy something. It is all I can do; it is senseless and inevitable. The sooner I am done with it, the better. Nonexistence is preferable to the negativeness of existence. Sleep is preferable to deceit.

> *God—if you're listening—forget it.*
> *I'd like to say I don't mind the pain*
> *And it's all worth it or something—*
> *But I do, and it isn't*
> *You see I've finally found out what you had in mind—*
> *Which was NOTHING!*
>
> *After all, what could be fairer?*
> *You left the whole thing up to us.*
> *We make up the questions—*
> *We make up the answers—*
> *That way we can never be wrong!*
> *Of course we can never be right, but*
> *Who needs to be right?*
> *The fact of the matter is—*
> *The fact of the matter!!!*
> *It doesn't matter*
> *It doesn't matter*
> *It doesn't matter*
> *Write that on the blackboard of your mind*
> *500 times.*
> *It is nothing but a cruel joke*
> *See how I laugh*
> *An idiotic human delusion*
> *See how I—laugh?*[5]

—Jacque Weiss

---

[5]Printed by permission of the author.

Two challenges now present themselves. First, from the range of alternatives set forth above, can you choose one that reflects the way you think or feel about things? If not, can you construct a statement of your own that more accurately represents your point of view? Now, can you share your personal stand with others who are also at this threshold of philosophical beginnings?

Second, there is the tougher, long-range challenge to subject all of the alternatives to a more systematic and critical analysis by applying the philosophical concepts to be presented in the forthcoming chapters of this book. The ten popular statements do not purport to cover all the possibilities. They often cut across the formal categories established by philosophers. Nevertheless, the statements lend themselves to philosophical analysis, and what is spoken or written in the ongoing world of everyday affairs can be criticized and evaluated for its deeper content and meaning.

Those who attempt to develop and defend their own patterns of thought and action will find themselves directly confronted by philosophical issues and deeply involved in philosophical activity. The invitation to philosophy that unfolds in the pages to follow should provide an exciting starting place for anyone ready to embark on the philosopher's quest.

Case Study and Discussion Questions

Case Study

In this prologue it has been suggested that philosophers ask the same sorts of questions that children ask but in a more careful and sophisticated fashion. It is a natural activity but one that we are not always encouraged to pursue.

1. In addition to the questions already listed in this prologue, what are some other questions children often ask? (You might want to engage a few children in conversation.)

2. Reflect on your own experience and give specific reasons why you stopped asking these kinds of questions. Why do we lose our childhood curiosity and settle for more "matter-of-fact" issues?

Discussion Questions

1. Those who argue that philosophy is irrelevant or impractical or far too abstract are likely to summarize their criticism in the observation that "philosophy bakes no bread." What do these critics mean, and what do you find acceptable or unacceptable in their claim?

2. How might you defend or refute the claims of those who maintain that "ignorance is bliss" or that "too much thinking gets us into trouble"?

3. Neil Postman, a critic of contemporary society, has written: "Thinking is not a performing art, so it does not play well on TV." What might he have meant by this statement? What do you think of it?

4. Which of the ten personal statements *best* corresponds with your current philosophy of life? Provide a reasoned defense of that position.

Suggested Readings: A Personalized Selection of Readable and Provocative Titles

Bloom, Allan. *The Closing of the American Mind.* New York: Simon & Schuster, 1987.

Bronowski, J. *The Ascent of Man.* Boston: Little, Brown, 1973.

Camus, Albert. *The Stranger.* New York: Random House, 1954.

Fromm, Erich. *The Art of Loving.* New York: Harper & Row, 1974.

Greene, John C. *Darwin and the Modern World View.* New York: New American Library (Mentor Book), 1963.

Hesse, Hermann. *Siddhartha.* New York: New Directions, 1951.

James, William. *The Will to Believe.* Cambridge, MA: Harvard University Press, 1979.

Johnston, William. *The Still Point: Reflections on Zen and Christian Mysticism.* New York: Fordham University Press, 1977.

Jung, C. G. *The Undiscovered Self.* New York: New American Library (Mentor Book), 1974.

Kopp, Sheldon B. *If You Meet the Buddha on the Road, Kill Him!* Palo Alto, CA: Science & Behavior Books, 1972. (Also a Bantam paperback, 1976.)

Matthews, Gareth B. *Philosophy and the Young Child.* Cambridge, MA: Harvard University Press, 1984.

Merton, Thomas. *The Seven Storey Mountain.* New York: Harcourt Brace Jovanovich, 1978.

Pirsig, Robert M. *Zen and the Art of Motorcycle Maintenance.* New York: Morrow (Bantam Book), 1974.

Postman, Neil. *Amusing Ourselves to Death: Public Discourse in an Age of Show Business.* New York: Penguin, 1985.

Quinn, Daniel. *Ishmael: An Adventure of the Mind and Spirit.* New York: Bantam/Turner, 1992.

Sartre, Jean-Paul. *Existentialism and Human Emotions.* Secaucus, NJ: Citadel Press, 1971.

Schmidt, Paul F. *Rebelling, Loving and Liberation: A Metaphysics of the Concrete.* Albuquerque, NM: Hummingbird Press, 1971.

Schumacher, E. F. *A Guide for the Perplexed.* New York: Harper & Row, 1977.

Skinner, B. F. *Walden Two.* New York: Macmillan, 1948.

Stace, W. T. *Religion and the Modern Mind.* Philadelphia: Lippincott (Keystone Book), 1952.

Watts, Alan W. *The Book: On the Taboo Against Knowing Who You Are.* New York: Collier, 1966.

CHAPTER 1
What Is Philosophy?

A. Questions to Consider

- With what types of questions does philosophy deal?
- How can philosophy help us to understand the world and our lives better?
- How does philosophy differ from other disciplines?

B. Defining "Philosophy"

A straightforward definition of philosophy would surely prove helpful at the outset, but the term is not easy to define. For Socrates and his Greek contemporaries, philosophy was, quite literally, "the love of wisdom." Others describe philosophy as "a rigorous attempt to understand" or "a persistent and organized attempt to see life steadily and see it whole." There is little agreement on a plain and simple definition that will satisfy everyone. Some regard philosophy as the name for a subject area of study; some prefer to use the term to identify an individual's general approach to life; others see philosophy as the identification of the presuppositions and assumptions underlying a subject matter (for example, the philosophy of science, the philosophy of history, and so forth); still others think of philosophy as a set of techniques to clarify the way language is used.

A clear and cogent answer to the question "What is philosophy?" might reasonably be deferred until one has had an opportunity to see what philosophers do and hear what they have to say. In the meantime, it can be proposed, tentatively, that philosophy is an activity undertaken by human beings who are deeply concerned about who they are and what everything means, and that a philosopher is a person who perceives in some measure the ways in which the various experiences and awarenesses of existence form a pattern of meaning. This is the broad and inclusive definition of philosophy that sets the framework for the subject matter of this book. In this light, philosophy is more than a purely technical enterprise of analyzing words, concepts, and logical thought processes. It is more than a peculiar game played by academic specialists. Rather, philosophy, without apology, forcefully directs attention to the relentless efforts of human beings to achieve an organized view of themselves and the universe in which they live. At its most inclusive, philosophy is as broad as life and as deep as human understanding.

C. The Fields of Philosophy

One way to approach philosophy is to describe the several branches that have emerged as the traditional fields of study in the discipline. Each of three well-established areas of philosophical study is identified by the major question it asks: How do we know? What is real? What is good, right, or beautiful? Labels have been assigned to these broad areas of philosophical investigation. A simple diagram shows how the study has been divided.

The question "How do we know?" is the central focus in the field of philosophical activity known as **epistemology**. Analyses and speculations in this field of endeavor result typically in theories of knowledge. Epistemology is characterized by attempts to deal with the age-old problems of explaining how it is possible for human beings to know anything and what opportunities and limits accompany the human effort to explain or understand. Epistemologists seek to clarify and refine the process of knowing. Closely related to epistemology are the study areas of truth, logic, and perception.

The question "What is real?" is the prime concern of those in the field of **metaphysics**. What truly exists and how what exists is ordered or organized are characteristic problems that metaphysicians try to solve. Some of the classic efforts of philosophers have been directed toward the identification of the underlying or basic nature of the world. Another activity of metaphysicians has been to elucidate the quality of the primordial substance—is it spirit, or energy, or particles, or timeless matter? Early Greek philosophers were tantalized by the challenge to name and describe the original and indivisible "stuff" of the universe.

The questions "What is good?" "What is right?" and "What is beautiful?" are dealt with in the area of **axiology**. In this field philosophers wrestle with their concerns over what "should" or "ought" to prevail in the world. That is, they are dealing with the nature and application of **values**. Discussions of values that determine good and bad in human conduct are the concern of **ethics**. Discussions of values that determine what is artistic or beautiful are the concern of **esthetics**. Axiology ranges over a wide landscape of philosophical problems, but it usually touches heavily on issues relating to the good person, the good society, and the good life. Social systems, political arrangements, and moral codes are typical concerns of the philosophical realm surveyed by the axiologist.

The division of philosophy into distinct fields is only a simplifying device. The lines of demarcation are not sacred, and they are not inviolate. For example, what a person knows may be linked irrevocably to what is assumed to be real. What a person believes to be good may depend on what that person thinks he or she knows. Some of the most famous philosophers over the years have been those who undertook to connect in a grand synthesis their interlocking views on epistemology, metaphysics, and axiology. The problem for the student may be simply a matter of where it is most reasonable to start.

As the chapters to follow will demonstrate, philosophers do become involved with an exceedingly wide range of topics and concerns. That they do so, however, does not mean that the philosophical perspective is exactly the same as the perspective of other studies. For example, philosophy shares with science and religion an interest in and concern about the world and the meaning of human life. But there are some differences in the aims and the approaches of these three important disciplines.

Science has much in common with philosophy. Both exhibit a passion for truth, and both emerge from an inquiring and reflective attitude. Scientists, however, focus their attention on limited fields of interest where they attempt to describe particular facets of the world so that the world may be interpreted in systematic terms. The sciences describe, predict, experiment, and ultimately try to provide comprehensive theories that fit and explain factual observations. Philosophy may use the descriptive materials and the theories of science to enhance or support a position, but philosophy goes further by constantly challenging the basic assumptions of science and by forever asking questions about the underlying nature, meaning, and possibilities of things.

It has been said that **religion** begins at the point where a person moves beyond philosophical speculation into the arena of personal commitment and action. Religion is more than a knowledge or understanding of something; it implies the response of a person's whole being to that on which he or she feels dependent. Religion stresses **faith**, devotion, and worship. In contrast, the emphasis in philosophy is on understanding and wisdom. The study of philosophy, then, because of the kinds of questions it raises, may help people build their religious convictions on foundations that are intellectually mature and defensible, but the goal of philosophy is not commitment or salvation. The philosopher is inclined to insist on careful reasoning and continuous examination of basic assumptions. Philosophy strives to keep the crucial questions open to intellectual review and public discussion.

The distinctions between science, religion, and philosophy can be illustrated by comparing the perspectives taken on the contemporary controversy over abortion. In confronting the issue of abortion, the scientist focuses attention on the physical condition, its causes and consequences, and the effect that the practice might have on personal or social well-being. The religionist stresses the rightness or wrongness of the practice in light of personal moral commitments or supernatural principles viewed from the perspective of ultimate meaning or value. The philosopher directs attention to how the term "abortion" is used, what the word or practice means in different contexts, how arguments for and against abortion are constructed and defended, and how abortion fits or does not fit with other ethical, metaphysical, or personal worldviews. All are legitimate concerns in the controversy over abortion. It is important to recognize that the philosopher's questions are more likely to address the clarity of language, the processes of thought, and the character of the basic assumptions or presuppositions in the arguments. It is not that the philosopher is indifferent to the sensitive issue but rather that he or she wants to be as clear as possible about what the issue really is.

D. Two Approaches to Philosophy

Two principal methods are used to introduce students to the field of philosophy. The first is the historical approach; the second is the issue approach. The former concentrates on the contributions of acknowledged philosophers, who are usually studied in chronological order. This method has been the traditional way of teaching philosophy. It views philosophical thought in a developmental frame of reference. Characteristically, attention is focused on the original works of those who are judged to be key writers. There are many advantages to the historical approach, and it continues to be a strongly supported and quite legitimate way to study philosophy. However, the historical approach and the issue approach are not incompatible: The pursuit of one leads naturally to the pursuit of the other. The only controversy arises over the most appropriate place to begin.

The issue approach, the one featured in this book, stresses involvement in the activity of philosophizing. We start with issues or questions about which students may have already formed some opinions. We emphasize modern problems and modern philosophical discussions. The issue approach is based on the conviction that interest in philosophical inquiry can be excited more readily and that the going will be less tedious if, at the very outset, students plunge into the sea of ideas, where they must begin to think or sink.

But, you may well ask, don't I need some background before I can discuss intelligently the momentous questions posed by philosophy? Of course you do. But the foreground is important too, and that is where most of us find it sensible to start. Building a personal philosophy of life; asking questions and seeking answers that make a personal difference; clarifying and identifying assumptions; making distinctions; seeking out new perspectives because of concern with finding meaning in life—these are what make philosophy an intensely intimate activity.

"Philosophic study means the habit of always seeing an alternative." This statement, by the American philosopher William James, introduces another aspect of the issue approach to philosophy. The issue approach exposes students to a provocative variety of positions taken by philosophers on major questions. By examining this diversity of ideas, students are forced to speculate about the range of the possible. The aim is to stretch the mind, to explore the realm of the conceivable. By scanning the horizon in many directions, students can more firmly fix their own positions or the positions of others.

In this book one of the conceptual devices used for surveying the field of philosophy is the **continuum**. A continuum is a range of possible alternatives between two logical extremes. The continuum **concept** is introduced in the early stages of philosophical study as a tool for comparing ideas that differ from one another to a greater or lesser degree. To show what a continuum is, we can use two familiar physical concepts. The concept "white" describes the highest concentration of light. The concept "black" describes the total absence of light. Between white and black, there is a full range (a spectrum) of possible intensities of light. The spectrum can be represented by a continuum of light intensity. The continuum provides a scale along which various degrees of light intensity can be named and along which the relationship between the various degrees can be specified. A graphic representation of the continuum might take the form of a half-circle, as shown.

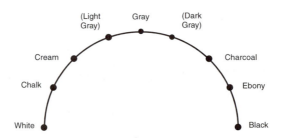

In philosophy, continua can be constructed to represent the range between such concepts as theism and atheism, freedom and determinism, absolutism and relativism. But a caution should be introduced at this point. Continua need be accepted only as beginning tools. There is nothing philosophically sacred or ultimately "true" about the continuum concept. In fact, some philosophers argue that understanding is distorted or precluded when ideas are viewed as totally opposed to one another. Others object to the implication that intermediate positions can exist between extremes. If, after careful consideration, the continuum concept proves to be untenable, it should be abandoned without regret. But whether accepted or rejected, the concept should be understood.

The issue approach to philosophy seeks to challenge and involve students. Strong emphasis is placed on the open mind and the inquiring perspective. Students often complete an extensive educational program without being given a fair opportunity to scrutinize their beliefs, explore their motives, test their values, or compare their convictions. Even if for no other reason than enlarging intellectual experience, a systematic effort to examine the bases on which ideas are claimed to be meaningful and defensible is a worthy undertaking. And if it be feared that philosophy questions everything and settles nothing, some reassurance may be found in the words of the late English journalist-critic G. K. Chesterton, who remarked: "Merely having an open mind is nothing. The object of opening the mind, as of opening the mouth, is to shut it on something solid."

E. Two Kinds of Philosophy

The work of philosophy begins typically with the identification of basic beliefs and assumptions. Key concepts are analyzed and defined; alternative positions are compared and critically evaluated. This is the starting point, the point at which fundamental questions are asked and a distinctive direction or perspective is given to the enterprise. Here, claims are made about the way to proceed so that conclusions may be reached.

Once the broad foundations for the philosophical undertaking have been laid, supporting evidence is gathered and then criticisms and objections are carefully considered. Relevant arguments or evidence from different fields of experience are brought to bear in the effort to determine what can or cannot be incorporated into the eventual synthesis of ideas. The adequacy of a given philosophical proposal is then tested by submitting it to public review so that its structure can be inspected or its implications evaluated.

In modern philosophy a dispute often arises over the exact nature or scope of the philosopher's work. The controversy may center on the distinction made by the philosopher C. D. Broad between **critical philosophy** and **speculative philosophy**. The following continuum may clarify the differences in emphasis and objectives of contemporary philosophical endeavors. In crude, simple terms it might be argued that critical philosophy is where one begins, and speculative philosophy is the farthest point to which one can go.

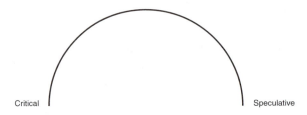

Critical   Speculative

Critical philosophers contend that their primary function is to analyze statements and to identify the precise meanings and the mutual relations among concepts. They insist that if we are ever to proceed beyond fuzzy meanings or unreliable knowledge words must be used carefully and consistently, and language must be clear and precise. Critical philosophers accept an obligation to clarify the meanings and determine the relations of fundamental concepts. In their view philosophy provides a service not furnished by any other discipline. Even in the fields of mathematics and science the philosopher stands apart and makes a special contribution. For example, the physicist may employ concepts such as "matter," "motion," or "time" and have a better understanding of what these concepts mean than the ordinary person, but the physicist need examine such meanings only as they relate to his or her own specific purposes. It is the function of the critical philosopher to study the nature of concepts *as such* and to make sure that those concepts are used accurately and consistently by the physicist or anyone else.

Critical philosophers also accept responsibility for examining and criticizing the fundamental beliefs or basic assumptions held by people as they organize their worlds or express their convictions. Take, for example, the common assumption that there is a *necessary* connection between a cause and an effect. To most of us, this assumption appears unquestionably obvious. But David Hume in the eighteenth century strongly criticized it. We observe one event following another, but no matter how often two events occur together or how repeatedly one kind of happening follows another, the *necessary* connection is never established. What we in fact experience—first the flash of lightning, then the clap of thunder—forces us to give up the familiar idea of **cause** as a necessary connection between events and permits us to speak only of a conjunction, or regular sequence, of events. This kind of analysis, appraisal, and constant challenging of basic premises is a central concern of critical philosophers. Their most rigorous test is to subject initial assumptions or statements of belief to all possible objections.

Thus we see that critical philosophy restricts the philosophical enterprise to a separate and distinct field of intellectual activity—one so important and so technical that it recruits specialists trained to analyze, evaluate, and propose alternatives to the concepts used by either experts or amateurs in any realm of human thought or endeavor. In this light, philosophy tries to keep the rest of us honest by insisting that we remain true to our premises, precise in our use of concepts, and logical in drawing our conclusions.

Critical philosophy draws fire from those who argue that its approach is too narrow, that it results in sterile word games, or that it renders philosophy useless and trivial by sucking all the vital juices out of human experience.

Speculative philosophy is more in line with what the average person believes philosophy to be. Speculative philosophy may be less exact, but it is surely more exciting, for it seeks the broader vistas, asks more provocative questions, and concerns itself with piecing together wholes—regardless of whether or not the language is clear or the logic precise.

Speculative philosophy is defended as being more practical because it attempts to construct a "big picture"—one that gives human beings some perspective from which to launch their aspirations, calm their frustrations, and satisfy their psychological or even their spiritual needs. Speculative philosophy does not categorically avoid value questions, religious implications, poetic expressions, or artistic sensitivities. The object of speculation is to put enough of the big parts together so that life takes on meaning and integration and possibly direction.

The eminent philosopher A. N. Whitehead explains it this way: "Speculative Philosophy is the endeavour to frame a coherent, logical, necessary system of general ideas in terms of which every element of our experience can be interpreted."[1] Speculative philosophers may strive for clarity or consistency or precision—but *not* at the expense of significance. Intuitive judgments, ethical prescriptions, visionary projections, and existential declarations are among the philosophical expressions to which the term "speculative" might apply.

Until very recently, most philosophers in the Western European tradition exhibited a profound concern for the speculative side of their work. Many of them attempted to integrate various knowledges, feelings, awarenesses, and hopes into an overarching pattern that gave them power to reflect on the total. There were numerous efforts "to see life and to see it whole."

Contemporary dissatisfaction with speculative philosophical systems stems from the accusation that they are overambitious, hopelessly unverifiable, and beyond the reach of reasoned criticism. Their critics claim that in sacrificing precision for significance the speculative philosophers often become **dogmatically** entrenched in self-validating systems that change slowly—*if* at all—in the face of contrary evidence or more rigorous logic.

Some philosophers, in their reaction to sloppy thinking and in their conviction that clarity and precision are of paramount importance in the contemporary world, would confine philosophy to the critical end of the continuum. Others, dismayed by the fragmentation of human experience and the lack of meaning in modern activities, would push philosophy toward the

---

[1]Alfred North Whitehead, *Process and Reality: An Essay in Cosmology* (New York: Free Press, 1969), p. 5 (paperback).

broader, speculative end of the continuum. Still others would argue that the philosophical enterprise is both critical and speculative, since speculation must be restrained by critical analysis, while one's analysis is to some extent dependent on one's broader understanding of the world. We will not in this book resolve the issue between the critical and the speculative philosophers. Our effort will be directed toward exposing a wide variety of alternatives. We will present critical and speculative views, hoping that the tension this presentation generates in students will motivate them toward deeper philosophical investigation.

F. Conclusion

Philosophers emphasize the framing of significant and meaningful questions. However, answers—or what appear to be answers—are what the student of philosophy is most likely to confront in the early going. But answers can be used as a starting point in the philosophical effort to develop a *reasoned* view of life and the universe. Answers can be critically analyzed for their clarity and reasonableness; they can be rigorously compared with alternative answers; and they can be evaluated on the basis of their overall adequacy. Analysis, comparison, and evaluation—these are the tools with which the ground of philosophy is surveyed and the mine of philosophy worked. Both questions and answers are like raw ore—of questionable worth until sifted, graded, refined, or fused into alloys. By carefully stating their explicit reasons for favoring particular answers, students are led directly to the heart of philosophy. Clear and critical thinking is expected. But it is not enough for students of philosophy merely to make their own thoughts lucid and consistent. There is the further challenge to test the adequacy of their ideas in an atmosphere of constructive criticism from the philosophers whose works they encounter, from their teachers, and from their fellow students.

One of the best ways to learn to think critically is to read critically. As you read the writings of philosophers you should ask the following questions (some of which are borrowed from the Adler and Van Doren book listed in this chapter's "Suggested Readings").

1. What format does the philosopher use to present her ideas? Philosophers have used different styles of writing to develop their positions, such as dialogue (Plato, Anselm), essay (Locke, Hume), and question-answer (Aquinas).

2. What question is the philosopher trying to answer? For example, Plato spends the first half of the *Republic* answering the question "What is justice?" The second half finishes his answer to a second query: How do you produce a just person?

3. What are the assumptions and controlling principles at work in answering the question (whether stated or not)?

4. How does the philosopher develop her thesis? What connections are made? What supporting arguments are given?

5. Is the philosopher consistent with her assumptions in developing the argument?

6. How are terms being used? Be particularly careful with familiar words, since it is easy to wrongly assume that an everyday word is being used by a philosopher with an "everyday" meaning. (A good example of this is Descartes's use of "clear and distinct ideas" in his *Meditations*.) Furthermore, sometimes a philosopher is inconsistent in the use of a term; in his book *The Structure of Scientific Revolutions* Thomas Kuhn has been accused of using his key word "paradigm" in a few dozen different ways.

7. Does the philosopher's work ring true to human experience and observation? This is not necessarily the best test, but it is often a good place to start in your critical analysis.

By training your mind as you read, you will develop good philosophical skills and habits. You might even find yourself turning your honed mind back on your own ideas.

Case Study and Discussion Questions

Case Study

It frequently happens that when people appear unconcerned about the world's problems or remain unshaken in the face of personal tragedy or disappointment, we say they are being "philosophical" about life.

1. In light of what has been presented in the early part of this book, how would you distinguish between a person who is being "philosophical" in the popular sense of the word and one who might more justifiably qualify for the title "philosopher"?

2. To what extent might these same two persons display attributes or attitudes that are similar?

Discussion Questions

1. In what specific ways might the study of philosophy assist those in pursuit of a higher education?

2. In what special ways might a philosopher contribute to a debate over the use of animal furs for human clothing? Over the use of new technology in human reproduction (for example, in vitro fertilization and cloning)? Over the legalization of physician-assisted suicide?

Suggested Readings

Adler, Mortimer, and Charles Van Doren. "How to Read Philosophy." In *How to Read a Book*. New York: Simon & Schuster, 1972, 270–295.

Barrett, William. *The Illusion of a Technique: A Search for Meaning in a Technological Civilization*. New York: Anchor Books, 1979.

Bontempo, Charles J., and S. Jack Odell, eds. *The Owl of Minerva: Philosophers on Philosophy*. New York: McGraw-Hill, 1975.

Broad, C. D. *Introduction to Scientific Thought*. Totowa, NJ: Littlefield, Adams, 1959.

Dewey, John. *Reconstruction in Philosophy*. Enl. ed. Boston: Beacon Press, 1957.

Durant, Will. *The Story of Philosophy*. New York: Pocket Books, 1957.

Goodman, Nelson. *Ways of Worldmaking*. Indianapolis: Hackett, 1978.

Hook, Sidney. "Does Philosophy Have a Future?" *Saturday Review* (November 11, 1967): 21–23, 62.

Johnson, A. H. *Philosophers in Action*. Columbus, OH: Charles E. Merrill, 1977.

MacIntyre, Alasdair. "Philosophy, the 'Other' Disciplines, and Their Histories: A Rejoinder to Richard Rorty." *Soundings* 45 (1982): 127–145.

Nagel, Thomas. *What Does It All Mean? A Very Short Introduction to Philosophy*. New York: Oxford University Press, 1987.

Plato. *Five Dialogues*. Translated by G. M. A. Grube. Indianapolis: Hackett, 1981. (Includes three of Plato's dialogues: *The Apology, The Crito*, and *The Phaedo*.)

Rorty, Richard. *Philosophy and the Mirror of Nature*. Princeton, NJ: Princeton University Press, 1979.

Russell, Bertrand. *The Problems of Philosophy*. New York: Oxford University Press (Galaxy Book), 1959.

Schlick, Moritz. "The Future of Philosophy." *Publications in Philosophy*. College of the Pacific, 1931–1932.

Sprague, Elmer. *What Is Philosophy? A Short Introduction*. New York: Oxford University Press, 1961.

Whitehead, Alfred North. *Adventures of Ideas*. New York: Free Press, 1967.

CHAPTER 2
Philosophical Thinking

A. Questions to Consider

- In what ways is language important to the thinking process?
- Do symbols serve to reveal or obscure the truth?
- What does it mean to think "critically"?
- Are there reliable rules for sound reasoning?
- Is there more than one way to arrive at a logical conclusion?
- Must an argument be logical for a conclusion to be true?
- How do you go about criticizing a philosophical statement?
- What are some of the common logical mistakes that people make in their thinking?

B. Introduction

Philosophy has been broadly characterized as the search for an enlightened worldview. In this endeavor, philosophers typically try to identify and analyze the basic assumptions that people depend on (but are rarely aware of) to make sense out of their lives and their experiences. But a more specific and more technical responsibility assumed by philosophers is the task of clarifying concepts and constructing defensible arguments.

Philosophical thinking is distinguished from ordinary thinking. It is characterized by its attempt to be conceptual and abstract. The stress is on the deeper-level meanings and the symbolic representations that attend the human effort to understand. Rather than directing its attention to the concrete events and experiences of the world, philosophical thinking examines the underlying structure of human thought. Particular sensations or individually distinct events, while they may be examined as **data**, are not the main point of interest. The specific size, shape, and movement of balls on a pool table become the special subject of philosophical concern when questions are raised about **cause**, tactics, or what it means to play a game of pool.

Philosophical thinking also demands that we be as accurate and precise as possible about the definition and use of words. Words are the common currency of communication. Words are the basic foundation on which human beings build a system of mutually agreeable abbreviations for sharing experiences, feelings, desires, and aspirations. But words are also combined and arranged to formulate **concepts** or *ideas* that can be used to exchange meanings at a more general and complex level. Philosophical thinking encourages us to examine, share, and evaluate those broader ideas that we believe to be significant. In this regard, philosophy moves toward a position of rationality or **reason**, in which spontaneous emotion, idiosyncratic experience, or unthinking and automatic verbal expressions do not dominate.

Finally, philosophical thinking is marked by the compelling obligation to give reasons for whatever we affirm or conclude. Anything a philosopher says or writes is subject to critical analysis, comparison, and evaluation by all who care to join in the dialogue. Philosophical positions must be publicly proposed and defended.

So, philosophers are people marked by the habit of wrestling with the deeper meanings of concepts and the wider connections of ideas. They find significance in the act of **reflection**—in the pursuit of thoughts and feelings beyond the requirements of the moment and beyond the limits of what is comfortably close at hand. The different methods and techniques of reflection they use need to be analyzed and compared.

Some philosophers insist that ideas should follow each other in a rigorous, formal, logical way. Others put their trust in feeling or **intuition** as a source of knowledge or belief. Eastern philosophers in particular may be wary of any form of abstract conceptualization, believing it preferable to let the mind alone, to surrender to the flow of experience. But with few exceptions philosophers agree that it is appropriate to reflect on what is real or what might be the best way to live a life and then discuss it.

The processes and the products of reflection are expressed in **language**. In speaking or in writing, philosophers attempt to be clear and compelling about those things that matter to them and about which they have thought deeply. They express and elaborate their own ideas, and they consider and criticize the ideas of others. In a word, they communicate. They engage in an ongoing dialogue about what they judge to be critical issues. Personal, private, and unexpressed points of view may be individually satisfying—even ultimately paramount—but philosophers typically talk to one another and express to a wider public their views about alternative ways to think, act, or exist. Ideas are presented, defended, and shared. Because the philosophical approach involves analysis, comparison, and evaluation, it is in the arena of public exposure and open criticism that true philosophy is practiced. Socrates was a true philosopher; his life was an example of philosophy in action. His special passion was to promote serious dialogue between thoughtfully concerned human beings.

C. Language and Discourse: From Symbols to Arguments

Philosophers devote a great deal of time and energy to the study of the forms and functions of language because effective communication and meaningful dialogue are founded on the clear and rigorous use of mutually intelligible **symbols**. A symbol is simply something that stands for or represents something else. Words and numbers are symbols, and symbols are the building blocks of any language. There must be reasonable agreement on the form and organization of symbols if philosophical dialogue is to be fruitful. There must be such agreement if everyday speaking and writing are to be anything but gibberish.

In the prologue, clarity was listed as one of the goals of philosophical study. Clarity can be achieved only if there is reasonable consensus on the way in which language is to be used. Clarity of expression depends on the careful selection and precise use of words. What is called critical thinking depends on the consistent organization of the units of language into ordered and intelligible discourse. At this point we may begin to recognize and appreciate the crucial importance of grammar and syntax in the process of human communication. To be understood, even poorly or partially, we must play the game of using structured symbols. To philosophize—to identify assumptions, to clarify positions, to exchange meanings—we must concern ourselves with the use and abuse of words and with the way arguments are structured and evaluated.

Our attention is again directed to words. As symbols, words "stand for" other things, such as objects, events, and actions. When we communicate, we nearly always use words. We may add gestures, facial expressions, or tonal emphasis, but the words carry the basic message. The clarity of our ideas (and even their meaning) is intimately connected with the manner in which we express them. If our choice of words is inappropriate or our use of them vague or ambiguous, then clarity of expression will not be achieved.

Words, then, are the basic tools of thought. Just as a carpentry project can be ruined by using the wrong tools, so a thought can be blurred or distorted by using the wrong words. But how can we tell when the words are "right"? This question draws us into the complex field of **semantics**. Semanticists study the meanings of words. They are concerned with the symbolic units of language (the words) and how these units are defined, organized, and agreed on in a system of exchanged meanings. For example, in a given statement does the word "communism" refer to the theory developed by Marx, to the political system in China today, or to the shared relationships in an experimental commune? When people say "love conquers all," does the word "love" mean physical attraction, romantic idealization, or cosmic compassion? Semanticists also warn us against confusing a word for a thing; they remind us that words simplify and abstract from complex, ever-changing reality.

Beginners in philosophy must direct special attention to the meanings of words, many of which are used in one way by people carrying on an ordinary conversation and in a quite different way by philosophers. In everyday communication, to demand that every word be critically analyzed and defended may have the effect of obstructing or terminating the effort to establish human connections; in philosophy, the precise use of carefully defined terms sets the foundation for the exploration and exchange of significant ideas.

Words are combined into phrases and sentences. Sentences having the properties of **statements**, or, as they are sometimes called, **propositions**, are key elements in the philosophical process called logical reasoning. A statement is a declarative sentence that asserts or claims that some condition or relationship exists. It expresses meaning and must be either true or false. Not all sentences contain statements. Some sentences express commands. Others frame questions—and questions have a special importance in philosophy. But philosophers put much effort into the construction of sentences that do contain statements or propositions. Then they analyze the ways in which statements or propositions are related to one another to provide a basis for conclusions or generalizations. Declarative sentences—sentences that assert or claim that something is indeed so—become elements that may be organized into what logicians call arguments. An **argument** is a list of two or more statements, one of which is designated the **conclusion** and the rest of which are designated **premises**. The conclusion states the point being argued for, and the premises state the reasons being advanced to support the conclusion. Here are two different patterns of argument in which it is easy to identify the premises and the conclusion:

The clouds are getting darker overhead.

The wind is becoming stronger.

The barometer is dropping.

Therefore, a storm is on the way.

John is shorter than Gene.

Gene is shorter than Phil.

Therefore, John is shorter than Phil.

An argument can be further defined as any group of propositions (statements), one of which, it is claimed, follows from the others, which are regarded

as supplying the evidence for th
philosophical activity that deal
evaluating arguments purported
thinking. Critical thinking is a pr
thinking is usually judged by th
and presented in a systematic
arguments are poorly presented, we are often accused of cloudy thinking
help us think more critically about statements that occur frequently in arguments, we might raise the following questions:

Is the statement consistent with everyday experience and perception? Does what is said actually reflect what happens in the world?

Would the statement appear reasonable or adequate to an impartial third party? Are biases, prejudices, and selective perceptions clearly recognized and avoided?

Is the statement ambiguous, obscure, or internally contradictory? Is it vague or lacking a clear referent, or does it relate ideas that are mutually exclusive?

Is the statement consistent with other statements that we have already accepted as true? If not, must the new statement be abandoned or must the earlier statements be reevaluated?

Are there exceptions or counterexamples that make the truth of the statement questionable? What percentage of the relevant cases fit? How strong is the contrary evidence?

Is the statement acceptable in light of the common use of language? Is there fairly widespread agreement on the definitions and uses of words?

Does acceptance of the statement mean accepting consequences that are unreasonable or undesirable? Does the statement lead to a conclusion that is absurd or that clearly denies considered judgments from previous reasoning or experience?

Are there alternative statements that are equally or more clearly pertinent and reasonable? Would a different statement make the point more accurately and adequately?

These questions provide a basis for analyzing critically such statements as the following:

The truth will make you free.

You can't change human nature.

Pleasure is the only ultimate value.

Violent revolution in underdeveloped countries is necessary and desirable.

Human beings are inherently selfish and competitive.

Moral people look out for themselves first.

Man is condemned to be free.

Science is the only valid way of knowing.

Beauty is in the eye of the beholder.

Good and evil are two sides of the same coin.

Let us examine more closely the relationship between what is commonly called critical thinking and what philosophers call **logic**. The study of logic is a study of the rules of reasoning by which people arrive at conclusions. Logic is defined popularly as the science of reasoning, but that is not entirely accurate. The term "reasoning" merely identifies the practice of drawing conclusions from premises. There are two distinctive processes of reasoning: psychological and logical. The psychological process of drawing conclusions from premises is called **inference**. The psychological process is difficult to describe, but we know that human beings do it all the time; it is somehow related to the activities of the human brain and nervous system. Logical reasoning, in contrast, takes place only when evidence is stated in the form of propositions and those propositions are formally related as premises and conclusion.

On the basis of my current state of health, my childhood frustrations, and my interest in geopolitics, I may conclude (infer) that the world will come to an end tomorrow. I have my reasons! But unless the evidence can be organized into declarative sentences and the resulting propositions ordered in the correct form of an argument, my conclusion cannot be evaluated logically. Philosophers are concerned with the structure of logical reasoning, and they attempt to discriminate between valid and fallacious forms of reasoning. Logicians are not primarily concerned with the psychological aspects of the process of inference. Psychologists or neurologists might study the mental or physical processes leading to a person's acceptance of a particular belief or opinion, but logicians are interested in the relationships among propositions and in the logical order of the argument. They are concerned with the formal correctness of the completed structure of the argument. Logicians study the methods and principles used to distinguish correct from incorrect arguments. It is their intention to be formal and objective.

A warning is in order. Distinguishing between **reason** and **rhetoric**—two concepts that are all too frequently confused—is important. Reason implies some sort of orderly thought process that can be traced, analyzed, and judged by intellectual standards. Reason claims to increase human knowledge or understanding, often apart from its practical applications. Reason may be valued for its own sake because it illuminates meaning, order, and perspective. Reason emphasizes the passion for clarity and truth; it stresses criticism and the search for sound arguments. Rhetoric, on the other hand, is a form of communication designed to persuade, to motivate people toward a predetermined action or opinion. Rhetoric is the skillful use of language in an effort to elicit a particular response. Rhetoric is a means; it takes the form of intellectual coercion or psychological persuasion. Rhetoric tends to be uncritical and dogmatic.

The distinction between reason and rhetoric raises some sticky semantic questions, but it is a similar distinction to that sometimes made between "education" and "propaganda." Education seeks to give persons the power to make decisions and the knowledge to make choices on their own. Propaganda is designed to produce a predictable opinion or response, whether or not responders understand what they do or why they do it. Over the years philosophy has been tilted toward the broader view—toward reason and education.

Logical reasoning is one of the most important areas of contemporary philosophical study. The traditional way of classifying logical arguments is to designate them either inductive or deductive. Different criteria are employed in evaluating each type, and we shall consider them separately.

D. Inductive Reasoning

Induction refers to the process of drawing conclusions from specific evidence. It is a process of reasoning in which conclusions are typically drawn from the observation of particular cases. Inductionists claim that we can experience directly only what is concrete and particular. Particulars are the individual units of perception or experience rather than the general or universal aspects. When we generalize about these particulars, we go beyond the immediate experience of those particulars. Consequently, a conclusion reached through the inductive process is never absolutely certain. In induction, reasoning proceeds to a conclusion that is not confined to the scope of the premises but is somehow additional to, or beyond, them. Inductive logical procedure is tightly linked to the concept of **probability**. The conclusion is based on the evidence, but the conclusion is never absolutely *certain*. It is only probable: After all, there is the possibility of discovering new evidence. Courtroom drama on television and in the movies often illustrates this point.

The inductive probability of an argument is the likelihood that its conclusion is true as long as the premises are factual. Inductive arguments are "strong" or "weak." The claim is that their premises constitute *some* evidence for their conclusion. The greater the weight of the evidence, the stronger the argument. The terms "valid" and "invalid" and the concept of "validity" are not appropriately applied to inductive arguments. Inductive logic is concerned with tests for measuring the inductive probability or strength of arguments and with the rules for constructing strong inductive arguments. This method of reasoning has been identified with scientific activity, but we shall discover that the scientific method involves much more than the strict application of inductive logic.

We use induction constantly in our daily lives to guide our choices. We "learn from experience" by classifying particular events into "kinds" or "classes" and then discovering how these kinds or classes of things are related to one another. We are then in a position to make predictions about what is likely to happen in the particular situations that occur in our lives. A child is bitten by an ant, is subsequently bitten by a flea and a mosquito, and is later stung by a bee. The child comes to the conclusion that insects cause pain. A generalization about small creeping and flying organisms ("insects cause pain") is established that becomes a principle by which the child acts toward a certain class of creatures. Later knowledge and experience may modify the child's concept or confirm it, but, in either case, specific experiences have led to the general idea.

One of the more obvious advantages of inductive thinking is that it helps human beings to frame their expectations of the future on the basis of what they know about the past and the present. Conclusions about what is most likely to happen in the future are guided by the accumulation of available evidence. Inductive logic gives the power to project forward in time and predict what will probably occur. It is this kind of reasoning, for instance, that is used by the weather forecaster to predict the likelihood of rain tomorrow and by the pollster who attempts to foresee the result of an election. Inductive logic is a most valuable human tool. It stresses the effectiveness of basing conclusions on the careful and extensive accumulation of pertinent evidence.

One of the arguments presented earlier in this chapter showed the inductive form. The factual premises were listed and the probable conclusion followed:

The clouds are getting darker overhead. (premise)

The wind is becoming stronger. (premise)

The barometer is dropping. (premise)

Therefore, a storm is on the way. (conclusion)

Another example differs only in that it argues from past particular cases to a *particular* case in the future:

The first grape in this bunch tasted sour. (premise)

The second grape in this bunch tasted sour. (premise)

The third grape in this bunch tastes sour. (premise)

Therefore, the next grape in this bunch will also taste sour. (conclusion)

Now examine the following inductive generalization: "Practice makes perfect." How is this generalization derived? We survey many particular cases of competent performance—concert pianists, tennis champions, expert typists, skilled bricklayers, chess masters, successful airline pilots, professional golfers. We observe that long, intense practice is part of every one of these different activities. In other words, practice is a common factor in all cases. We then go beyond our specific observations and induce the general principle that "practice makes perfect." Assuming that this is a fair example of how the inductive process works, it should be clear that inductive thinking is subject to serious hazards and limitations. It is not a simple, straightforward matter to make reliable inductive inferences from particular cases to general conclusions.

Before deciding that the statement "Practice makes perfect" is a **reliable** inductive generalization and not a hasty generalization, we would have to raise and answer certain questions. Must people practice to perfect *all kinds* of skills? Does the generalization apply, for example, to a child prodigy in mathematical calculations? These questions point to a distinction that is made between two kinds of **causes**. A necessary cause or condition exists if, in its absence, an effect cannot occur. It is *one* of the factors needed to produce a given effect. A sufficient cause or condition is one in whose presence an event *must* occur. The generalization "practice makes perfect" implies that practice is not only a necessary cause of skilled performance but also a sufficient cause of it; *anyone* who practices long and hard on the piano can become a concert pianist. But does this implication square with what we know about piano players? Another question arises. In some or even all cases of expert performance, can there be two common factors rather than just one—for example, practice *and* natural ability? The problem immediately becomes very complex.

In this brief introduction to logical reasoning, no attempt will be made to cover all the rules and procedures for checking the correctness or reliability of all inductive generalizations or conclusions. There are, however, a few preliminary guidelines:

1. How *complete* is the evidence on which the conclusion is based? What proportion of the total number of relevant cases has been examined?

2. How *reliable* is the evidence? How sure is it that the facts have been observed carefully? It should be clear that the reliability of the conclusion can be no greater than the accuracy and objectivity of the evidence on which it is based.

3. Since it is usually impossible to inspect all relevant cases, is the sample selected *representative*; that is, are the examined cases *typical* of the total population of cases?

4. Have *negative instances,* cases that do not fit, been actively searched out and taken into account?

5. Are there *alternative theories* (different conclusions) that can equally well or better relate and explain the facts?

Critique of Inductive Reasoning

Even simple inductive logic presents some serious difficulties. Facts do not speak for themselves; they do not flash lights to show their interrelationships to an impartial observer. Any concept, then, that organizes or relates the facts or any generalization made about those facts is additional to the facts themselves.

This limitation of strict induction is expressed in the maxim "There is nothing as practical as a good theory." Human knowledge in general and orderly thinking in particular depend on concepts and theories by which the particular facts selected from the countless number available are given relevance or meaning. Facts and experiences must be selected according to some criterion that dictates what is pertinent and what is irrelevant. In other words, there must be a **theory** that makes it possible to draw conclusions from the evidence. Many scientists besides Darwin possessed elaborate collections of living and extinct organisms but failed to see how the specimens could be related significantly and used as evidence for a theory of evolution. Inductive logicians are hard pressed to explain the foundations of their theories and generalizations.

E. Deductive Reasoning

The basic principles of **deductive** logic are fairly well established. There is widespread agreement on the definitions of its basic concepts, and the rules of procedure are precisely formulated. The defining characteristic of a *valid* deduction is its certainty. If the conclusion is necessary—that is, if it is forced by the premises—the argument is certain.

A deductive argument involves the claim that its premises provide all the evidence required for a conclusion. Additional evidence does not affect the credibility of a valid deductive conclusion. A deductive system of argumentation is a closed system; it cannot advance beyond the scope of its premises. Consider this point in the light of the following deductive argument:

All human beings are mortal. (premise)

Socrates is a human being. (premise)

Therefore, Socrates is mortal. (conclusion)

There is nothing in the conclusion that was not already contained in the premises. Deductive arguments are typically analytic. They are analytic in the sense that they analyze, or separate out, something that has already been included in the premises, and then they state it in the conclusion.

In deductive arguments, premises, in the form of statements or propositions, are often established as self-evident or "given," which means that no proof is necessary, and the premises are accepted as obvious *before* any reference is made to the facts. Such premises, whether accepted for logical or for intuitive reasons, set the foundation and prescribe the limits for the deductive reasoning process that follows.

Instead of labeling arguments "strong" or "weak" or even "correct" or "incorrect," the deductive logician applies the terms **valid** and **invalid**. A valid argument is one that has the property of being legitimately derived from premises by prescribed logical deduction. To be valid, the argument must—without ambiguity or exception—follow the established rules. Any flaw or error in the logical procedure immediately renders the argument and its conclusion invalid. The task of deductive logic is to clarify the nature of the relationship that holds between premises and conclusion in valid arguments and to propose techniques for discriminating valid from invalid arguments.

One pattern of deductive reasoning is found in the **syllogism**. A syllogism is a precise and standardized form of argument that contains two premises and a conclusion. Two types of syllogisms will be introduced. First is the categorical syllogism, which consists of three categorical propositions. A categorical proposition is a statement that consists of only two terms and relates a class of things (called the subject) to another class of things (called the predicate). In a categorical syllogism, the three propositions together supply exactly three terms, each of which appears twice and is used in the same sense throughout the argument. Following is an example:

All firefighters are brave.

Max is a firefighter.

Therefore, Max is brave.

This is a valid syllogism because the conclusion is forced by the premises. The terms establish clear and definite categories for the argument and are related to one another in a manner that conforms with the definition for a categorical syllogism set forth above.

Another type of syllogism is the hypothetical syllogism, which exhibits a somewhat different form. The hypothetical syllogism is expressed conditionally using if-then propositions in the premises:

If a person is a firefighter, then he or she is brave. (major premise)

Max is a firefighter. (minor premise)

Therefore, Max is brave. (conclusion)

Because this straightforward argument obeys the logical rules for deduction applied to hypothetical syllogisms, it is valid. Again, the conclusion is forced by the premises. If the premises are accepted as given, then the conclusion *must be* the case.

Because hypothetical syllogisms are employed so frequently in everyday discourse, examples will be given to show how the rules of reasoning are applied. The task is to identify the critical parts of hypothetical syllogisms and to describe the basic criteria for judging them to be valid or invalid. A familiar example will start things off:

If a person is a firefighter, then he or she is brave. (major premise)

Max is a firefighter. (minor premise)

Therefore, Max is brave. (conclusion)

The major premise contains two key terms, "firefighter," and "brave," which are linked or related to each other in a particular way. The first key term (firefighter) of the major premise is called the **antecedent**, and the second key term (brave) is called the **consequent**. The minor premise introduces a third term (Max) and relates it to one of the terms in the major premise. The validity or invalidity of the syllogistic argument is determined by the way the terms of the minor premise relate to the terms of the major premise. When the minor premise affirms the antecedent of the major premise, the argument is valid. When, however, the minor premise affirms the consequent of the major premise, the syllogism is invalid. Hypothetical syllogisms are also valid when the minor premise denies the consequent of the major premise; they are invalid when the minor premise denies the antecedent of the major premise. Using our familiar example, we can diagram and describe the four syllogistic forms and identify the valid and invalid arguments.

Form 1 (Valid. The minor premise affirms the antecedent of the major premise.)

If a person is a firefighter, then he or she is brave.

Max is a firefighter.

Therefore, Max is brave.

In the diagram, the most inclusive term (brave) in the syllogism is represented by the larger circle. Everything brave is encompassed by this circle. The smaller circle includes *all* firefighters. The smaller circle is completely enclosed by the larger one. Max, as a firefighter, is necessarily included in the smaller circle. If Max m*ust be* in the smaller circle and the smaller circle is totally enclosed by the larger one, then Max *must be* in the larger one. The conclusion is forced by the premises. Max *must be* brave. The antecedent is affirmed, and the argument is valid.

Form 2 (Invalid. The minor premise affirms the consequent of the major premise.)

If a person is a firefighter, then he or she is brave.

Max is brave.

Therefore, Max is a firefighter.

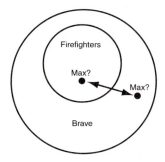

In this form, the larger and smaller circles exhibit the same relationship to one another as in Form 1. But while it is clear that Max is in the larger circle, it is by no means certain that Max is in the smaller circle. It cannot be stated unequivocally that Max is a firefighter. He is brave, but he could be a brave police officer. Here the minor premise affirms the consequent of the major premise. Doubt about Max's classification puts the conclusion in question and renders the argument invalid.

Form 3 (Invalid. The minor premise denies the antecedent of the major premise.)

If a person is a firefighter, then he or she is brave.

Max is not a firefighter.

Therefore, Max is not brave.

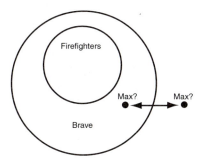

Here it is certain that Max is *not* in the smaller circle, but it is not clearly established that he is even in the larger one. Max *could be* either inside or outside of the larger circle. For this reason, Max's classification is in doubt, and the fact that the minor premise denies the antecedent of the major premise makes the argument invalid.

Form 4 (Valid. The minor premise denies the consequent of the major premise.)

If a person is a firefighter, then he or she is brave.

Max is not brave.

Therefore, Max is not a firefighter.

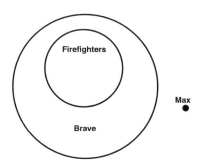

In this last diagram, it is established that Max is totally outside of the larger circle. *All* firefighters are inside the larger circle. Therefore, Max cannot possibly be found in *either* of the circles. The minor premise denies the consequent of the major premise, and the argument in this form is valid.

These are but simple first steps in the field of deductive logic, and they are taken here primarily to demonstrate how deductive reasoning differs from inductive reasoning. The differences are fundamental and can be summarized as follows.

Inductive Arguments	*Deductive Arguments*
1. If all of the premises are true,then the conclusion is *probably,* but not necessarily, true. Such an argument is considered *strong.*	**1.** Given the premises, if the rules of reasoning are followed, the conclusion *necessarily* follows. Such an argument is considered *valid.*
2. The conclusion contains information not present in the premises.	**2.** All of the information is already-contained (at least implicitly) in the premises.

Now additional questions arise concerning deductive logic. First, what does deductive logic have to do with truth? It has been shown that deduction is concerned primarily with the formal structure of argument and with validity. But establishing a proposition as a major premise in no way guarantees its truth. An argument can be valid even though the experiential "truth" of its premises cannot be demonstrated. The truth of the argument's three propositions may have to be decided using criteria that are external to the argument itself. Using our working example again, we can ask critical questions that bear on the truth of its propositions.

If a person is a firefighter, then he or she is brave.

Max is a firefighter.

Therefore, Max is brave.

Are *all* firefighters really brave? Are they always brave? Is it clearly established that Max is, indeed, a firefighter? The "truth" of the conclusion depends on demonstrating, by using criteria outside of the argument itself, that the major and minor premises state with accuracy the actual state of affairs. Finally, is the conclusion, which in our working example is clearly forced by the premises, a reasonable one in light of what else may be known about bravery, firefighters, and Max? A valid conclusion may also be an unacceptable conclusion. Remember that although the question of truth is always relevant to the judgment of a *sound* argument (that is, one that has valid form and true propositions), it is not relevant to the judgment of a *valid* argument.

Another kind of question can be directed to deductive arguments. Do the terms and propositions of the argument have any meaning? Does the argument make any sense? What useful purpose does it serve? These questions cannot be answered from within the framework of the formal argument. External criteria suddenly impinge on the process when the issue of "meaning" is raised.

Propositions may be true (factual) or not; they may be meaningful or not. The following syllogism, because it conforms to the rules of syllogistic reasoning, is valid.

If anything is glynx, then it is flurgh.

Pzyok is glynx.

Therefore, pzyok is flurgh.

The terms used in this argument are neither true nor false. They have no acceptable definition and are, therefore, meaningless or nonsensical. Yet the argument is valid. Once the major premise has been established as a starting proposition, the question of truth or meaning is (at least for a time) set aside. The question becomes, "Does the deductive reasoning proceed *validly* to a conclusion?" Deductive logicians may prefer that beginning premises be true and significant, but they are primarily concerned with the logical procedure.

In mathematics, the formula $2 + 2 = 4$ is accepted as a self-evident proposition. Those who question the proposition cannot proceed very far in their understanding of even simple arithmetic. But what, exactly, is 2? Like the other elements in the proposition, it is a pure symbol. It is not a *thing* or a feeling. It has no specific reference to an object or an action. It is an arbitrary symbol that must be accepted at face value, along with the other symbols to which it is related in clear and consistent ways, so that mathematical reasoning can advance through ever more involved and intricate logical processes. But the truth, and surely the meaning, of the proposition 2 + 2 = 4 may be incomprehensible beyond the scope of the reasoning process itself. Yet to deny that 2 + 2 = 4 excludes one from the all-important field of conventional mathematics. The beginning propositions must be taken as self-evident and inviolate so that clear and consistent reasoning can take place. Students of algebra recognize the necessity even as they move on to a greater appreciation of the intricacies and wider applications of mathematical principles.

In recent times, a whole new field called **symbolic logic** has grown up in which logicians have introduced many new and special symbols that can be related to one another in ever more precise and consistent ways. Modern symbolic logic has become a powerful tool for analysis and deduction partly because it developed its own highly technical system of symbols—its language. This language permits the clearer exposure of logical arguments that are often obscured by the use of ordinary language. It is easier to divide arguments into those that are valid and those that are invalid when they are expressed in a special immaculate symbolic language because such problems as vagueness, ambiguity, and metaphor do not arise. However, there is a pitfall associated with using technical symbolic language. If vagueness, ambiguity, and the like are not eliminated before symbolization occurs, they lock themselves into place, with the possibility that they might not be detected as questionable elements in the system. Deductive logicians take special care to avoid criticism on these points.

Critique of Deductive Reasoning

We have cautioned that inductive arguments should not be accepted without critical examination. Deductive thinking has its dangers also. The deductive thinker runs the grave risk of focusing attention on the validity of an argument while neglecting to examine with sufficient care the reliability of the statements (premises) on which the argument depends.

The propositions that become major premises are often just "given." Reasoning can proceed whether or not the propositions are factual, whether or not they have any humanly significant meaning. Serious and systematic thinkers have found themselves in fundamental disagreement on the best or most productive starting propositions.

The seductive danger in syllogistic thinking is illustrated in the following syllogism, which, by the rules of deductive logic, is valid.

Whatever deters crime is socially desirable. (major premise)

Capital punishment deters crime. (minor premise)

Therefore, capital punishment is socially desirable. (conclusion)

The argument is valid, but is the conclusion true? There are strong grounds for doubting the truth of both the major and minor premises. And if either premise is doubtful, the conclusion is doubtful.

F. Informal Fallacies

An error in logical reasoni̶n̶ ... ment is wrong or if the langu̶a̶... the conclusion of that argume̶r̶... "fallacy" is also used to refer to an argument that persuades for psychological or emotional reasons rather than for logical ones. If the selection or arrangement of words is contrived so that the effect is to trick or delude another person, we also call that a fallacy. The trouble with so many statements or arguments that are fallacious is that on the surface they may look good; they seem to carry weight and conviction. It is not until they are analyzed from a rigorously logical point of view that their inadequacies can be exposed.

Formal fallacies are those that occur when there is something wrong with the form or structure of an argument or in the way the rules of reasoning are followed. This problem has been addressed in the foregoing discussions of inductive and deductive logic.

Informal fallacies are errors related to the *content* or clarity of statements that may or may not be used as propositions in a formal argument. Whether intentional or unintentional, statements containing informal fallacies abound in everyday discourse, and the forms they take are so numerous that no attempt will be made to present a comprehensive list at this level of study. Just a few of the more common and more seductive types of informal fallacies will be illustrated at this time. If the goal is to sharpen one's reasoning skills, some of the more obvious mistakes should be noted and avoided.

Amphiboly. A form of confusion that results when the grammatical construction of a statement makes the meaning unclear. (This is sometimes called "syntactical ambiguity.")

Example: The archivists examined an original flag that had led Union soldiers into battle at the Civil War Library & Museum in Philadelphia.

The statement, because it is carelessly structured, is not entirely clear. There could be two quite different meanings. The fault lies in the loose grammatical construction.

Semantical ambiguity. A form of confusion that results when a word or phrase can have two or more different meanings. (The word "ambiguous" comes from two Latin words that mean "to drive on both sides.")

Example: The trustees asked security personnel to stop drinking on campus.

The phrase "to stop drinking" could be understood in two very different ways. The substitution of a less ambiguous phrase would clarify what is meant.

Equivocation. This could be classified as a form of semantical ambiguity. Often it is employed to establish a conclusion by using a word in two different senses in the same argument.

Example: Anyone who is considered old enough to join the army and fight for his country is a mature person; and anyone who votes must be mature, too. So, anyone mature enough to fight is mature enough to vote.

In this example, the term "mature" is used in two quite different ways. When a term in a statement or an argument is related to other terms, it is logically demanded that the meaning of that term remain unchanged.

Post hoc fallacy. The incorrect assumption that merely because two events occur together or in a time sequence, one is the cause of the other.

Example: Evelyn carried a rabbit's foot, so naturally she won the race.

The cause-effect relationship between winning the race and carrying a rabbit's foot is not at all certain. Other possible contributing factors are completely ignored.

False dilemma. The assumption is improperly made that an issue has only two sides or that there are only two alternative choices in a situation.

Example: People are either Christians or atheists.

Placing people in two mutually exclusive categories in no way describes the actual situation in the world. The content of the statement does not square with the evidence.

Argumentum ad ignorantiam. The mistaken argument that what one person asserts is true because another person cannot disprove it, or that an assertion is false because another person cannot prove it to be true.

Example: God exists because you cannot prove that God does not exist.

The inability to prove a particular statement has no bearing at all on whether or not its opposite stands proved. Evidence, not ignorance, is required to make a statement acceptable.

Argumentum ad hominem. The faulty assumption that if you discredit the person, you thereby discredit his or her argument.

Example: What can he know about patriotism? He speaks with a foreign accent.

No evidence for a relationship between patriotism and a person's manner of speaking is established. Attaching the emotional connotation of "foreign accent" to a person cannot legitimately be used to distract attention from the issue of patriotism.

Begging the question. We beg the question when the argument is based on the very conclusion we are trying to prove. The argument merely moves in a circle and says the same thing twice.

Example: Learning is important because everyone should acquire knowledge.

This is not a meaningful statement. It is not a premise; it does not advance an argument. Learning and acquiring knowledge are synonymous, and reasoning does not go beyond the initial statement. It is like saying what is already obvious: Learners should learn.

Hypothesis contrary to fact. The very questionable claim that one can know with certainty what *would* have happened if a past event or condition had been different from what it actually was.

Example: If my father had been rich, I would be a successful surgeon today.

The initial proposition does not describe the actual situation that existed in the past. It is purely imaginative and does not set a factual basis for the reasoning that follows but turns into a speculative apology that illogically asserts to know what *would* have happened if what *had* happened *had not* happened. The logical inconsistency here is easy to detect.

Straw man. Misrepresenting a statement or an argument, or substituting another one, in order to attack the original statement or argument more easily.

Example: Go ahead and build your nuclear power plant. I guess you don't care about the environment.

Arguing for or against nuclear power plants is not necessarily an indication of one's ecological concerns; but it is easier to attack a lack of concern for the environment than it is to argue the merits or demerits of nuclear power.

False obversion. The misuse of contrasts and opposites; the faulty assertion that if a statement is true, its opposite must therefore be false.

Example: Children learn easily; therefore, adults learn with difficulty.

Even though "children" and "adults" are set up as mutually exclusive or opposite terms, the capacity for learning among adults is not established simply by characterizing the learning capacity of children.

False conversion. The switching of subject and predicate in a statement with the result that the new statement does not meet the requirements for correct reasoning.

Example: All patriots salute the flag; therefore, all who salute the flag are patriots.

When one term is set up to totally encompass another in an affirmative way, it is unacceptable and illogical to switch suddenly and make what was originally the enclosed term into the encompassing term.

Testimonial. The strategy of directing attention to a well-known or attractive person in order to create a positive image of a product or cause that might be temporarily associated with that person.

Example: I always buy Bulgarian motor cars because on TV my favorite movie star says they are well made.

An impression (in this instance, a *positive* one) is created by focusing attention on a side issue that has no necessary connection with the main thrust of the argument. In the typical advertising testimonial, it is highly unlikely, and certainly not proved, that a movie star knows very much about the product he or she recommends.

Bandwagon. Appealing to common practice (whether actual or alleged) in order to get others to do something or to share the same point of view.

Example: Chew Bozo Bubble Gum—ten million people can't be wrong.

While many advertisers use this fallacious form of reasoning, the truth or merit of an idea or a behavior is not dependent on the number of people who believe it is true or worthy to practice.

Reification. The practice of treating a word or a concept as if it were a thing with a life or power of its own.

Example: Science will turn all of us into robots.

This proposition gives a personalized life and power to what is usually regarded as a collective concept covering many activities and attitudes. The fallacy lies in making an object or a force out of what is a general and abstract concept. Science does not *do* anything. Scientists do.

Fallacies can be innocent fun. We equivocate when we make a pun: "The army made me a private, but it did not respect my privacy." We express a hypothesis contrary to fact when we tease an opponent by saying, "I could have won that tennis match if I had really tried." Some logicians have even argued that there may be times when the use of an informal fallacy is legitimate. But fallacies can also lead us to misinterpret a situation or misjudge a person, a practice that may have serious consequences. False conversions like "Crooked politicians support high taxes; therefore, any politician who supports high taxes is crooked" may result in judging a person guilty by association. The false dilemma "All women are either feminists or victims of male chauvinism" fails to describe the world as it actually exists. The initial recommendation of the logician stands firm: Be clear about what you want to say, and be careful how you say it.

G. Conclusion

A chapter on philosophical thinking can only point to a traditional aspect of philosophy that has in modern times assumed a new vitality, usually under the rubric "critical thinking." It is important for those attracted to the field of philosophy to recognize that critical thinking and logical reasoning will present intellectual challenges and require special competence in "close-order" thinking. If students contemplate the pursuit of philosophy as an academic major or a professional career, they must face the likelihood that certain areas of philosophical study will demand intellectual skill and an intensive knowledge of various logical procedures in what has become a very technical and intricate discipline.

For those just beginning their explorations in philosophical territory, a few general remarks may help to keep expectations more realistic. Philosophical thinking demands that we be accurate and precise in the use of symbols and words. Structured language is essential to the process of communication, the mutual exchange of meaning. Clarity and consistency are among the criteria by which philosophical activity is judged. Logical reasoning is a time-honored philosophical trademark.

In the attempt to be clear and honest about what they have to communicate, those who take seriously the admonition to "think critically" come to realize that they must be very intimate with words in order to understand their deceptions and their limitations. Yet, despite fundamental differences and disagreements in basic philosophical postures, the study of the principles of sound reasoning does provide an excellent starting point for those who wish to understand and exchange ideas about significant issues and alternatives.

Our observations lead us to the inductive conclusion that the ability of people to reason logically provides no guarantee that they *will* reason logically. We propose a syllogism that students can analyze and evaluate in terms of its validity and its truth:

To think clearly, people must not let their emotions interfere with the process of logical reasoning.

But most people do allow personal feelings to intervene in the course of reaching inductive and deductive conclusions.

Therefore, most people do not think clearly.

Case Study and Discussion Questions

Case Study

The inherent suspicion of formal reasoning that characterizes some of the Eastern perspectives on the world is illustrated by the thought-provoking statement that "what can be expressed verbally is not Zen." The pronouncement conveys the idea that abstract symbols such as words and numbers are believed to erect a barrier to true understanding because they dissect and distort what is real and inclusive and interdependent—what is beyond words. Nevertheless, even such Eastern views are often expressed in words and transmitted in conventional symbols. This does not mean that the mystical elements in perspectives such as Taoism or Zen Buddhism can be fully and accurately translated into rational Western language, but it does underscore the philosophical obligation to treat words and concepts with special care.

1. What kinds of symbols, concepts, and arguments might be most useful in trying to understand a posture that differs so much from the views traditionally considered in the study of Western philosophy?

2. Is there any merit in the deep suspicion of formal reasoning that characterizes many of the Eastern views about humans and the world?

Discussion Questions

1. When so many of the close personal relationships between human beings seem to be based on subtle emotional factors, is it or is it not desirable to insist on logical exactness in all of our interpersonal communications?

2. What are the best reasons for demanding that a formal education include rigorous practice in the construction of sound arguments?

3. In an age of technological complexity, what are the advantages and disadvantages of putting everything into a form that can be handled precisely by a computer?

4. What are some examples of the informal fallacies commonly used by advertisers and politicians in their efforts to influence the attitudes or behavior of people in modern American society?

Suggested Readings

Barry, Vincent E. *Invitation to Critical Thinking*. New York: Holt, Rinehart & Winston, 1984.

Beardsley, Monroe C. *Thinking Straight: Principles of Reasoning for Readers and Writers*. 4th ed. Englewood Cliffs, NJ: Prentice-Hall, 1975.

Caton, Charles E., ed. *Philosophy and Ordinary Language*. Urbana: University of Illinois Press, 1963.

Chase, Stuart. *The Tyranny of Words*. New York: Harcourt Brace, 1959.

Copi, Irving M. *Introduction to Logic*. 7th ed. New York: Macmillan, 1986.

Damer, T. Edward. *Attacking Faulty Reasoning*. 2d ed. Belmont, CA: Wadsworth, 1987.

Fischer, David Hackett. *Historians' Fallacies: Toward a Logic of Historical Thought*. New York: Harper & Row, 1970.

Hook, Sidney, ed. *Language and Philosophy: A Symposium*. Washington Square, NY: New York University Press, 1969.

Langer, Susanne K. *Philosophy in a New Key: A Study in the Symbolism of Reason, Rite, and Art*. 3d ed. New York: New American Library (Mentor Book), 1951.

Michalos, Alex C. *Improving Your Reasoning*. Englewood Cliffs, NJ: Prentice-Hall, 1970.

Rorty, Richard, ed. *Linguistic Turn: Recent Essays in Philosophical Method*. Chicago: University of Chicago Press, 1971.

Rosenberg, Jay F. *The Practice of Philosophy: A Handbook for Beginners*. Englewood Cliffs, NJ: Prentice-Hall, 1978.

Ruggiero, Vincent Ryan. *Beyond Feelings: A Guide to Critical Thinking*. 2d ed. Palo Alto, CA: Mayfield, 1984.

Russell, Bertrand. *The Problems of Philosophy*. New York: Oxford University Press, 1955.

Scriven, Michael. *Reasoning*. New York: McGraw-Hill, 1976.

Toulmin, Steven, Richard Rieke, and Allan Janik. *An Introduction to Reasoning*. New York: Macmillan, 1979.

Whitehead, Alfred North. *Symbolism: Its Meaning and Effect*. New York: Capricorn Books, 1955.

CHAPTER 3
Perception and Truth

A. Questions to Consider

- Can I trust my senses to tell me about the world, or are my senses too often deceived?
- How can a physical organ like the brain produce intangible concepts and ideas?
- Do my thoughts accurately represent things the way they actually exist?
- Do things exist when they are not being perceived? If a tree falls in the forest and no one is there to hear it, does it make any sound?
- What does it really mean to say that a statement is true?
- What means are at our disposal for ascertaining the truth?
- Is truth something that must be discovered, or is truth a human invention?
- Can something be true today but not tomorrow?
- Is something true because I believe it sincerely?
- Does understanding the nature of truth make any practical difference in our lives?

B. Introduction

As a way of leading into the three major substantive areas of traditional philosophy, we will stop here to consider briefly two important philosophical issues that people have faced repeatedly in their attempts to make sense of their lives and their world. The issues are concerned with the "process of perception" and the "nature of truth." A consideration of the alternatives proposed under these headings will direct attention once more to the core problems in philosophical study.

Both of the issues present themselves whenever there is an attempt to make a distinction between *appearance* and *reality*. Intense philosophical investigation has been directed toward resolving the human dilemma expressed in the often-voiced statement "Things are not what they seem." Attempts to explain the differences between what the world "looks like" and what it "is" have evoked thoughtful responses for centuries. Is there or is there not something more basic underneath or beyond what we commonly observe to be so? Is there or is there not something structured and certain behind or inside of what is often experienced as cloudy or changeable? Attempts to answer questions like these lead directly to deeper levels of philosophical inquiry where philosophers make special efforts to clarify the distinction between perception and external reality.

It is appropriate, therefore, that in an introductory book designed to be as concise as possible, the problem of perception and the problem of truth be confronted in the same chapter. The study of either one typically involves a consideration of the other. Furthermore, a preliminary discussion of the alternative views held on perception and truth should aid in understanding the complex epistemological and metaphysical positions to be analyzed later.

C. Perception

As it is commonly used today, the term "perception" refers to the psychological process by which we become aware of ordinary objects such as rocks, trees, and tables when our sense organs are stimulated. For most of us, seeing and hearing are such familiar processes that we accept them uncritically as "natural" activities and seldom analyze the dynamics involved. But in philosophy, **perception** may have several meanings, for here it is necessary to describe more precisely the nature of the relationship or "connection" between the knower and the known. The exact character of the relationship is a matter in fundamental dispute.

We will first look at the extreme and middle positions: then we will present two positions that attempt to mediate on either side of the center.

1. A Perception Continuum

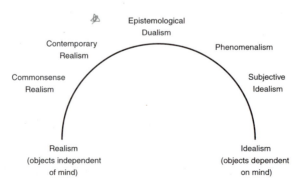

2. Theories of Perception: Alternative Views

a. *Commonsense realism.* Commonsense **realism**, or what is also called **naïve realism**, is the view of perception held by those, such as the eighteenth-century Scottish philosopher Thomas Reid and the twentieth-century British philosopher G. E. Moore, who believe that when they perceive an object, they experience that object exactly as it actually exists. If an object is perceived as yellow, round, soft, tart, and fragrant (for example, a grapefruit), commonsense realists conclude that what they have perceived are the actual color, shape, texture, taste, and smell of the object exactly as that object is materially constituted. There is no distinction between what the senses detect and what is grasped mentally. The object exists in its own right separate and apart from the human perceiver, but what that person experiences or perceives is the object itself. No distinction is made between how an object *appears* and what that object really *is*. This is the straightforward and uncritical view of perception that many people take for granted and apply with confidence in their everyday lives.

Critiques of Commonsense Realism

1.

Commonsense realism is often charged with being naïve because it does not provide an adequate explanation for certain recurrent perceptual experiences such as dreams, hallucinations, and mirages. Commonsense realism does not recognize what many of us have learned: that we must often make an important distinction between what our senses convey to us and what we know to be the case. On a dry summer day we notice that the highway in the distance before us appears to be wet, but we have learned that, when we move forward for a closer look, we often find no trace of water on the road.

2.

On critical examination, commonsense realism discloses some disconcerting contradictions. Either it suggests that a perceived object exists in the mind as a material thing (which tends to contradict the view that the object has a separate and independent existence) or it asserts that objects themselves may have contradictory properties (such as a straight stick that appears to be bent when it is partially immersed in water).

b. *Epistemological dualism.* When certain kinds of deeper-level questions were asked about perception, the naïve realists found it difficult to provide satisfactory answers. The inability of commonsense realism to address a growing list of disturbing questions led to the development of a more complex theory to explain the connection between the knower and what is known. Epistemological dualism, or what is also called the **representative theory of perception**, is a theory originally proposed by John Locke, an English philosopher of the seventeenth century who undertook an extensive and systematic analysis of the elements in the perceptual process. According to Locke, there is a real world of objects that exists "out there" apart from and independent of a human being. But there is also a world of *ideas* that exist in their own right as psychological entities in the human *mind* (and "mind" cannot be equated with the physical organ called the "brain"). Both objects and ideas exist, and they are separate and distinct from one another. Locke argued that in the human process of perception, external objects stimulate the sense organs. The resulting sensations trigger ideas or conceptions in the human mind, and, in this way, the mind perceives, or makes connection with, what exists externally. The mind produces a conceptual picture or idea of an object. The epistemological dualist views the human sense organs as cameras that take "pictures" of objects. But just as a photograph of a child is not the same as the child itself, a mental image is not the same as the external object it depicts. It is a representation. The sense organs "copy" or "represent" the things in the world outside, and then the human mind develops or processes the sensations and in so doing produces ideas about external things. The dualism is evident. External *things* exist as objects; internal *representations* or "pictures" exist as subjective ideas in the mind.

Critiques of Epistemological Dualism

1.

Epistemological dualism is subject to the same criticism directed at commonsense realism; our senses do not always take clear, sharp pictures. But the theory faces the additional objection that minds do not always organize and interpret perceptions in consistent and mutually verifiable ways, as experience with the Rorschach inkblot test points out.

2.

The camera analogy used in the representative theory of perception has other shortcomings. What the camera "sees" depends on the location of the camera with respect to direction and distance from the object of perception. If direction and distance are varied, pictures of the same object will not coincide. Climbers in the Himalayas noted that the native Sherpas applied different names to a single mountain when its features were viewed from different sides. The people of the local area, with nothing but their different "pictures"' to guide them, apparently did not realize that they were looking at one and the same mountain. Representations, in and of themselves, provide insufficient grounds for interpreting and communicating about the world of objects.

c. *Subjective idealism.* At the opposite extreme from realism on the perception continuum is found the position identified as **subjective idealism**. This theory of perception, which also goes by the name of **mentalism**, was proposed by George Berkeley, an eighteenth-century Irish philosopher.

Dissatisfaction with the position that there are two separate realities is shown in the effort to develop a **monistic** theory—one based on the conviction that there is but one underlying reality. Berkeley agreed with Locke that all we can know are the ideas produced by sensations. But Berkeley raised a crucial question: If all we can know are the ideas produced by sensations, what possible grounds do we have for inferring the actual existence of external objects that cause sensations in the first place? How can we be sure that our ideas "copy" any *thing* at all? Berkeley could find no justification for asserting the independent existence of objects or external things. All that we perceive are the sensations from which our minds construct ideas. Perception is viewed as the process by which sensations are interpreted and organized by the mind to produce ideas. Ideas are all that the mind has to work with. The reasoning mind arranges and relates the ideas in a pattern of perception. Berkeley argued that what a person perceives as "real" is made up entirely of ideas in the mind. His conclusion is summarized in what has become a famous maxim of the subjective idealists: "To be is to be perceived."

If subjective idealism is carried to an extreme and proposed as a theory of perception applying to a single individual—to the *one* subject who perceives—it results in what philosophers call **solipsism**. This position maintains that there is only one perceiver—myself. Therefore, reality is limited to what I, the solipsist, perceive it to be. The world ceases to exist when I, the only perceiving subject, stop thinking about it. To most people this position appears fantastic and excessive, so to avoid the excesses of solipsism the cautious subjective idealist relies on some outside source for ideas. Berkeley avoided the absurdity of the extreme position by introducing God as the ultimate source of ideas. Reality consists of ideas, but ideas have a continuous existence because God continually has them "in mind."

> *There was a young man who said, "God*
> *Must think it exceedingly odd,*
> *If he finds that this tree*
> *Continues to be*
> *When there's no one about in the Quad."*[1]
>
> —*Ronald Knox*

> *Reply.*
> *"Dear Sir: Your astonishment's odd:*
> *I am always about in the Quad.*
> *And that's why the tree*
> *Will continue to be*
> *Since observed by*
>
> —*Yours faithfully,*
> —*God."*
> —*Anonymous*

---

[1]Reprinted by permission of A. P. Watt & Son, Literary Agents of Monsignor R. A. Knox's Estate.

Critiques of Subjective Idealism

1.

Subjective idealism has not been a very popular theory of perception in Western philosophy. Some theorists hold that science gives only knowledge of correlations among perceptions and has no need to assume the existence of external objects. But the average person believes that science has extended our knowledge and improved our lives by dealing very directly with a real world of objects. Furthermore, the world of practical affairs is conducted on the assumption of a natural universe of material things that exist in their own right and that human beings must take into account.

2.

Another objection to idealistic theories of perception is raised when it comes to the problem of proof. It is argued that if there is no outside material reality to which we can refer, then we can never be sure that any two people perceive the same thing in the same way and that no common denominator can be established for assessing the accuracy or inaccuracy of our perceptions. Furthermore, if to be is to be perceived, how do we know that the mind, which does the perceiving, exists? Those who defend idealistic theories are often found to express quite different—and quite contradictory—views.

d. *Phenomenalism—mediating idealism and dualism.* Immanuel Kant, the famous eighteenth-century German philosopher, fully appreciated the impact that the ideas of the scientific revolution had had on life and thought in Western civilization, but he was convinced that in the stampede to explain everything in scientific terms, something of critical importance had been neglected. He argued that the philosophical claims of **idealism** that had been so strongly championed by Plato many centuries before were now being ignored or denigrated in mankind's love affair with science. The effort to restore the balance between the legitimate demands of both experiences and ideas is illustrated in Kant's theory of perception, in which the claims of science and reason are reconciled. Kant's theory of perception has come to be called **phenomenalism**.

Kant argued that external things exist but that human beings do not perceive those things as they really are. Human beings can never perceive a thing-in-itself, the **noumenon**. There is no way to know or prove what a thing really is out there by itself. All that can be known is how the thing *appears*, the **phenomenon**. The noumenon stimulates the senses, but the raw sensations are translated by the mind into concepts. What is perceived is not the object (the thing-in-itself) but only the phenomenon, the *idea* of the object produced by our minds. Thus, Kant began his theory of perception by making a distinction between the *form* of knowledge and the *content* of knowledge. The form is the way the mind structures what is fed in. The content comes from sensory experience. The senses provide data such as colors, sounds, and smells, but these data are discrete and singular. Senses do not reveal relationships or categories or causes or laws. It takes the mind to integrate and interpret the data presented by the senses.

Kant argued that the mind was constructed of structural categories by which the sense data are ordered into patterns that can be recognized or known. Because these structures, or forms, must be present *before* the data of the senses can be organized into meaning, Kant concluded that they must be **a priori**. That is, structured categories for organizing and interpreting experience exist in their own right *prior* to the introduction of the specific content of sensory stimulation. Just as a container must have a certain shape to hold a liquid, the mind must have a certain form in order to hold knowledge. To know an object involves more than a succession of sensory stimulations. It requires the ordering of these sensations by a priori categories of the mind that are intuitive and thus independent of sensations. It is because forms preexist as intuitions in the human mind that human beings can claim to perceive. Perception depends on form as well as content. Both reason and experience play a part. "Conceptions without perceptions are empty; perceptions without conceptions are blind."

Kant faced the same sort of problem that bothered his predecessor, Locke. But Kant's phenomenalistic theory places a far greater stress on the claims of idealism. It insists on the fundamental role of ideas in accounting for human perception.

Critiques of Phenomenalism

1.

Phenomenalism must face the objection that the *content* of knowledge depends on sense organs that are far from perfect. Furthermore, it cannot assure us that everyone's senses are activated by the same stimuli. If everything that people can know is reduced to sensory stimuli, and if we can never know things as they really are, in and of themselves, how can we be even reasonably sure that our perception and the resulting knowledge are not fundamentally illusory? The phenomenalist appeal to a priori forms does not solve the problem because there is no agreement on what the a priori forms are.

2.

What difference does it really make whether we distinguish phenomena from noumena? Of what importance or relevance is this distinction if the noumena remain totally beyond the reach of perception and thus can never be known?

e. *Contemporary realism—mediating realism and dualism.* Modern theories of perception are very complex, and many technical disputes arise. But contemporary realists, such as E. B. Holt and W. P. Montague, tend to accept the view that the external, or objective, world is actually present and that it is open to human sensory experience. Moreover, they agree that in the process of perceiving an object, that object is not changed. What we experience with our senses, what the scientists detect with their instruments, is not changed by the activity of observation. It is true that our awareness is *selective*, but that does nothing to modify or constitute the object being perceived. In this view, perception *reveals* things to a human organism—things to which that organism may adapt or toward which it may take some action. Perception is viewed as a *process* by which connections are made between the functioning nervous system and the outside world. Through sensory stimulation, the brain comes to infer the properties of things. Contemporary realism as a theory of perception postulates (1) a world of objects, (2) a conscious organism or functioning brain, and (3) a natural process by which the object and the organism are connected.

Contemporary realists typically propose theories that are subject to modification as a result of new evidence or experience. They tend to be suspicious of closed systems or absolute conclusions. They attempt to develop theories from which the most productive inferences can be drawn and from which the most confident action can proceed. Perception is viewed as one aspect of mankind's reciprocal interaction with its natural environment, and the theories of explanation rely heavily on the application of the scientific method to the problems that are confronted. (See "The Scientific Method" in Chapter 4.)

Critiques of Contemporary Realism

1.

Contemporary realists are open to the charge that their theories are nothing more than camouflaged dualism and are thus subject to the same criticisms leveled at dualistic theories. How can a physical event cause a mental event? If objects are truly separate and independent, how can they in any sense affect an organism and cause a reliable perception? Unless the "connection" between object and perceiver is more thoroughly explained, the whole process of perception remains a vast mystery.

2.

Further dissatisfaction with contemporary realism is expressed by those who are not content with any theory that does not rest on unshakable foundations. These critics find the trial-and-error experience of fallible human beings to be an unsound basis for the construction of reliable explanations. Answers based on inference from experience are highly variable and provide no grounds for certainty. If awareness is selective and validation is pragmatic, there is little hope of counteracting human bias.

If a theory of perception does not refer to some clearly fixed, nonhuman criterion, then that theory cannot discriminate between adequate and inadequate proposals and cannot claim any true explanatory power.

It should now be clear that to evaluate the theories of perception, some other fundamental philosophical questions must be asked. Too many interconnected issues are as yet unresolved. Attention can be directed to upcoming discussions of the nature of truth, the broader theories of knowledge, and the nature of what is ultimately real. Theories of perception are based on crucial assumptions, many of which have yet to be identified and analyzed.

D. Truth

Truth is a difficult concept to define because the word "truth" has long stood as a symbol for such a variety of our deepest concerns and highest aspirations. Stubborn zeal has characterized the human search for truth. Especially in Western civilization there has been strong support for the conviction that the hunger for truth is one of humankind's noblest passions. Science and religion alike claim to seek and to profess the truth. But what *is* truth? When this question is examined carefully, it becomes apparent that there are quite different ways of viewing truth. Three alternative stands on the nature of truth will be explored in this chapter.

1. A Truth Continuum

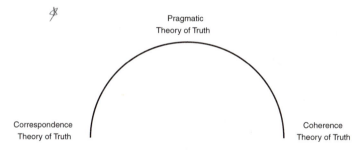

2. Theories of Truth: Alternative Views

a. *The correspondence theory.* "True" and "false" are terms typically used to assess the quality of a statement. **Correspondence theory** holds that a statement is true if it *corresponds* to objective reality; that is, an expression of truth is one that states a fact or describes an event as it really and independently exists. The fact or event is "there," and its independent existence is affirmed by the experience or perception of a human being. Proof that it is "really there" is established by one or more other human beings who also experience or perceive it and who then confirm the original statement. If I say, "There is an airplane flying overhead," you can look up and see whether my statement is correct. If you see the airplane, you will no doubt conclude that I have spoken the truth. We will be in agreement that something actually exists in the air above us and that the word "airplane" accurately describes what it is. Further discussion might reveal that we disagree on the particular *kind* of airplane it was or on the speed of its flight, but my original statement that there was indeed an airplane flying overhead would not be judged false.

Scientists constantly direct our attention to the "facts," or the data, and stress the need for accurate perceptions. Scientists then insist on the objective verifiability of our observations, which means that the same facts we have reference to must be observable by others. Disagreement about the existence of pertinent facts or differences in the reported perceptions of those facts means that any statement made about the facts is open to serious question.

These disagreements—and the doubts that result—increase the possibility that the statement may not be true. Under such conditions, the statement might indeed be judged false. But, in the final analysis, supporters of the correspondence theory of truth argue that accurate perceptions or observations are a sufficient basis for reporting the existing state of affairs and that accurate perceptions precisely stated cannot result in reasonable disagreement.

The correspondence theory of truth is likely to figure prominently in the arguments to prove the commonsense theory of perception and certain aspects of the perception theories of contemporary realism and epistemological dualism.

Critiques of the Correspondence Theory

1.

Certain difficulties with the correspondence theory are encountered when we expand the hypothetical illustration involving the airplane. Suppose a third person were to look into the sky and say, "The two of you have poor eyesight. That is not an airplane; it is a hawk." Now who is most accurately describing what is actually up there? We know that each person does not have the same visual acuity. We also believe that at times (in dreams, for example) people see what is not really there. Perception can be distorted. If each of us persists in our conviction, how is it possible to decide who is speaking the truth? Few people would be satisfied with bringing the issue to a vote and letting the majority decide, for one of the things that the history of science has tended to demonstrate is that the majority is often mistaken on points of fact.

2.

The correspondence theory does not help us to resolve questions of truth in those fields where there are no "facts," in the sense of things capable of being verified or measured by objective criteria. There is no way of demonstrating whether or not the principles of love or justice are true. There is no basis on which the correspondence theory can assert the truth or falsity of the belief that a human being possesses an eternal soul. Or take the case of a theory such as evolution, which is defended by citing verifiable and measurable "facts." How do we decide whether or not the theory of evolution "corresponds" with those "facts"? Evolution itself is not an object or a thing "out there" that we can perceive as existing or not existing.

The correspondence theory has another weakness. Within the theory itself there is no way to judge the adequacy of the generalizations being used. Since most of our knowledge consists of generalizations, this is a serious short-coming.

---

b. *The coherence theory.* The **coherence theory** of truth maintains that truth is a property exhibited by a related group of consistent propositions. A particular statement, or **proposition**, is true if it is totally integrated with other statements or propositions already established as part of the whole system. New propositions can be added to the conceptual foundation to form a more intricate pattern. As long as a new proposition can be incorporated in such a way that it does not contradict or invalidate the basic propositions (or any propositions derived therefrom), then the new proposition can be affirmed as true; what does not fit cannot claim to be true. The coherence theory can be described as the "hang-together" theory.

Mathematics illustrates the theory of coherence. A mathematical system is built, step by step, from a certain number of basic propositions. Plane geometry affords a familiar example. Using Euclid's geometry as a model, Plato developed a coherence theory of truth. He believed that he had discovered a means for attaining truth that owed nothing to observation or sensory experience beyond what could be represented in a symbolic or diagrammatic way. Plato was persuaded that he had discovered the true and perfect world of ideal (or non-sensible) **Forms**, which are connected to one another by eternal and necessary relations that the reasoning mind alone can trace. This world of ideas, when grasped by thought, reveals a complete system of immutable and necessary truth.

Scientific theories also exhibit a pattern of coherence. In general, a theory is acceptable only if it is consistent with already established laws or principles. For example, although there are claims that extrasensory perception (ESP) has been experimentally demonstrated, the theory is not widely accepted because it fails to cohere with many of the organized principles on which physical science relies. The same would apply to phenomena such as UFOs.

The coherence theory is illustrated in the world of everyday affairs by the person who wants some center to his life—some reliable categories to use in ordering and classifying the confusion. Countless stimuli attack him. Contradictory opinions and judgments are imposed on him. Without some established criteria by which he can discriminate, organize, or judge, he feels lost and directionless. If he can find one or more basic propositions worthy of his allegiance, he then has the power to integrate his experience, separate what is worth keeping from what is not, and organize his knowledge. In short, using the principle of coherence gives him a way to organize and view his life.

Kant's phenomenalistic theory of perception would place heavy reliance on the kind of proof afforded by the coherence theory of truth. The coherence theory might also be called on to defend the part of Locke's perception theory of epistemological dualism that deals with mental representations or ideas.

Critiques of the Coherence Theory

1.

One of the difficulties encountered in the coherence theory is that it sometimes relies on beginning postulates or assumptions whose "truth" cannot be demonstrated or proved. No "proof" can be offered that one set of starting assumptions is ultimately better than another. Within the coherence tradition itself, philosophers have violently disagreed about the basic postulates on which coherence systems of truth should be constructed. Plato's basic assumption that ideas are fixed and unchanging stands in dramatic contrast to the assertion of Pierre Teilhard de Chardin, late Roman Catholic priest and paleontologist, that evolutionary change is the fundamental characteristic of all things. Plato and Teilhard erected their coherence theories on radically different foundations. Even if coherence is the criterion of truth, a person could, by putting faith in a particular coherence theory, run the risk of being unalterably wrong because the starting premises were inadequate or incorrect; thus, one's *whole system* of "true" facts may actually be wrong. Yet how could a person distinguish being *consistently* true from being *consistently* false using only the coherence theory? Furthermore, since it takes two propositions to apply the coherence theory (something has to cohere with something else), there is one proposition to which this theory cannot be applied—namely, that truth means coherence.

2.

Coherence theorists not only fail to agree on a starting point, but when they get around to integrating propositions from many and different areas of experience, they also reach no consensus. Religious and scientific worldviews continue to express irreconcilable contradictions and inconsistencies—no matter how beautifully coherent each may be as a separate system.

c. *The pragmatic theory.* We now shift our attention to a criterion of truth that seeks to avoid both the limitations and the extremes of either the correspondence or the coherence theory. The distinctively American approach to the problem is expressed in the philosophies of men like C. S. Peirce, William James, John Dewey, and C. I. Lewis and is called **pragmatism**.

Pragmatism takes the stand that what works is what is true. Truth can be defined only in terms of *consequences*. According to the pragmatist, a statement is true if it accurately describes a situation or relationship on which a person can act in order to achieve a desired result. In this view human beings in their ongoing activities create truth. As James put it, "Truth is *made,* just as health, wealth, and strength are made, in the course of experience." Truth is judged in terms of its effectiveness in assisting people to integrate their knowledge, predict the course of events, or achieve a desired goal. The pragmatist is content to find truth in the successful completion of an invention (for example, a computer), in a theory by which a course of events can be more accurately predicted (for example, a theory of personality development), or in the organization of life experiences into a pattern that satisfies human needs or desires (for example, a democratic form of government). For the pragmatist, truth has a "cash value." It pays off.

The pragmatic theory of truth is humanity-centered; people make truth. Pragmatists do not concern themselves with absolute or ultimate truth. For them truth does not possess an independent existence; it is not "out there" waiting to be discovered. Pragmatists adopt the position that truth is being continuously shaped by human thought and action as particular hypotheses are subjected to the practical test of action and its consequences. They often point to the activities carried out in a scientific experiment as an example of truth making.

The pragmatic theory of truth has been called on in many cases to prove the claims of contemporary realism as a theory of perception. Final judgment rests on the answer to the question "Does it work?"

Critiques of the Pragmatic Theory

1.

Many people are totally dissatisfied with viewing truth as tentative and changeable. They find no security or hope in a theory of truth that is not solidly grounded in the stable nature of things. If the nature of what is so is not definite and clearly identifiable, it has no right to be parading under the banner of "truth."

2.

More sophisticated critics point out that there is no necessary connection between what is ultimately true, on the one hand, and what just happens to work or what it is useful to believe, on the other. They note that the human mind is small and its days brief, and they argue that there is more to the universe than what stumbling seekers might happen to find or what nearsighted viewers might happen to see. In short, they maintain that humankind is not the measure of all things and that truth cannot be based on the fallible judgments of finite human beings. These critics might accept the proposition that "what is true works" while rejecting the pragmatic assertion that "what works is true."

One does not necessarily have to choose only one of these alternatives. In fact, most of us probably use each of them at one time or another. On the same day a person might employ the correspondence theory to determine whether the announcement of a solar eclipse is true, then decide the truth of a claim made about God's action in the world by appealing to the coherence theory, and, finally, use the pragmatic theory to test the truth of her belief that a loose wire is responsible for the malfunction of her stereo.

E. Conclusion

Truth and perception are issues that have long attracted the interest of philosophers. The discussion in this chapter may have prompted the suspicion that a particular point of view taken on one of these issues is associated with a specific stand on the other. That may well be the case. An overall philosophical perspective typically exhibits a number of predictable relationships among the kinds of answers proposed to a variety of more limited questions. It is hard to divorce one's stand on the nature of truth from one's stand on the kind of activity involved in perceiving the world.

It may also have occurred to the reader that truth theories and forms of logic can exhibit interesting parallels. The correspondence theory of truth and inductive logic have some common philosophical characteristics. Similarly, the coherence theory of truth and deductive logic are usually expressed in certain philosophically compatible ways.

The discussions of logic, perception, and truth have better prepared us to study even broader questions about the nature, source, and validity of knowledge. These issues will be explored in the next chapter.

Case Study and Discussion Questions

Case Study

In the Declaration of Independence, many of the founding fathers of the United States of America signed a statement that read in part as follows: "We hold these truths to be self-evident, that all men are created equal, that they are endowed by their Creator with certain unalienable Rights, that among these are Life, Liberty and the pursuit of Happiness."

1. Which theory of truth do you think provides the basic justification for the concept "truth" as it is used in the above citation?

2. Is it "self-evident" that all people are "created equal"?

Discussion Questions

1. What view of perception offers the most reasonable means by which human beings can make their way in a complex world?

2. Does it or does it not make sense to insist that how each person "sees" things depends entirely on that person's unique time, place, and subjective judgment? on one's cultural background?

3. Which theory of truth offers the best defense for the argument that "the truth will make you free"?

4. Is the search for truth a compelling human aspiration, or should human beings heed Sartre's advice to settle for an error that is liveable?

5. Would any one of the theories of truth adequately help us to determine the existence of God, Napoleon, *and* Antarctica?

Suggested Readings

Armstrong, D. M. *Belief, Truth, and Knowledge*. New York: Cambridge University Press, 1973.

Austin, J. L. *Sense and Sensibilia*. New York: Oxford University Press (Galaxy Books), 1964.

Ayer, A. J. *Language, Truth, and Logic*. New York: Dover, 1952.

Berkeley, George. *Three Dialogues Between Hylas and Philonous*. Edited by Robert M. Adams. Indianapolis: Hackett, 1979.

Bradley, Francis Herbert. "On Truth and Coherence." In *Essays on Truth and Reality*. Oxford: Clarendon Press, 1914.

Brown, James I. *Observation and Objectivity*. New York: Oxford University Press, 1987.

Dretske, Fred I. *Seeing and Knowing*. Chicago: University of Chicago Press, 1969.

Fish, Stanley. *Is There a Text in This Class?* Cambridge, MA: Harvard University Press. 1980.

Gadamer, Hans-Georg. *Truth and Method*. 2d ed. Translation revised by Joel Weinsheimer and Donald G. Marshall. New York: Crossroad, 1991.

Hirst, P. J. *Perception and the External World*. New York: Macmillan, 1965.

James, William. *Pragmatism and the Meaning of Truth*. Cambridge, MA: Harvard University Press, 1978.

Locke, John. *An Essay Concerning Human Understanding*. New York: New American Library (Meridian Book), 1964.

Merleau-Ponty, Maurice. *The Phenomenology of Perception*. Translated by Colin Smith. Atlantic Highlands, NJ: Humanities Press, 1962.

Ornstein, R. E. *The Psychology of Consciousness*. 2d ed. New York: Harcourt Brace Jovanovich, 1977.

Quine, W. V., and J. S. Ullian. *The Web of Belief*. 2d ed. New York: Random House, 1978.

Russell, Bertrand. *The Problems of Philosophy*. New York: Oxford University Press, 1959.

Ryle, Gilbert. *The Concept of Mind*. New York: Barnes & Noble, 1975.

Swartz, Robert J. *Perceiving, Sensing and Knowing*. Berkeley: University of California Press, 1977.

White, Alan P. *Truth*. New York: Doubleday (Anchor), 1970.

CHAPTER 4

Epistemology: How We Know

A. Questions to Consider

- Do people actually *learn* something new, or do they merely become aware of what they already know?
- Can something be true "just for me" or does truth mean "true for everyone"?
- Are there different *ways* by which we come to know different *kinds* of things?
- Does the scientist have the only reliable method for knowing anything?
- How is it possible to argue or even communicate with those who claim they "just know"?
- By what standards shall I judge the accuracy or usefulness of a way of knowing?
- Is knowledge a "picture" of reality or a plan of action for controlling it?
- Is it possible to know anything for sure?

B. Introduction

Epistemology is the branch of philosophy concerned with the nature, sources, limitations, and validity of knowledge. It deals specifically with theories of knowledge, systematic efforts to explain the nature and content of thought and to describe the process by which human beings acquire reliable knowledge. The term "epistemology" identifies the philosophical activity directed toward questions about how and what a knower knows.

Epistemology is intimately involved in the development and analysis of criteria (the plural form of the word **criterion**). Criteria are the standards by which something is measured or judged. To establish a basis for comparing and evaluating judgments about the accuracy or extent of human knowledge, the philosopher must analyze the various criteria used in the process of knowing. The nature of what can be known and the process of knowing it can be fruitfully discussed only if we can establish precise criteria. Each of the alternative theories of knowing presented in this chapter should be critically analyzed to determine the adequacy of the basic criteria on which it depends.

For many human beings, the simple and direct way of knowing through trial and error results in an epistemology that is relatively unsophisticated by philosophical standards. It simply works, and why or how it works is not something to be analyzed or pondered. This is not a bad way for most of us to ricochet through life and accumulate from personal experience what we think of as knowledge. However, trial-and-error procedures involve the distinct possibility that the consequences might be disastrous or fatal. Trying again may not turn out to be a viable option. Trial and error has its staunch adherents, but there has been a long and intensive search for other ways of knowing that are more rigorous, more systematic, and more dependable.

In fact, since at least the time of Plato (in his *Theaetetus,* for instance) the classic philosophical definition of knowledge has been "*justified* true belief." That is to say, knowledge is more than mere opinion that may or may not be correct. Knowledge involves beliefs or assertions for which you have reasons or "warrant." In one of his dialogues, Plato illustrated the difference between a mere opinion (that turns out to be true) and knowledge by comparing a blind man who comes to a fork in the road and just happens to take the right path to his destination and a man who can actually see which path will lead him to his destination.

As this chapter will demonstrate, philosophers give different justifications or warrants for their assertions. For instance, some insist on logical demonstration, while others depend on sense experience. There are those who argue that our beliefs make up a web of interpretations that organize our experience; pull on one belief and the whole web moves. That means that the project of finding warrant for our beliefs, whether through reason or experience, becomes problematic since the criteria for recognizing adequate interpretations from inadequate ones seem to be spun out of the same silk. If there are no nonarbitrary criteria by which we can judge all systems of belief, then we seem to be left with relativism—no knowledge (in the classic sense), just each to his own web.

C. An Epistemological Continuum

To provide an initial contrast from which further analysis may proceed, we present a sample continuum featuring three theories of knowledge that have made strong claims for priority in Western philosophy. The issue can be framed between the epistemological alternatives proposed by the empiricists and the rationalists, with the scientific method occupying a position somewhere between the two.

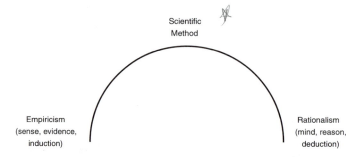

All three might agree that knowledge comes from the relation of mind to experience, but they differ on the issue of where to place the primary emphasis. Other epistemological postures will be presented following the initial comparison of empiricism, rationalism, and the scientific method.

D. The Classical Positions

1. Empiricism

The search for knowledge that is both absolute and certain has been fervent and continuous. However, since at least the time of Aristotle, there has been a strong epistemological tradition based solely on human experience, not directed toward the possibility of achieving absolute knowledge. This tradition is exemplified in the doctrine of **empiricism**. Empiricists argue that it is unreasonable to set a goal of absolute and all-inclusive knowledge—especially when there is close at hand the power to increase practical knowledge by slower but dependable methods. Empiricists are content to build a system of knowledge that has a high probability of being true even though its absolute certainty cannot be guaranteed. Empiricists find that high probability is a stable and realistic foundation for the knowledge accessible to human beings.

Empiricists insist that human knowledge is acquired from experience—that it is **a posteriori**, or postexperiential. If we were trying to convince an empiricist that something exists, the empiricist would say, "Show me!" On points of fact she would have to be assured by her own experience. If we told her that there is a tiger in her bathtub, she would first demand that we tell her how we arrived at such a conclusion. If we explained that we saw the tiger in the bathtub, the empiricist would listen to this report of our experiences, but she would accept it only on the grounds that she or someone else could check the accuracy of our claim by taking a firsthand look for herself.

Two aspects of empirical theory are brought out in the illustration. The first is the distinction between the knower and the thing known. The knower is the subject, and the thing known is the object. There is a real world of external facts and objects that the person can perceive. Second, the truth or verification of facts or objects depends on their being experienced by other human beings. To be meaningful to the empiricist, statements about the existence or nonexistence of anything must meet the criterion of public verifiability.

A more complicated problem arises when statements are made about objects or events no longer available for direct verification. When it is asserted that George Washington chopped down his father's cherry tree, empiricists would have to be convinced of at least three things: first, that the words "George Washington" and "cherry tree" refer to the kinds of things that one does experience; second, that someone was there and actually observed the event; and third, that if empiricists had been there themselves, they also could have observed the event.

Another aspect of empiricism is its dependence on the principle of *regularity*. Knowledge of the natural world is based on a perception of the regular way in which things behave. Nature is orderly. By describing the way things have happened in the past or by describing the uniform ways in which similar things behave in the present, the empiricist feels justified in making predictions about the *probable* behavior of things in the future.

Besides appealing to regularity, the empiricist invokes the principle of *resemblance*. Resemblance means that those phenomena that are experienced as identical or similar really are enough alike to warrant making generalizations about them. If we learn that one banana is tasty and nutritious, we want to be reasonably sure that the next object that looks and tastes like what we call a banana is not going to be fatally toxic. The more experience we have with banana-like things, the more reliable is our knowledge about what bananas are and what they mean in our experience. Resemblance involves the human ability to abstract likenesses from distinctive objects or perceptions.

Typically, empiricists base their theory of knowledge on the experiences provided by our five senses. John Locke, who has been called the father of British empiricism, proposed a theory of knowledge in which the features we have discussed are combined in a clear fashion. Locke claimed that the human mind at birth is like a smooth wax tablet (*tabula rasa* in Latin) on which sensory data etch themselves. As life progresses, more and more sensory impressions are transcribed. From the combination and comparison of sensations, complex ideas are produced. Locke viewed the mind as a receptacle that receives and stores sensations. Knowledge results from the natural activity of the mind as it combines basic sensations. It is like a pantry with one opening (the senses) through which cans (sensations) enter to be kept and rearranged on the shelves.

Those who insist that all knowledge can be reduced to sensory experience and who further insist that what cannot be traced to specific sense experiences is not true knowledge are called **sensationalists**, or **radical empiricists**. Modern radical empiricists might paraphrase Locke in the following manner: Knowledge is the result of a complex neurochemical process in which external objects stimulate one or more sense organs and cause a material or electrical change in the physical organ called the brain.

Critiques of Empiricism

1.

Empiricism is grounded in experience. But what does the term "experience" mean? At times it refers only to the stimulation of the senses. At other times it appears to refer to a sensation plus a judgment. As a concept, experience does not directly refer to the objective reality so dear to the empiricists. The critics point out that there is nothing inherently or necessarily self-evident about facts. Facts do not of themselves point out their interrelationships to a neutral perceiver. When critically analyzed, "experience" is found to be far too ambiguous a term on which to base a systematic theory of knowledge.

2.

A theory that places such a heavy emphasis on sense perception does not make adequate allowance for the fact that human senses are limited and imperfect. Our senses are often deceived, a fact that even the empiricists themselves recognize. Empiricism is not well equipped to separate fact from fancy.

3.

Empiricism gives no certainty. What is only probable knowledge is, by the same token, wholly questionable knowledge. Unless we mount guard and have an unbroken sequence of sensory experiences, we can never be sure that the automobile we drove into the garage at night is the same one we drive out in the morning.

2. Rationalism

Advocates of **rationalism** are intent on attaining knowledge that is absolute and certain. In their pursuit of such knowledge they start with propositions that are self-evident. The basic axioms on which they build their system are derived from ideas that are claimed to be clear, distinct, and certain to the human mind. The human mind has the capacity to "know" these ideas, but human beings do not create them or learn them through experience. The ideas are somehow "there" as part of basic reality, and the human mind, because it partakes of this reality, thereby contains the ideas. It is in this sense that the mind **reasons**. The rationalist argues that since the mind comprehends principles, the principles must therefore "exist"; that is, they must be true and real. If principles do not exist, it is impossible for human beings to conceive that they do. Principles are regarded as **a priori**, or preexperiential, and therefore principles are not developed from experience; on the contrary, experience can be understood only in the light of principles.

Plato provided the classical expression of rationalism. In a dialogue called the *Meno*, he argued that, in order to learn something, one must discover a truth one does not already know. But if the person does not already know the truth, how can he possibly recognize that it is the truth? Plato contended that a person cannot tell whether a proposition is true when he learns it unless he already knows it to be true. Furthermore, a person cannot *learn* what he *does* know since he already knows it. The conclusion is that people do not learn anything; they only *remember* what they already know. All the basic and universal principles are preexistent in human minds. Sense experience can at best merely stimulate memory and bring to consciousness the knowledge that is in the mind all the time.

Plato's theory of knowledge is integrated with his stand on the nature of what is ultimately real. For him, basic reality is composed of ideas, or principles. These ideas he called **Forms**. Beauty, truth, and justice are among the Forms that exist absolutely and changelessly—for all time and for everyone. People can come to know the Forms through the process of rational intuition—an activity peculiar to the "mind." The proof that Forms really exist is established by the fact that we can conceive of them. Thus, Plato viewed knowledge as a discovery that takes place during the orderly process of rational thought.

Geometry is one of the rationalists' favorite illustrations. It is argued that the basic axioms of geometry (for example, "a straight line is the shortest distance between two points") are clear and distinct ideas that human beings "just know." From the basic axioms a system of subaxioms can be deduced. The result is a formal and consistent network of propositions that are logically included within the limits set by the original self-evident axioms.

René Descartes, a seventeenth-century mathematician and philosopher, made a strong case for the rational approach to knowledge. Living in a period of ideological ferment, he had an intense desire to establish his beliefs on a foundation of absolute certainty. To accomplish this goal, he undertook to subject his knowledge to a most exacting test. He applied the method of rational doubt. He decided that if he found any reason to doubt a category or principle of knowledge he would set that category or principle aside. He would accept only that to which he could raise no objections.

Descartes considered the knowledge produced by the senses, but, because he admitted that the senses can be deceived (as in dreams or hallucinations), he was forced to conclude that sense data are unreliable. He tested his belief in an all-powerful God, but here too he found he could conceive of a God who might deceive human beings. Rigorously pursuing his goal of absolute certainty, Descartes was forced to question the reliability of perceptions, feelings, beliefs, and traditionally established truths as acceptable sources of knowledge. They were all judged to admit of possible exceptions. They were flawed. The only thing that he could not doubt was his own existence; he could not doubt that he was doubting. Even if he was deceived into thinking that he existed, he reasoned that the deceit itself implied someone being deceived. Descartes's rock of certainty was expressed in the Latin phrase *cogito, ergo sum* ("I think, therefore I am").

The story is told of an American philosopher whose class was studying the problem of existence. The students were asked to read Descartes's *Meditations*. The next day a worried and haggard student came to the professor with the complaint that he had been up all night trying to decide whether or not he really existed. "Tell me, please tell me, do I exist?" The professor considered the question and then asked, "Who wants to know?"

In his attempt to explain why the one truth (I think, therefore I am) is true, Descartes concluded that he had been convinced because of the clarity and distinctness of the idea. On this ground he reasoned that all truth can be recognized by the clarity and distinctness with which it occurs to the mind: "Whatever is clearly and distinctly conceived is true."

What has been demonstrated by these examples of rationalist philosophy is that absolutely certain and reliable knowledge is believed to derive not from sense experience but rather from the realm of the mind. (And in rationalism "mind" is *not* synonymous with "brain.") Both Plato and Descartes claimed that true knowledge is already within us in the form of ideas, which we do not acquire (learn) but which are innate. Rationalists further maintain that the world we come to know by the method of rational intuition is the real world. Truth and falsity reside in ideas and not in things.

Critiques of Rationalism

1.

Rational knowledge is constructed out of ideas that are neither visible nor tangible. The existence of self-evident or innate ideas has not been affirmed by all human beings with equal force and conviction. Furthermore, there is a notable lack of agreement among rationalists themselves on the basic truths from which they reason. Plato, St. Augustine, and Descartes developed quite distinctive rational theories.

2.

Relatedly, genuine starting points, like Descartes's *cogito, ergo sum*, do not tell us too much and cannot get us very far. To develop a body of truths from such skimpy beginnings, rationalists are accused of smuggling in ideas from other sources (such as experience or tradition). Often these ideas are principles that are "self-evident" only to a particular culture or group.

3.

Many thoughtful people have found it extremely difficult to apply rationalistic concepts to the practical world of affairs. The tendency toward abstractness and the tendency to doubt or negate the validity of sensory experience have been roundly criticized. Sophisticated critics are likely to complain that the rationalist treats ideas or concepts as if they were somehow objective "things." To devalue sensory experience, to de-emphasize the importance of physical entities, and then to substitute a nebulous set of abstractions is judged to be a highly questionable method of acquiring reliable knowledge.

4.

Rational theories fail to account for the vast change and increase in human knowledge over the years. Many ideas that were self-evident at one time are no longer accorded any respectability. At one time in history, the idea that the earth is the center of the solar system was almost universally accepted as a self-evident proposition.

E. The Scientific Method

It is a widely held view that science is basically an inductive-empirical method for obtaining knowledge. There is some justification for this popular assessment, because scientists do put great store in specific facts, observations, and sense data. However, a careful analysis of the **scientific method** reveals that what the scientist does in the search for knowledge is more accurately described in terms of a particular combination of empirical and rational procedures.

Scientific epistemology is both complex and controversial, but an effort will be made to present a concise philosophical analysis of the scientific method as a distinctive theory of knowledge.

Simply stated, the scientific method is one way of going about the business of acquiring knowledge. A definite sequence of procedures is followed in order to find specific kinds of answers to specific kinds of questions. Perhaps the epistemology of the scientific method can be discussed most profitably by directing our attention to a typical formula in which the sequential steps in the thought process are arranged. While there are many different versions of the "scientific method," the bare outlines of the procedure can be described in the following six steps:

a.   Awareness and definition of a problem.

b.   Observation and collection of relevant data.

c.   Organization or classification of data.

d.   Formulation of hypotheses.

e.   Deductions from the hypotheses.

f.   Testing and verification of the hypotheses.

Let us consider each of the six steps separately so that our analysis can be incisive and especially so that we can point more directly to the empirical and the rational elements in the scientific way of knowing.

a. *Awareness of a problem.*   The world that the scientist looks on is made up of an almost infinite number of separate facts and events that in and of themselves exhibit no meaningful order. It is only when people encounter obstacles as they seek to deal intelligently with that world that thought takes shape. In other words, people somehow create problems and propose what they think are answerable questions. Without a clearly defined problem, there is no way of knowing what particular facts to collect. The scientific method stresses at the outset the clear and precise statement of a problem.

The initial phase of the scientific method assumes a world of empirically observable objects and events, but people impose on that world an order or context by which a limited range of perceived facts can be given meaning. The rationalist's claim is supported at this stage by the argument that it is reason that structures and guides investigation. Reason provides a "sense of the problem," without which it would be impossible to order or arrange facts in any intelligible way. If there is no question, how can there be an answer?

b. *Observation and collection of data.*   Observation and the collection of data is the most familiar step in the scientific method. It is because so much of the specific activity of scientists is directed toward the gathering of data that many have come to equate science with fact-collecting. The meticulous observations made possible by ingenious instruments give dramatic support to the conception of science as a basically empirical and inductive procedure. The reliance on direct or indirect sense perceptions and the demand for precise observation conspire to keep our attention on the empirical aspect of scientific investigation.

c. *Organization, or classification, of data.*   The organization, or classification-of-data, phase of the scientific method stresses the arrangement of facts into groups, kinds, and classes. In all the particular sciences, the attempt to enumerate, analyze, compare, and contrast the relevant data depends on the establishment of systems of classification. The special study that develops and elaborates adequate systems of classification is called **taxonomy**, and modern scientists work continually to perfect their specialized taxonomies. But it is important to remember that categories or classes are not facts. Rather, they are the conceptual boxes into which the facts are inserted so that those facts can be organized according to their relevance and thus be given general names and meanings. Both empirical and rational elements are evident at this stage in the procedure.

d. *Formulation of hypotheses.*   Facts do not speak for themselves. In the world confronted by science, a group of molecules or cells does not jump up and down, wave, whistle, and declare, "Look at me! Here! I am a rock, or a tree, or a horse." *What* a thing *is* depends on the labels assigned to that thing. *How* a thing comes to be *explained* depends on the conceptual relationships with which it is viewed. This fact brings us to one of the most difficult aspects of scientific methodology: the role of the **hypothesis**.

Hypotheses are tentative statements about relationships between things. These hypothetical relationships are proposed in the form of working guesses, or theories, according to which it is hoped that *explanations* will become possible. Hypotheses are typically suggested on a trial-and-error basis. They may be merely reasonable hunches, or they may be extensions of previously verified hypotheses to new data. In either case, hypotheses serve to frame the data in such a way that a presumed relationship is set up and a *possible* explanation suggested. A hypothesis is usually stated in the form of an "if X, then Y" proposition. *If* human skin lacks pigmentation, *then* it will burn quickly when exposed to the direct rays of the sun. This hypothesis offers a tentative explanation of at least some of the relationships between skin pigmentation and sunlight. The hypothesis also tells us what conditions must prevail and what observations are needed if we wish to verify our original working guess.

In the concept of the hypothesis, so crucial to the scientific method, we can find both empirical and rational elements. There must be empirical data in the form of observable and measurable facts, and there must also be conceptual categories by which the *kinds* of data are logically separated and arranged so that probable interconnections can be suggested.

e. *Deductions from hypotheses.*   Those who think of science as a method of strictly inductive reasoning that proceeds directly from facts to explanations should pay special attention to the function of hypotheses. Hypotheses establish logical propositions from which it is possible to infer, or *deduce*, relationships between the particular things being investigated. Furthermore, hypotheses can assist us in predicting and discovering new facts. The deductive reasoning that is so necessary to the hypothesis stage points out that much of what we call scientific knowledge is theoretical rather than empirical in nature and that prediction is dependent on a form of syllogistic logic.

f. *Testing and verification of hypotheses.*   **Verification** in science means testing alternative hypotheses by actual observation or experimentation. Final reference is made to the facts. If the facts do not bear out one hypothesis, another hypothesis is selected, and the process is repeated. The last court of appeal is, however, the empirical data; scientific generalizations, or laws, must meet the test of experience. At this point, one might not be surprised to find the pragmatist applying the test of consequences as the ultimate criterion in evaluating the scientific method: Does it work? Neither do the rationalists surrender the field during the verification phase. They point out that a hypothesis is scientifically acceptable only if it is found to be *consistent* with previously established and verified hypotheses (refer to the coherence theory of truth).

To summarize: The scientific method is a theory of knowledge by which people seek particular kinds of answers to particular kinds of questions. The method emphasizes a rigorous sequence of procedures by which a continuously expanding and self-correcting body of knowledge is achieved. The scientific method rests on the assumption that there are discoverable regularities in the relationships among phenomena and that the human sense organs (or the instruments by which they are refined) are basically adequate. Through the systematic organization and verification of observations, people are able to accumulate a growing body of knowledge that has a very high *probability* of being true. The scientific method does *not* claim to be a method by which one can arrive at any changeless or ultimate knowledge.

Critiques of the Scientific Method

1.

The scientific method arbitrarily limits what we can know to those things that can be studied by the tools and techniques of science. If a chemist employs the postulates and techniques of her special discipline, she can learn only about those things that can be framed in chemical terms. To claim that science is the only valid way of knowing would be to maintain that the world is only as large and as significant as this one method by which it is known.

2.

The sciences permit many interpretations to be made about a thing or an event. Each interpretation may be true as far as it goes. Various hypotheses may be proposed that have equal validity in explaining a given set of facts even though each hypothesis may use a different language or a different system of classification. The unity and consistency of scientific knowledge are not as obvious as many people think they are.

3.

Science describes the mechanisms of *nature—how* things are causally related—but it never tells us *what* things are, much less *why* they are the way they are. Scientific verification is basically pragmatic; it is indeed useful to know "if X, then Y," but we also want to know what reality *is* and *means*—the *reason* for things. On these points science remains silent.

F. Other Epistemological Theories

1. Analytic Philosophy

Analytic philosophy is the general label given to a vigorous philosophical movement that emerged in the late nineteenth and early twentieth centuries. It stresses aspects of philosophy that are neither speculative nor **metaphysical** and stands as a distinctive and widely supported contemporary alternative. Encompassing the varied contributions of thinkers like Bertrand Russell, Wittgenstein, Ryle, Ayer, and a host of others, analytic philosophy is difficult to summarize. However, there is a shared concern with the use and function of language. The consensus is that philosophical problems are, at least in part, linguistic problems, and, if such problems are to be confronted directly, there must be a rigorous clarification of the language employed. Whether statements take a grammatical or a mathematical form, the symbols used must be precise and logically related. Knowledge results from the consistent integration of mutually acceptable systems of symbols.

Analytic philosophy received strong impetus from the **logical positivists**, who asserted that there are only two types of meaningful statements: empirical propositions and analytic propositions. Empirical propositions can be verified by reference to experience in the world. Analytic propositions are statements whose truth or falsity is determined by the definitions of the words in the statement; these would also include the truths of mathematics and logic. All other statements are regarded as meaningless. Metaphysical, ethical, and religious statements are generally classified as meaningless. Positivists maintain that statements not framed as either precisely verifiable empirical propositions or rigorously logical analytic propositions are simply nonsense. They argue that much of what has been said—and continues to be said—in the name of philosophy can be dismissed as nonsensical. Examples of meaningless statements include the following: "God exists"; "Life has a purpose"; and "The unexamined life is not worth living." Since most metaphysical and ethical statements do not qualify as either empirical or analytic propositions, they are obviously meaningless. Such statements can only reflect the subjective feelings of individuals (compare the **emotive theory** of value); they have no discernible reference to objective reality, and they cannot be given a logically intelligible structure.

There are few logical positivists today. The position is too extreme. For one thing, logical positivists could not even accept their own working premise and remain consistent, since their working premise was neither an analytic nor an empirical proposition. For another thing, although we cannot verify the existence of quarks or black holes through direct sensory experience, we would not say that scientific assertions of their existence are meaningless. But the revolutionary trend continues in the method of contemporary analytic philosophers called **linguistic analysis**. Linguistic analysis stresses the idea that the *method* we use for investigation has profound implications for the way we think. The emphasis is clearly epistemological, and the work done by philosophers of this persuasion tends to be restricted to problems involved in the use of symbols.

Modern analytic philosophy can be divided roughly into (1) philosophy of science and (2) **ordinary-language philosophy**. These two branches share the following attitudes. They contend that the special function of philosophy is to clarify concepts. They believe that the clear description of symbols and statements helps us avoid the temptation to accept metaphysical presumptions that can be so easily converted into unjustifiable **ontological** commitments. Philosophers of science and ordinary-language philosophers distinguish among the various uses of language, and they attempt to discriminate among types of language employed in different sorts of investigative procedure. They analyze the difference between substantive issues and conceptual issues. In other words, they maintain that what we say about what the world is may be quite different from what we say when we discuss *ideas*. For example, there is a difference between saying "The noise of the explosion gave me a headache" and saying "Noises cause headaches." In the first instance we are speaking of an event in the world. In the second case we are dealing with the ideas involved in the relationship between cause and effect. Analytic philosophy subscribes to the view that it is the philosopher's special task to study the concepts that are integrated into a structured pattern of communication rather than to talk loosely and fruitlessly about reality or values in and of themselves.

In the particular case of the philosophy of science, it is the philosopher's role to look over the shoulder of the scientist and examine carefully the descriptive concepts and statements to see that they are precisely defined and consistently related. The meticulous methods of symbolic logic are often used in this sort of watchdog activity. Rather than concerning themselves with the subject matter of scientific research or the particular techniques of scientific observation and description, the job of philosophers of science is to raise certain kinds of questions that must be answered at the conceptual level. When and under what circumstances is it legitimate to generalize from particular findings? What exactly is meant by a "scientific law"? What does it mean to say that something is "caused"? Is observational language adequate for all science, or must nonobservational language be used sometimes when making reference to hidden or suspected processes? The philosopher of science is thus seen to have a unique function—one that is distinct from scientific investigation per se.

Ordinary-language philosophy does not lend itself to such an uncomplicated definition. The ordinary-language philosopher agrees that philosophy is not a *realm* of inquiry; it is a position regarding a *method* of inquiry. But here the emphasis shifts to an analysis of language in everyday use. One way to characterize ordinary-language philosophy is to trace a typical sequence of language-related propositions:

A word is a sound or a squiggle.

The meaning of a word is its use.

The use of a word is a concept.

Thought depends on language.

Language is a social convention; private language is impossible.

Reference to particulars is prior to reference to generalizations.

The objectivity of ideas lies in the agreement on the rules for the usage of words.

The objective or public aspects of language are crucial because thinking is the use of words in a reciprocally intelligible way, and knowledge is the ability to do something based on prior conceptualization.

An analysis of the actual everyday employment of words will reveal the metaphysical and axiological distortions to which they have been subjected.

It is said that the analytic philosopher talks about language, not about the world. But in a deeper sense, the analytic philosopher is concerned primarily not with mere words but with the work that people do with them.

Critiques of Analytic Philosophy

1.

Analytic philosophy is not philosophy in the traditional, or generally accepted, sense. The traditional philosopher, in addition to seeking clarity of expression, seeks for vision and for new ways of understanding humanity and the universe. The study of language remains a legitimate activity, but clarification is not synonymous with knowledge, and analysis does not produce or reveal meaning. The models offered by analytic philosophers tend to limit the range and depth of philosophical discourse. What cannot be logically structured is disqualified from consideration. Many of our most serious and persistent questions are thereby excluded from the realm of philosophical inquiry.

2.

Language analysts concern themselves with word games and techniques rather than values and beliefs. Therefore, they tend to leave substantive knowledge, reasonable action, and applied ethics to scientists, politicians, theologians, or anyone else. Linguistic analysis becomes aloof, ingrown, and sterile—like the "criticism of criticism" in literature—and often appears to be a kind of exclusive recreation engaged in by an intellectual elite disillusioned about its ability to cope more directly with the human problems of a living world.

3.

Linguistic analysts try to maintain the view that there is no necessity in *things*, only in language. But they tend to deal with words as though they were *causes*. In spite of their protestations to the contrary, linguistic analysts frequently attempt to settle issues of *reality* in terms of language as if somehow language *caused* reality. This involves them in metaphysical questions after all—an involvement that they began by repudiating.

2. Authoritarianism

The viewpoint characteristic of **authoritarianism** presupposes that knowledge is possessed by someone or something outside the individual. To attain knowledge, the individual must rely on this outside agency and accept what that agency teaches or proclaims. The church, the state, the family, the culture, or the expert represent the more common sources of knowledge to which people turn. Authoritarianism stresses the sources of knowledge rather than the method by which knowledge is attained.

a. *Culture and tradition.*   Few people deny that much of what they know comes to them from the culture or society in which they grow up and participate. It is more than coincidence that the French speak French and that New Zealanders speak English. Human beings are social animals who learn. Particularly, they learn those things formally taught or informally communicated by the groups in which they live their lives. A great deal of the collected knowledge of specific cultures is available to people. In the process called **socialization**, or enculturation, the skills, attitudes, and beliefs of a person's society become part of his or her very personality and operate as authoritative sources of knowledge. If human beings had to start from scratch and invent their own knowledge, it would be hard to conceive of a pattern of life very far removed from that of the primates.

The accumulated knowledge developed and perpetuated by a culture constitutes that culture's **tradition**. Tradition expresses itself in standardized ways of perceiving and thinking that, because they are inculcated in the emerging personalities of any society, have a necessarily coercive effect on the way particular groups of people "know"—that is, know both themselves and their broader environment. The advantage of tradition as a source of knowledge is that it provides continuity, stability, and a base for consensus and correction that transcends the capabilities of any single individual. Those who argue for the authority of tradition are likely to conclude that the older ways or beliefs are the surest—they have stood the test of time. On the basis of a survival-of-the-fittest assumption, those beliefs have proved their superiority.

b. *Majority opinion.* Democracy carries the implication that what the majority knows or believes must be somehow better or truer than what only a few stand for. Here again is an appeal to authority. What is true for the largest number is also true for any individual. The majority is assumed to represent the most reliable source of knowledge.

c. *Prestige and expert opinion.* One of the standard devices used by book publishers in this country to interest the public in a book is to print blurbs on the dust jacket that indicate the educational or social standing of the author as well as the author's claim to professional competence. This device is an attempt to establish the author as an authority. And many people, because they want to know something they do not already know, seek out those whom they believe to be experts in a given field. In an effort to increase our knowledge, every one of us puts trust in those who are "in a position to know." In today's complex world most of us freely admit our dependence on "experts." It is hard to imagine how it could be otherwise if we are trying to become educated people.

d. *Charismatic authority.* **Charisma** refers to a quality reported to be the possession of a limited number of human beings who, because of something "dynamic" or unexplainable in their personalities, are able to capture the allegiance of others. Not because of their social prestige or their stores of information but because of some intangible and indefinable power, these people establish their authority in the lives of their fellow mortals. People as different as Gandhi and Hitler have been perceived as charismatic leaders. Whether or not these people claim to be authorities, they are characteristically looked on as fountainheads of knowledge, power, and right; "If it were not so, I would have told you." Charismatic leadership seems to depend on a more or less total emotional commitment from a body of followers. Those who are convinced as a result of their intensely personal experiences with charismatic leaders become disciples. For them, truth and right are embodied in the person of the leader, who is the source and proof of both. Knowledge is attained through one's surrender to charismatic authority.

Critique of Culture and Tradition

Reliance on the authority of culture and tradition is misplaced because not all cultures have survived, and those that have survived show marked differences in both the amount and the kind of knowledge they possess and especially in the nature of the beliefs and practices that have been established as basic and unchangeable. An appeal to the authority of traditional knowledge offers no explanation for the fact that cultures do, in fact, change, and it cannot account for the appearance of *new* knowledge. Furthermore, those individuals who do innovate or show great sensitivity to what is new or different are often the ones most oppressed by the weight of tradition. The sixteenth-century philosopher-scientist Bruno was burned at the stake for his early acceptance of a modern view of the universe.

Critique of Majority Opinion

The principal difficulty with the majority-opinion point of view is that the accumulation or advance of knowledge has often depended on a stubborn minority (often a minority of one). At one time almost everyone believed that the earth was flat.

Critique of Prestige and Expert Opinion

There is a danger in accepting ideas not because of their intrinsic merit but because of the person who expresses them. Another peril exists when we accept the statements of those we respect even though they are commenting on a subject not within the area of their established competence (as when an athlete recommends breakfast cereal or a movie star discusses foreign policy). And even when we are extremely careful to give weight to only the facts and opinions expressed by those who are experts or authorities in their fields, how can we be sure that what they say is true? No field of knowledge is free from internal controversies or new and different interpretations. A justified inductive appeal to authority requires that the authority be a genuine expert in the area in question, that there be a consensus among the experts, and that one could come to the same conclusion given enough time and expertise.

Critique of Charismatic Authority

Deeply felt attachments to a charismatic authority have no doubt been amply satisfying to a host of human beings. But what about those who have not had the experience, those who seek knowledge along rational or scientific lines, or those who are not satisfied with secondhand knowledge? If the question "Why is one authority's word any truer or more ultimate than that of another?" is raised, we are forced to introduce noncharismatic criteria to evaluate conflicting claims.

3. Intuition

The discussion of charisma forces attention to another way of knowing. The charismatic authority is the source of knowledge for followers, but how does the authority attain his or her knowledge in the first place? One answer to this question is found in the idea of mysticism.

Mysticism can be defined as the belief that the most reliable source of knowledge or truth is **intuition** rather than reason, sense experience, or the scientific method. The mystic maintains that immediate and true knowledge is attained through a direct awareness that does not depend on systematic mental activity or sense impressions.

A reasoned explanation of mysticism is difficult and probably unfair, for the mystical awareness, while true and basic for those who have had it, is held to be incommunicable. The literature of mysticism is full of references to "the inner light," "spiritual rebirth," "the peace that passeth all understanding," and "the unnameable name." The literature often reports an awesome and indescribable feeling of the oneness of all things. More formally, it might be said that mystics perceive intuitively—that they experience total responses to total situations. However described, the experiences of the better-known and more influential mystics are characterized by a feeling, or intuition, of meaningful synthesis between self and reality, with the result that life discovers its center and the springs of knowledge run pure and fresh.

A more common type of experience occurs when suddenly, for no apparent reason, a person becomes aware of meaningful relationships or feels a new depth and clarity in existence. At one time or another this may have happened to most of us. It is not unusual for a person to experience, in some special moment, the feeling of being sure—an awareness of reality somehow distilled and free of sham and irrelevancy. This experience is sometimes called **insight**; Maslow refers to it as a "peak experience." The difference between the person who has a flash of insight and the true mystic may be simply a matter of degree (although there is great disagreement on this point), but the difference may also depend on the extent to which the experience becomes the core and meaning of life. Many people value their particularly lucid moments, but few find that these events basically alter their everyday patterns of life.

4. Revelation

Revelation is a distinctive way of knowing in which what is *revealed* (knowledge or truth) is somehow beyond or separate from what is perceived by the senses or logically thought out. The idea is that there exists a store or source of knowledge external to human beings, and that at least some of that knowledge can be communicated to individual persons by unusual means not open to the ordinary channels of investigation. Frequently revelation is described as the communication of the Divine Will to human beings, of God breaking through to mortals in a very unique way. Knowledge may come like a bolt of lightning or by way of "a still, small voice." In either case there is the suggestion of a distinctly different dimension a person comes to know. Historically, the Christian religion has placed strong emphasis on revelation and its epistemological authority. Prophets and lawgivers are believed to have shown exceptional sensitivity to this special dimension of knowing.

Critique of Intuition and Revelation

Knowledge obtained through intuition or revelation is subject to criticism on the grounds that it is not always consistent, that different people have quite different awarenesses of the nature of truth, that there is no criterion for determining which is the better of two conflicting doctrines, and that for a vast number of human beings knowledge based on intuition is incommunicable (even if it is true) and therefore not generally available. Those who do not experience intuition or revelation and those who cannot accept the word (authority) of those who claim such experience must and do rely on some alternative way of knowing. Additional problems connected with religious knowing are examined in Chapter 7.

5. Existentialism

Those who adopt an **existential** posture typically express the conviction that human beings can never be certain of anything beyond the sheer fact of their own existence. If knowledge is defined as something with an independent structure and logical consistency, then the existentialists' insistence that it must originate with and remain dependent on unique and improbable human "knowers" renders it impossible. What human beings assert that they know is wholly capricious and unreliable. The subjective quality of the process of knowing is seen by the existentialist as inevitable. When we claim to "know" something, the "knowing" seems to be rather an intuitive grasp that has, or can be given, personal significance. There is nothing stable or objective about it. It is neither rational nor empirical in the traditional sense. To state that one knows is merely to express a personal affirmation that may shift or change at random with no outside criteria by which it may be evaluated or criticized. It boils down to this: Truth is what I affirm it to be. It is for this reason that there can be no existential theory or *system* of knowledge. It is for this reason that nonexistentialists are likely to apply, and existentialists not likely to reject, the label "irrationalists."

Atheistic existentialists seem to be completely disillusioned about the possibility of knowing or finding "truth." A person may respond or act, but in no way can that person be certain about anything. These existentialists tend to deny that life has, or can have, any more than a subjectively chosen meaning. Religious existentialists also exhibit extreme pessimism about the acquisition of reliable knowledge or fundamental truth. They are likely to argue that human beings cannot know; they can simply believe. And belief is a nonrational "leap of faith." A person affirms himself or herself by a jump into darkness. There is no way to know for sure where or why. The only justification for such a leap is "This I am."[1]

6. Zen

Zen Buddhism is one of the Eastern philosophies that puts little store in intellectual theories of epistemology. Although it is risky to use Western language to characterize an Eastern philosophical posture, the Zen way of knowing appears to favor the intuitive and the mystical elements in the process. The goal in Zen Buddhism is to achieve an enlightenment (satori) that transcends the formal categories of reasoning as well as the generalizations resulting from the amassing of discrete experiences in the sensory world. Any system of formal or objective "knowing" is devalued on the ground that it provides only an abstract picture of total reality and thus distorts rather than aids comprehension. The futility of trying to attain precise and structured knowledge is illustrated by the case of a man who paints lines on his plate glass window in order to locate more accurately specific points of interest in the vast panorama outside. The more coordinates he paints on the window, the more the panorama is deformed and segmented, and the less he or anyone else can see of the magnificent view.

For the followers of Zen, total reality simply exists. "Knowledge about" that reality separates one from direct "acquaintance with" all-inclusive "Being." The human experiential vision should be total and peripheral rather than partial and narrowly focused. The Western compulsion to structure and divide knowledge is viewed as a misguided attempt to describe the indescribable—to substitute a wall and a door for the "gateless gate." In the worldview of Zen, the wise person, or sage, is one who ceases to make objective distinctions and becomes identified with the underlying oneness of that which is. Such an antiknowing posture is likely to be seen by Western philosophers as a type of skepticism.

Critique of Existentialism and Zen

The rejection found in existentialism and Zen of all ways of knowing is too subtle to make sense to the average person. Human beings continue to ask what they assume to be answerable questions. The posture of antiknowing is fatalistic, defeatist, and unreasonable. The avid pursuit of systematic knowledge has brought about demonstrable and desirable results. Humankind had to seek, and organize, and build knowledge to raise itself from the level of

---

[1]Further aspects of existentialism are considered in Chapter 6.

bestiality. Precise, consistent, and communicable knowledge has promoted human mastery of the environment, raised standards of living, and enriched experience. Without an active and ordering intellect, a human being would simply not amount to anything. Antiknowing thus becomes a barrier to human evolution.

7. Skepticism

Some worldviews encourage an attitude of fundamental distrust or colossal indifference toward the whole field of epistemology. How we attain knowledge is judged to be a futile or irrelevant question.

> *Myself when young did eagerly frequent*
> *Doctor and Saint, and hear great argument*
> *About it and about: but evermore*
> *Came out by the same door where in I went.*
> *—Rubaiyat of Omar Khayyam*

It may be admitted that belief, action, and feeling have their place in human existence, but certain and dependable knowledge (should such a thing exist at all) is inaccessible.

The term **skepticism** is applied to the view that knowledge is beyond reasonable proof, highly uncertain, or totally impossible. These three levels of skepticism are found in philosophical works. The first type is characterized by an attitude of suspended judgment. All assumptions or conclusions are questioned until they pass the test of critical analysis. The prescription is to hold off until all the evidence is in. Socrates practiced this type of skepticism by insisting that we always question our answers. His stand lays claim to philosophical merit because it helps to free people from superstition, prejudice, and error and opens the way for intellectual progress. This sort of skepticism is closely related to agnosticism, which is a profession of ignorance rather than a denial that there is valid knowledge. The **agnostic** stresses the point of view that, at least for the present, human beings must remain ignorant of the real nature of such ultimates as matter, **mind**, and God. Belief is suspended until such a time as knowledge claims can be validated or confirmed.

A second type of skepticism is found among those who hold the view that knowledge deals only with experience or phenomena and that the mind is unable to know the real source or ground of experience. This brand of skepticism is found in Kant's **phenomenalism**, where it is maintained that the best we can do is deal with the surface appearances of things (the phenomena) because the real nature of things, what things really are in and of themselves (the noumena), is forever inaccessible to us.

The third type of skepticism is revealed in the extreme stand that human beings can never attain certain or reliable knowledge about anything. These hard-core skeptics echo the forceful assertions of Gorgias, a well-known orator and philosopher of ancient Greece: Nothing exists; there is no such thing as true knowledge; even if there were such a thing, a person would not be able to recognize it; and even if he or she recognized it, it could not be communicated to anyone else. In this adamant expression of skepticism we encounter a devastating rejection of the whole field of epistemology.

As a group, skeptics tend to emphasize the follies and excesses present in attempts to attain knowledge. They remind us of four things: (1) knowledge is a human achievement; (2) human faculties are weak and limited; (3) the human senses and human reason are both equally unreliable; and (4) even the experts exhibit a great diversity of theories and opinions. On the positive side, skepticism often precedes and stimulates philosophical reflection. It stresses the importance of keeping an open mind, considering alternatives, proceeding with deliberate caution, and avoiding the perils of **dogmatism**. Elements of skepticism are evident in the epistemological inquiries of Descartes, Kant, Locke, and, especially, Hume.

While there is a place for philosophical skepticism, then, there is also a place for a kind of practical skepticism. In fact, all of us are skeptics at one time or another, and this is often good, for it keeps us from uncritically accepting statements made by politicians and salespersons.

Critique of Skepticism

Critics of skepticism point out that, while an admission of ignorance or an insistence on reasonable doubt may provide an antidote to dogmatism and irresponsible truth claims, total skepticism cannot be taken seriously as a philosophical postulate. To assert that knowledge is impossible implies that something is known about the nature of knowledge in the first place. Thus, a thoroughgoing skepticism is self-contradictory (like the statement "All generalizations are false"). Only a partial or pragmatic skepticism is reasonable for those who make statements about the nature or method of knowing.

Another problem with an uncompromising skepticism is that it fosters a noncommittal attitude that makes any intelligent and consistent human activity virtually impossible. Such skepticism just cannot serve as a workable basis or a feasible ideal for either personal or social life. Absolute skepticism turns out to be not only illogical but impractical as well.

8. Feminist Epistemologies

At the beginning of this chapter we noted that the classic definition of knowledge is "justified true belief." We have knowledge when the knower is able to give reasons or warrant for his beliefs. These justificatory criteria must be a priori, that is, they must transcend the social context and status of the knower. Without such justification we have only opinion at best. Some recent feminist philosophers have referred to this tradition as "pure" or "normative" epistemology. They propose, instead, what is sometimes labeled "naturalized" epistemology. They argue that pure epistemology begins with the wrong question: Can we have knowledge? Feminists assume that we already can and do have knowledge and, therefore, ask a different question: How do we obtain the knowledge we have? That is to say, what is the process of knowledge acquisition from the standpoint of, in this case, the female knower as opposed to the male knower?

Feminist philosophers do not always agree in their epistemological theories, but there are some common features. Their approach has come about in part because of empirically oriented data in the scientific studies of how we think and perceive. (This includes psychological theories, such as object-relations theory, which has influenced Evelyn Fox Keller.) The traditional approach to epistemology has been dominated by males, such as Plato and Descartes who, as Susan Bordo points out, sought to divorce the mind from the body; both Plato and Descartes argued that data from sensory experience are unreliable. But if human knowledge cannot be disembodied knowledge, then one cannot simply ignore the "standpoint" of the knower (to use a phrase of Susan Harding and others).

"Mainstream epistemology" has been inattentive to the subjective elements involved in knowing and has operated with the illusion that knowing is universal and perspectiveless. The feminist argues that this account was hardly questioned because it was propounded by philosophers who held dominant positions in society (namely, white males), who operated with the assumption that there was (or should be) a separation between the knowing subject and the known object, and whose theory of a universal knowing subject prevailed by simply cutting off "unacceptable" points of view. Such an epistemology was inadequate because it ignored the ways in which social values influenced knowledge and the social and political implications of its own analysis of knowledge. For example, science was assumed to be the disembodied report of value-free, context independent facts; this assumption went unexamined by the males who dominated the sciences and who benefited from maintaining this assumption. The feminist's corrective is to redefine adequacy: to have an adequate epistemology we must take into account the assumptions and values based on the identity of "our group" and the kinds of activities in which "our group" engages. This means that scientific knowing, for instance, is interactive and dependent knowing; it is a process in which the scientist is a member of a valuing community (not even free of political influences) and in which the knowing subject (the scientist) maintains a reciprocal and empathetic relation with the thing known (the object of scientific study). (This last point is developed by Keller in her study of the scientific research of Nobel prize winner Barbara McClintock; Keller's own work is sympathetic to Thomas Kuhn's *The Structure of Scientific Revolutions*.)

The feminist rejects the traditional idea that a philosopher's work is good to the extent that it is free of political influence. Without reducing epistemology to politics, we must still recognize that "**cognitive** authority" is linked with gender, race, class, sexuality, culture, and age. We must be aware of how knowledge is authorized and who is empowered by it. If we include in our knowing the perspectives of marginalized peoples, we will not be as inclined to allow assumptions to go unexamined; we can generate more critical questions and produce less partial and distorted accounts. In other words, instead of being left in a mire of relativism because we have to consider each "group's" epistemic perspective, some feminists argue that we will actually achieve greater objectivity in our knowing.

So one of the important voices that needs to be heard is that of the female knower, whose standpoint is affected by her roles as mother and caregiver, and by her experiences of giving birth, menstruating, working to produce products that are used (rather than exchanged), and oppression. By hearing those who have been marginalized and by questioning the emphases and purposes of "pure" epistemology, the feminist hopes minimally to democratize the production of knowledge.

Critique of Feminist Epistemologies

Since feminists are not in total agreement, critiques of individual works would be more appropriate; however, some feminist philosophers' concerns about "standpoint" accounts of epistemology give some idea of the kinds of critiques that are heard even among feminists. For example, if the adequacy of an epistemology is based on the social context and status of the knower, how can we establish a norm for the superiority of one epistemic stance over another? Again, if a philosopher develops her epistemology in reaction to an Enlightenment epistemology isn't she still thinking in terms of the dominant mind-set of the Enlightenment?

9. Postmodernism and Deconstruction

The most recent and significant developments in epistemology are critical of the authoritarianism of culture and tradition and have historical and conceptual links to the second type of skepticism discussed in section 7. These developments are often referred to as **postmodernism**.

In ancient and modern times it was usually assumed that there is absolute truth that applies to everyone, everywhere, at all times; truth is there waiting to be discovered through revelation, reason, experience, or intuition. Thus knowledge had to do with truth that rested on a stable foundation, such as God or universal reason. According to postmodernists, this assumption is misguided. They argue, instead, for anti-**foundationalism**: There is no universally applicable, objective foundation for knowledge—some unchanging thing to ensure an accurate knowledge of truth that exists for everyone.

In fact, there is no *one* way to look at *any*thing. Our lives are fragmented into a plurality of worldviews—those of "Eurocentric" white males, the research tradition of Western science, homosexuals, Africans, and so on. This reflects the fact that meaning and truth are not waiting to be discovered; they are social constructions created by groups that share a certain tradition or perspective. Some of these groups manage to gain a privileged status, silencing or marginalizing the worldview of others and insisting that their interpretation of things is the only universally true one. These privileged worldviews are metanarratives (or master narratives) that are used to oppress others by dictating interpretations of history (for instance, the correct understanding of the story of Christopher Columbus or of the Nazi Holocaust). In reality, a master narrative is just one of many equally viable interpretations. There are as many realities as there are perceptions, and there are many types of rationalities.

The postmodern argument that meaning and truth are social constructs is often based on a particular view of language called **deconstruction**, foreshadowed in the work of Michel Foucault and, later, most notably espoused by Jacques Derrida (whose ideas developed in response to the thought of Edmund Husserl, the founder of the modern school of **phenomenology**). Derrida built on the idea that words are signs that only arbitrarily represent ideas. For instance, the word "horse" is an arbitrary sign for the idea it signifies (let alone for the actual animal). It could just as well be "dopple," if we would all agree on that. In other words, deconstructionists argue that signs get their meaning because we use them in various ways in a specific linguistic-cultural framework. Different cultures, for instance, might use the same words in different ways to mean different things. Even if you repeat exactly what I say, there will be a slightly different nuance in the meaning. The context is always changing. Furthermore, deconstructionists call attention to the fact that language itself is not stable. For instance, language has an element of contradiction within it. Consider that words mean what they do because they are different from other words. For example, freedom means the opposite of enslaved. In a sense, you cannot have one without the other. When I scrutinize a text like the opening of the Declaration of Independence, I not only hear a call for freedom, but I also detect slavery lurking in the background (e.g., "all *men* [i.e., white, landholding males] are created equal").

So, words derive meaning by opposition to and exclusion of other words. This means that every text is a political creation, and the privileged texts (i.e., those that use certain words with certain meanings to the exclusion of other words and other meanings) are used to label or to justify racism, sexism, homophobia, and the like. To deconstruct the meaning of a text is to uncover the true agenda underlying what is said. Or, to put it in our contemporary idiom, we show how the use of certain words is "politically incorrect."

In the end, then, language does not represent truth; it is used to tell stories—narratives—that rearrange information to fit whatever world view a person or group is constructing. As Richard Rorty says, "Anything can be made to look good or bad by being redescribed." (What has been said of language is equally applicable to any symbol—whether it be a Nazi swastika, a Mercedes-Benz, a G.I. Joe doll, or Marilyn Monroe. As Derrida put it, "The world is a text.") A postmodernist like Rorty argues that we don't use language to represent reality; we use language to get what we want. In other words, each self is the source of its own "virtual reality." We create reality with words (and, if we are tolerant, we should respect the right of others to do the same). There is no ontological foundation for language outside of language. "There is nothing outside the text" (Derrida). Our language means what it does because it refers to other parts of our language, and that is changing all the time. Whose reorganization of language around a center gets top billing is part of a power struggle between competing groups in society. Knowledge is no longer just a matter of reason; it also has to do with the will to power. (For example, do we call what is growing in a woman's womb a fetus or a baby? Do we call the termination of a pregnancy an abortion or murder?)

If it seems that this philosophy text and this chapter on epistemology have entered into the realms of literature, that is precisely the deconstructionist's and postmodernist's point. Philosophy is giving way to literature. The question is no longer, "What is true?" The question is, "What is your story?"

Critiques of Postmodernism and Deconstruction

1.

A variation of the critique of **cultural relativism** applies to a postmodern epistemology. Is there any way to talk meaningfully about progress or a "better" story. In fact, if "what works to make me happy" is what knowledge is all about, how do we even define *"what works"*? Could this just be another case of "might makes right"? Are we really left to the individual self and its virtual reality? We do not seem to act like that from day to day when we rely on a Western scientific worldview, for instance, to inform us about almost everything we do.

2.

If Derrida is right and language is so fluid, how can I be sure that what Derrida wrote last week still means the same thing? Actually, Derrida accepts this application of his theory. But that does not seem to be a very productive way of going about our intellectual work.

G. Conclusion

The problems of epistemology are extensive and technical, but thoughtful persons often find it useful or interesting to make a rough initial distinction between "knowledge about" and "acquaintance with" a particular event, object, or condition. It makes sense to contrast what one can "know about" another person or a foreign country with how one is "acquainted with" or directly experiences that specific individual or place. Reading about the life of a famous movie actress is not the same as being her director or her husband. Watching a television special on poverty is not the same as living or working in a ghetto. "Knowledge about" a person puts that person into a conceptual pattern by which we can classify and compare him or her with other persons—and perhaps predict what he or she will do under specified conditions. "Acquaintance with" that same person requires that we become intimately involved in a relationship of loving, hating, sharing, grieving, rejoicing, and so on. "Knowledge about" tends to be objective, impersonal, logical. "Acquaintance with" tends to be subjective, personal, and involved.

If we accept John Dewey's illustration of a toothache and apply it in the first person singular case, the point can be made very clearly. The dentist surely knows more than I do about my toothache—its causes and its cure. But only *I* am intimately acquainted with the pain and inconvenience of this personal and unique bodily disorder. The dentist knows my toothache. He can describe its manifestations and prescribe treatment. He can predict the probable conditions and consequences of my ailment. But I *have* the toothache; I feel, or directly experience, it.

The basic distinction between two kinds of knowing may help us to sort out and evaluate conflicting knowledge claims, especially in areas where our personal experiences lead us to conclusions that may or may not be supported by objective evidence. For example, some people claim to know from their personal experiences that domination and aggression are the essential factors in human motivation. The distinction spotlights the contrast between empiricism and intuition on one side and scientific method on the other. "Knowledge about" gives us intellectual power with which to scrutinize our world and then organize it and predict what it will do. It is the only kind of knowing acceptable to scientists and logicians. "Acquaintance with" provides us with personal experiences that contribute to our sense of involvement or identity. These experiences are valued in and of themselves because of their intensity and immediate personal significance. The question remains whether the insights and hunches arising from personal experiences should be relied on as a form of independent, intuitive knowledge or should be considered as hypotheses that need to be examined on a scientific basis.

Another helpful way of thinking through the problems of epistemology is to distinguish between subjectivism and objectivism.

Subjectivism expresses the view that what is known about the world is dependent, at least to some extent, on the consciousness of a perceiver. Objects or ideas do not exist independent of the person through whom they are known. Knowledge shows up as the organization of experiences or ideas that are somehow conceived by the workings of a person's mind. Knowing is an inner or interior process that produces propositions concerning what can be affirmed. The extreme view of subjectivism is that the knowing or experiencing of conscious beings is what makes reality.

Objectivism reflects the view that things or ideas exist in their own right, independent of the knower or the conditions of their being known. A real world of some kind exists "out there," and the epistemological problem is to identify, describe, and explain the process by which what is external to persons (things, ideas, or values) can become something that persons assert that they know.

Epistemology raises more problems than it settles. Contemporary philosophers continue to debate the conflicting claims of empiricist, rationalist, scientist, language analyst, mystic, and skeptic. Subtle new combinations, technical innovations, and theoretical disputes add spice and profundity to an age-old question. It may be, as Bertrand Russell, the late controversial British mathematician-philosopher, suggests, that no one has succeeded in developing a theory that is *both credible and consistent*. The more believable theories appear to contain serious inconsistencies; the more logical theories appear to be unbelievable. Perhaps it is unnecessary to regard the theories as mutually exclusive. Perhaps one theory is really true and the others false. Or perhaps one theory is more basic or inclusive than others. Perhaps *all* disclose what is real and true. At least the postmodernist might say so.

Case Study and Discussion Questions

Case Study

In his provocative book *The Tao of Physics*, Fritjof Capra, a theoretical physicist, tries to show how present-day physics has almost completely abandoned any solid concepts of our world, with the exception of energy. He points to some astonishing parallels between modern theoretical physics and the Eastern wisdom found in such alternatives as Taoism, Buddhism, and Zen. Capra believes that Western physics and Eastern mysticism are separate but complementary roads to the same knowledge. The subjective and intuitive elements in Capra's epistemology for modern times are expressed first in a personal reflection and then in a professional statement that stimulate consideration for his way of thinking.

> I was sitting by the ocean one late summer afternoon, watching the waves rolling in and feeling the rhythm of my breathing, when I suddenly became aware of my whole environment as being engaged in a gigantic cosmic dance. Being a physicist, I knew that the sand, rocks, water and air around me were made of vibrating molecules and atoms, and that these consisted of particles which interacted with one another by creating and destroying other particles. I knew also that the Earth's atmosphere was continually bombarded by showers of "cosmic rays," particles of high energy undergoing multiple collisions as they penetrated the air. All this was familiar to me from my research in high-energy physics, but until that moment I had only experienced it through graphs, diagrams and mathematical theories. As I sat on that beach my former experiences came to life; I "saw" cascades of energy coming down from outer space, in which particles were created and destroyed in rhythmic pulses; I "saw" the atoms of the elements and those of my body participating in this cosmic dance of energy; I felt its rhythm and I "heard" its sound, and at that moment I knew that this was the Dance of Shiva, the Lord of Dancers worshipped by the Hindus.[2]

---

[2]Fritjof Capra, *The Tao of Physics* (Berkeley, CA: Shambhala, 1975, 1983), p. 11.
Reprinted by permission of Shambhala Publications, Inc., Boston.

In modern physics the universe is thus experienced as a dynamic, inseparable whole which always includes the observer in an essential way. In this experience the traditional concepts of space and time, of isolated objects, and of cause and effect lose their meaning. Such an experience, however, is very similar to that of the Eastern mystics.[3]

1. In what ways does this point of view challenge conventional knowledge about the seemingly stable qualities of the external world?

2. In what ways does Capra's position fit in with feminist epistemologies? with postmodernism and deconstruction?

Discussion Questions

1. Is modern television acceptable or unacceptable as a way for Americans to increase their knowledge of the "real" world? Is there as much "reality" in a carefully crafted video as there is in the event that the video is imaging?

2. Are there things that human beings need to know that remain outside the scope of scientific investigation?

3. In what ways does the historical record enhance or distort what human beings know about themselves?

4. What kinds of knowledge are most needed today to solve the problems of human existence on a crowded planet?

5. Do you believe that mystics have added significantly to the store of human knowledge?

6. How do we use the word "know" differently when we say we know that God exists; that elephants have trunks; that "I" exist; that the sun will shine tomorrow; that Abraham Lincoln was the sixteenth president; and that every event must have a cause?

7. Can a scientist ever achieve a complete and final verification of a hypothesis?

Suggested Readings

Alcoff, Linda, and Elizabeth Potter, eds. *Feminist Epistemologies.* New York: Routledge, 1993.

Ayer, A. J. *Language, Truth, and Logic.* New York: Dover, 1952.

Bacon, Francis. *New Organon and Related Writings.* Indianapolis: Bobbs-Merrill, 1960.

Belenky, Mary Field, Blythe McVickler Clinchy, Nancy Rule Goldberger, and Jill Mattuck Tarule. *Women's Ways of Knowing.* New York: Basic Books, 1986.

Bergson, Henri. *The Creative Mind: An Introduction to Metaphysics.* 2d ed. Secaucus, NJ: Citadel Press, 1974.

Bordo, Susan. *The Flight to Objectivity: Essays on Cartesianism and Culture.* Albany: SUNY Press, 1987.

Capra, Fritjof. *The Tao of Physics.* Berkeley, CA: Shambhala, 1975.

Cohen, Morris, and Ernest Nagel. *An Introduction to Logic and Scientific Method.* New York: Harcourt, Brace and World, 1962.

Conner, Steven. *Postmodernist Culture: An Introduction to the Theories of the Contemporary.* Oxford: Basil Blackwell, 1989.

---

[3]Capra, p. 81.

Descartes, René. *Meditations and Selections from the Principles of Philosophy*. Translated by John Veitch. La Salle, IL: Open Court, 1966.

Goodman, Nelson. *Of Mind and Other Matters*. Cambridge, MA: Harvard University Press, 1986.

Harding, Susan. *The Science Question in Feminism*. Ithaca, NY: Cornell University Press, 1991.

Held, Virginia. "Feminism and Epistemology: Recent Work on the Connection Between Gender and Knowledge." In *Philosophy and Public Affairs* 14:3 (Summer 1985).

Hume, David. *An Enquiry Concerning Human Understanding*. Edited by Eric Steinberg. Indianapolis: Hackett, 1977.

Keller, Evelyn Fox. *Reflections on Gender and Science*. New Haven: Yale University Press, 1985.

Kuhn, Thomas. *The Structure of Scientific Revolutions*. 2d ed. Chicago: University of Chicago Press, 1970.

Langer, Susanne K. *Philosophy in a New Key: A Study in the Symbolism of Reason, Rite, and Art*. 3d ed. New York: New American Library (Mentor Book), 1951.

Locke, John. *An Essay Concerning Human Understanding*. New York: Dutton, 1979.

Lyotard, François. *The Postmodern Condition: A Report on Knowledge*. Translated by Geoff Bennington and Brian Massumi. Minnesota: University of Minnesota Press, 1988.

Moser, Paul. *Empirical Knowledge*. Totowa, NJ: Rowman & Littlefield, 1986.

Norris, Christopher. *Derrida*. Cambridge, MA: Harvard University Press, 1987.

Pinker, Steven. *The Language Instinct: How the Mind Creates Language*. New York: Harper, 1994.

Plato. *Meno*. Translated by Benjamin Jowett. Indianapolis: Bobbs-Merrill, 1949.

Popper, Karl R. *The Logic of Scientific Discovery*. New York: Basic Books, 1959.

Quine, W. V. D. *Word and Object*. Cambridge, MA: MIT Press, 1960.

Russell, Bertrand. *The Problems of Philosophy*. New York: Oxford University Press, 1959.

Ryle, Gilbert. *The Concept of Mind*. New York: Barnes & Noble, 1975.

Suppe, Frederick. Foreword and Afterword to *The Structure of Scientific Theories*. Urbana: University of Illinois Press, 1977.

Toulmin, Stephen. *Foresight and Understanding: An Enquiry into the Aims of Science*. New York: Harper & Row (Harper Torchbook), 1963.

Underhill, Evelyn. *Mysticism*. 12th ed. Cleveland, OH: Meridian (World), 1970.

Waugh, Patricia, ed. *Postmodernism: A Reader*. London: Edward Arnold, 1992.

CHAPTER 5
Metaphysics: What Is Real?

A. Questions to Consider

- What ultimately constitutes everything that exists?
- Does the universe have a purpose?
- Is there anything beyond death?
- Is a human being basically a body, or a soul, or both?
- Is there order or regularity in the very nature of things?
- Does science show that a person is nothing but a highly evolved animal with a brain like an electronic computer?
- In the final analysis, who or what *am* I?

B. Introduction

Metaphysics raises the basic issues about the ultimate nature of reality. Metaphysics asks these questions: What is ultimately real? What are the general traits of everything that exists? What categories (terms, concepts, symbols) are necessary to describe the nature of what is? It is intriguing to realize that one of the philosopher's most difficult tasks is to define a two-letter word that we use many times each day: "is." What does it mean for a thing "to be"?

It is important to understand at the outset what is *not* included in the philosophical field of study called metaphysics. First, there is no claim that the term covers the broad range of topics labeled "metaphysics" in a secondhand bookstore. The New Age movement, occultism, spiritualism, black magic, or the preternatural are not the concern of the professional meta-physician.

Second, the word "metaphysics" must *not* be interpreted literally, which would imply that something exists "after" or "beyond" physics. Metaphysics is the study of *all* theories about the nature of reality. The metaphysical continuum ranges from idealism (mind and spiritual forces are ultimately real) to materialism (matter-energy and physical forces alone are real). There is no paradox, then, in the statement that materialism is a metaphysical theory maintaining that there is no reality beyond what physics describes.

The intimate relationship between metaphysics and epistemology should be apparent. Any theory of the nature of reality is necessarily related to one's stand on how human beings come to know what actually exists. Conversely, an assumption about the nature of reality can lead one to adopt a particular theory of knowledge. You will need to consider which is more fundamental in your personal philosophy: a conviction about the nature of reality or a commitment to a way of knowing what is real.

C. A Metaphysical Continuum

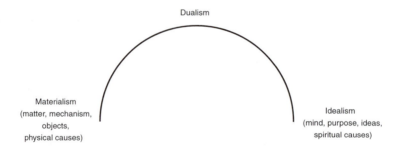

D. Worldviews: Alternative Theories of Reality

1. Materialism

"Materialist" in popular speech refers to a person who values money, success, things. When used to refer to a worldview, the term means something quite different. A metaphysical materialist holds that matter, or substance, or the stuff of the universe, is what is ultimately real. Modern **materialism** is likely to include the claim that energy or the space-time continuum is the basic category of reality. Strict materialists argue that life is nothing but a complicated physiochemical process. They hold that "mind" and thinking are nothing but the electrochemical activities of the brain. Since they believe that complex processes like life and thought can be explained wholly in terms of simpler physical or chemical processes, they are often called reductionists or **mechanists**; that is, they believe that every happening can be reduced to a mechanical process.

According to the materialist, every event is strictly determined by preced-ing physical events. Since the universe is seen as a closed, isolated system, exact knowledge of the state of the system at any given moment in time would enable us to predict every future event.

Many recent discoveries give support to the materialist worldview. Think of the discoveries in modern chemistry: drugs that speed up the higher mental processes; drugs that bring a schizophrenic back to reality; drugs that expand consciousness. Who would be surprised if tomorrow's newspapers announced that life had been artificially created in the laboratory? Antimaterialists have claimed that the ability of human beings for self-regulation—the ability to monitor their own behavior—points to a unique capacity of "mind." The materialist can now boast, however, of material systems that are self-monitoring, such as the computer chess champion.

How "real" are mind and consciousness, asks the materialist, when one sharp blow on the head eliminates them both? Stimulate a tiny portion of the brain with an electrical needle and speech is impaired or a childhood tune, long lost to memory, is recovered. Where are "mind," "self," and "existential meaning" during dreamless sleep, when only the body and the brain are *there?*

In the materialist worldview, mind (thinking) is an **epiphenomenon**, that is, an "extra"; thinking is to the brain as smoke is to a fire—only the fire and the brain *do* (cause) anything. Ideas, beliefs, and mental states are merely epiphenomena; they are only shadows or reflections cast by the material phenomena. Gilbert Ryle and Ludwig Wittgenstein view mental states, such as intentions, fears, and thoughts, as "dispositions to behave" in a certain way; they feel that such "dispositions" are simply underlying states of the body. Mental states that cannot be interpreted as dispositions to act, such as the experience of pain, are considered to reflect states of the central nervous system. Thus, the materialist's formula is to seek a neural change for every change in consciousness.

The theory of **evolution** can be marshalled in support of the materialist worldview. The universe has no purpose or direction. Humanity, life, and mind can all be explained by reference to mechanistic processes. Chance variations (mutations) occur, and in the struggle for survival the fittest of these survive and reproduce themselves; there is simply no need to appeal to a plan or purpose.

Karl Marx and Friedrich Engels developed a theory known as **dialectical materialism**. The political implications of this theory will be explored in Chapter 11. Here we can point out that the theory is "materialistic" in two senses. First, sense experience reveals the existence of a natural, material world, independent of Mind or minds. Aspects of reality that are not apparently matter in motion are "directly interwoven with material activity." Engels, however, referred to mechanists and reductionists as "vulgar materialists"; he held that all things change, and the dialectic of nature produces novel, complex entities (for example, living beings) that are just as "real" as the simpler forms from which they emerged (see **critical naturalism**). Second, Marx and Engels "turned Hegel upside down" by holding that the driving forces of history are material, economic structures, not ideas. Life determines consciousness, not the other way around. The ruling ideas in a society are the ideas of the ruling class. The ideology of the ruling class is no more than a rationalization for holding on to material power and is in conflict with the material interests of the oppressed classes—hence the dialectic of history: class struggle.

Traditional philosophers, said Marx and Engels, have only interpreted the world—the point is to *change* it.

Critiques of Materialism

1.

Materialists often use scientific evidence to support their world view. But do they, or can they possibly, talk about *any* proposition as true or false in purely mechanistic terms? For example, how can the statement "Scientific evidence supports materialism" be translated into physicochemical language or be reduced to an equivalent statement about brain processes?

2.

A. N. Whitehead, famous English philosopher and mathematician of the modern age, writes:

Many a scientist has patiently designed experiments for the *purpose* of substantiating his belief that animal operations are motivated by no purposes. He has perhaps spent his spare time in writing articles to prove that human beings are as other animals, so that "purpose" is a category irrelevant for the explanation of their bodily activities, his own activities included. Scientists animated by the purpose of proving that they are purposeless constitute an interesting subject for study.[1]

3.

Suppose a woman is lying on an operating table with the top of her skull laid back, and mirrors are so arranged that she is able to watch her brain functioning and to follow the explanations of its functioning reported by a brain surgeon. Would a materialist describe this situation as the brain observing itself and the brain understanding the brain? If so, would such a description do full justice to the event?

2. Idealism

The term "idealism" is unfortunate because in common speech it refers to a person motivated by high ideals; in philosophy, however, it refers to the worldview that Mind or Spirit or Ideas are the ultimate reality. It may assist the reader to think of idealism as "idea-ism."

---

[1]Quoted in Aubrey Castell, "The Self in Philosophy," *Pacific Philosophy Forum*, I (December 1962).

Idealism developed in the nineteenth century as reaction to and protest against the mechanistic worldview emerging from scientific discoveries. The idealist reformulated some of the traditional religious conceptions and attempted to give them a rational foundation. Whereas science-oriented philosophers envisaged a world order without purpose, moral laws, or spiritual forces, the idealists utilized these very categories as keystones in their philosophical construction.

We may start with a look at **subjective idealism**. Bishop Berkeley argued that there is no reason to suppose that matter and objects exist as the "dead things" out there described by materialists. Why not consider objects to be what we experience—sensations in our consciousness? If this sounds fantastic, try the following experiment: First, imagine you have no sight; the colors, shapes, and outlines of the "objective" world no longer exist, at least for you. Next, imagine you have no taste buds, no sense of touch, no hearing, no power to smell. What then is left of the vaunted objective world? In a word, remove the *subjective* (mind and senses), and there are no objects. Reality is our *experience* of things. If we are close to something, it is large; if we are distant, it is small. How can we say what size it "really" is? "To be is to be perceived."

Idealists recognize the difficulties of the subjective version of their theory. If I leave the living room at midnight with the fire burning brightly and return next morning and find only ashes, I cannot reasonably attribute the change simply to my perception, to my ideas. And yet there is no reality I can get hold of apart from my perception of it; the world *is* what *appears* to me to be, what I sense it to be. What it can possibly be other than as I perceive it, I have no way of knowing.

To avoid these difficulties, idealist thinkers developed a more comprehensive worldview: **objective idealism**. This theory holds that the world out there is **Mind** communicating to our human minds. Objective idealism was formulated by Plato in somewhat different terms. Plato maintained that individual things change and pass away; the material world is merely shadows. Underlying each bit of reality is a **Form**—the idea and structure of a thing that makes it intelligible to the human mind.

How can the scientist find order in the universe unless its underlying reality *is* Order? Again, use your imagination: Imagine a world of chaos—this minute the law of gravity operates; the next minute it does not. Now I sense my personal identity as "me" through last week and last year—now I sense myself as 300 other persons. Imagine, then, chaos. And contrast chaos with the orderliness that we actually experience. Can the materialist worldview of blind matter, of chance variations and combinations of electrons, really explain the formedness of the world?

Look again at the theory of evolution: chance variations and the survival of the fittest. Does this convincingly explain the movement over millions of years from simple to complex, from mindless worm to human intellect, from skin areas sensitive to light to human eye? These mechanisms may explain the *survival* of the fittest, but do they give a reasonable explanation of the *arrival* of the fittest? Is there not a goal or purpose working through the evolutionary process? If we must accept this inference, does it not follow that the underlying reality of the universe is Mind (God)?

The idea that evolution moves toward a goal that was set from the beginning of time is a teleological concept. **Teleology**, the claim that purpose, goal, or direction is part of the necessary nature of things, plays an important role in most idealistic worldviews. The case for a teleological interpretation of the evolutionary process is vigorously argued by Lecomte Du Noüy in his book, *Human Destiny*.

Is the idealist wrong in reminding us that materialism is an *idea, a* product of the human mind, and that any theory that reduces all of reality to physical mechanisms must somehow account for the fact that the theory claims to be *true*—not just a product of someone's brain? The idealist worldview may seem at many points to be abstract and unconvincing, but to deny the idealist's insistent claim that mind is somehow more than an electrochemical combustion would seem to deny the possibility of philosophizing at all.

Critiques of Idealism

1.

Idealists commit the **anthropomorphic** fallacy; that is, they project onto the universe, or reality-as-a-whole, characteristics that properly apply only to human beings. They make an illegitimate leap from minds to Mind, from ideas to Idea, from reasoning to Reason. The reasons idealists give for attributing human characteristics to ultimate reality are generous and ingenious, but they are not convincing.

2.

Aristotle criticized what he considered to be the one-sidedness of Platonic idealism. Form and structure *are* essential ingredients of reality, he argued, but everything (with the exception of God, who is Pure Form) has a material cause as well as a formal cause (not to mention an efficient cause and a final cause). In other words, all realities are formed matter, structures *of* matter. Did not Plato oversimplify the problem? Isn't Aristotle's position closer to common sense than Plato's?

3.

Who has ever encountered or experienced a mind or spirit independent of a matter-energy system? Scientific psychologists do not find it necessary to infer the existence of a mind or spirit in order to account for what *is* observed.

3. Metaphysical Dualism

Why not stand squarely in the middle of the continuum between materialism and idealism by accepting both matter and spirit as ultimately real? Why not adopt **dualism** as a worldview?

Dualism claims the merit of according with our common sense, our sense of being two fundamentally different things: a body that we inhabit and call our own and an "I," or a consciousness, altogether other than body. Descartes, the founder of modern philosophy, held to this view, that there are two ultimate substances, one material and the other spiritual. There are the body, a material substance, and the soul or mind, an immaterial substance.

In a voluntary act, I seem to experience my dual nature directly—first the thought (for example, to raise my arm) and then the bodily movement (my arm "obeys"). The example is trivial; what it points to is not: people as creators and builders. The hoe, the hut, the ceremonial song—indeed, the millions and ever-increasing flow of cultural artifacts—are all materializations of ideas. From time immemorial, human beings have experienced their dual nature. Not only the common sense of humankind but also reason itself has led human beings to the conception that the universe and all it contains is the materialization of an idea, an artifact of the Creator.

Metaphysical dualism finds expression in a variety of forms. It especially gives rise to the persistent "mind-body problem."

We have seen that Descartes taught that there are two ultimate substances: the mind, which he defined as a "thinking thing," and the body, which he defined as an "extended thing." No mind is extended, and no body thinks.

These utterly distinct realities are independent of each other, yet they seem to be connected. Bodies seem to produce mental sensations, and thoughts appear to move bodies. The problem is, How are they connected? (The problem is similar to attempting to move a chair by merely thinking about moving it. No matter how close the mind gets to the chair, the chair does not move. So, how do our thoughts "cause" parts of our bodies to move?)

Descartes's explanation is called **interactionism**. This is a theory of causal connection between mind and body, the exchange taking place, according to Descartes, in the pineal gland of the brain. Unfortunately, this does not solve the problem, since the brain is part of the body.

Other solutions have been suggested. One theory, **occasionalism**, argues that God continuously interferes to ensure that mental events accompany physical events. Another theory, suggested by the mathematician and philosopher Gottfried Wilhelm Leibniz, who lived a generation after Descartes, is that God predetermined a harmonious parallel between mental and bodily events; hence the theory's name—**preestablished harmony**. Of course, for the materialist and the idealist there is no problem, and the "solution" is simple—no connection is needed because there is ultimately only one reality.

Some philosophers view the relationship between mind and body as analogous to another variety of metaphysical dualism—namely, theological dualism, in which a spiritual being, God, is related to a physical reality, the world. The difficulties and views associated with this relation are even more varied than those that have to do with the mind-body problem.

Critiques of Metaphysical Dualism

1.

As we have seen, dualism raises the persistent "mind-body problem." How interaction between mind and body takes place remains a mystery.

2.

The weight of scientific evidence is solidly against the concept of mind as an entity and in favor of the concept of thinking, remembering, imagining, willing, valuing, and so on, as ways in which the unified organism functions. When a monkey solves a banana problem by fitting sticks together, it does so without benefit of an immaterial "mind." It is no more reasonable to posit a mind entity to account for thinking than to posit a lover entity and a hater entity to account for the fact that people behave lovingly and hatefully.

4. Critical Naturalism

In sharp contrast to all dualistic views of reality, **critical naturalism** is monistic, holding that there is only one reality, and that reality is nature. Humanity itself is one kind of naturalistic process among all the others. Critical naturalism is in agreement with materialism (which is also a naturalistic worldview) at two points. First, both worldviews reject all forms of supernaturalism. Second, both views reject the idea that there is such a thing as an independent immaterial substance, such as a mind, a spirit, or a soul; for example, thinking requires a brain, and where there is no living nerve tissue, there can be no consciousness, mental process, or self.

On the other hand, critical naturalism is called "critical" precisely because of its criticisms of materialism. Critical naturalism denies that reality is nothing but a mechanical process and holds that life generally and human activity specifically cannot be completely described in terms of physiochemical processes.

For a picture of reality, the critical naturalist would refer us to the findings of *all* the sciences. The concepts of the physical sciences are adequate for describing the nonliving aspects of nature, but the concepts of the biological sciences are necessary for an adequate description of living organisms. The reality of human beings, however, is not encompassed by the language of the physical sciences even when supplemented by the biological sciences; for a full portrait of human reality, we must turn to those sciences that focus directly on human beings: psychology, sociology, and anthropology.

Critical naturalism sees nature as an interrelated series of kinds, or levels, of reality, each with its distinctive characteristics. An adequate metaphysics will include different categories to describe what is happening on each level of reality. For example, water is composed of oxygen and hydrogen; when these chemicals are combined in a certain way, new qualities emerge, such as wetness, surface tension, drinkability, and so on. These qualities characterize the new whole and are not found in the separate parts. The whole, then, is more than the sum of its parts in the sense that it has emergent qualities.

Life is a distinct level of reality; a living organism can reproduce itself, seeks to maintain its structure when damaged, functions through metabolism, and so on. The laws of physics and chemistry apply to living things but cannot describe them fully; a distinct science, biology, with higher-level concepts is necessary.

A person is a more complex level of nature than is a single-celled organism. The emergent qualities of people include their capacities to think critically, have conscious purposes, laugh, predict, be self-aware, create culture, search for meaning, and even, perhaps, philosophize. The metaphysical categories necessary to describe these human capacities apply, so far as we now know, to no other living or nonliving thing in the universe.

The concepts of levels of reality and emergent qualities can perhaps best be understood in the context of the theory of evolution. Two billion years ago "reality" was nothing but physiochemical processes, becoming progressively more complex. No biologist or psychologist would have been needed at that point to give a complete, metaphysical account of existence. As time passed, however, there emerged into being living creatures with nervous structures of ever-increasing complexity, until "nature" finally evolved into the vast diversity that we now experience. An adequate worldview now demands terms and categories ranging from atomic nucleus, DNA, and tropism to self-identity, cognitive learning, and cultural change. However, insists the critical naturalist, that worldview does *not* require such categories as Mind, God, or World Purpose.

Critiques of Critical Naturalism

1.

The concept of emergent levels of reality may be an adequate *description* of how mind and consciousness came into existence, but it says nothing of *why* or *what* it all means. Critical naturalism refuses to take seriously the proposition that a purpose or goal may be operating through evolutionary processes. Is it reasonable to believe that purposeful, conscious beings "just happened" by "chance variations" in genetic structure?

2.

Critical naturalism prides itself on rejecting dualism but institutes its own dualism by holding that the unique characteristics of human nature are totally absent in nature itself. Critical naturalism recognizes that people have reasons, purposes, and values but asserts that the cosmic process that produced them is reasonless, purposeless, and valueless. Critical naturalism avoids the natural-supernatural dualism but introduces a dualism between human beings and nature.

3.
Critical naturalists reject the claims of religious experience, notably those of mysticism, on the grounds that the evidence proffered is diverse and contradictory. It is true that mystics often report their experiences in the language of their particular tradition. However, over against the world view of critical naturalism, they testify that the universe, far from being a mechanism indifferent to the human spirit, is essentially akin to it. From the standpoint of religious experience, the canvas of critical naturalism portrays an unnecessarily barren landscape.

5. Existentialism

The metaphysical alternatives presented up to this point in the chapter rest on a fatal assumption—according to the existentialists. Each of the preceding views, while disagreeing about what a human being *is*, assumes that human beings *are* something, that they have an *essence* or a *given* nature, and that this nature takes on character and relevance only in relation to a preexisting set of categories or conditions. To this, the existentialist stubbornly replies, "No!" Because existentialists refuse to frame their ideas in the light of any traditional objective categories of reality, their position is often dismissed as antimetaphysical.

The existential protest does, however, in the broader light of philosophical consideration, exhibit certain metaphysical leanings. The existential posture with regard to what is "real" develops initially and purely from the awareness or experiences of a conscious self, a human "I." Whatever can be labeled "real" must flow from the personal and concrete experiences of a unique human being. The origins are subjective; therefore, truth, meaning, and reality are subjective. The perspective is phrased starkly in Sartre's announcement: "Existence precedes essence." This helps us understand why the crucial concern of existentialists is not *what* one believes but rather *how* one believes. The basic philosophical thrust is not on what is "out there" but rather on "that which is aware." It underscores the fact that the metaphysical stance of the existentialist is unalterably subjective.

It is not surprising, then, that for the existentialist there is no essential or *given* human nature. There is no such thing as "man in general" or abstract "humanity." A person—a self-conscious "I"—cannot be defined in terms of any preexisting categories of thought or external systems of meaning. Each authentic individual confronts the raw fact of his or her own existence in a world in which *anything* can happen. He or she lives in a universe that is wide open and ultimately beyond rational explanation. It is in this sense that, for the existentialist, the world is "absurd." There is no necessary structure in things. There is no teleological principle at work in the universe; the world is without purpose or direction. The only significance it can have is what an individual person assigns to it. An authentic human being simply decides to live—alone and uncomforted, in "fear and trembling"—as he or she confronts the awesome.

Existentialists accept humans as irrational beings. Their answers to the questions "Who am I?" and "What does it all mean?" are purely subjective. Existentialists maintain that we are created continuously in the ongoing individual acts of choosing to be a person. Our thoughts, and especially our actions, say to us and to others, "*This* is what a person is." It is in this sense that as conscious human beings we are "condemned to be free." We are totally free. There are no rewards to be earned. There are no guarantees to be cashed in. We are self-created, and our continuing existence implies the courage to go on making conscious decisions without external assurances. Sartre summarizes it this way: "Man's project is to become God."

As persons, we are everything and nothing, sheer potentiality and possibility. We can make ourselves into animals or saints, conformists or rebels. We are thrust into the world to exist in ambiguity. Each of us must affirm our own definitions of ourselves. But this is still too impersonal. *You* exist; *I* exist. You and I in the frightful aloneness of our separate consciousnesses.

But existentialists also generate beliefs and make commitments. A commitment can be authentic or unauthentic. If I am a coward, I can claim that I am not responsible for my commitment—my childhood conditioning, my friends, my inborn temperament, my teachers are responsible for what I am and what I do. If I face my existence authentically, however, I must recognize that I and I alone *respond,* and the response I make is exactly my *responsibility.*

Existential commitment may be to God or to a deeply religious sense of the mystery of existence. The views of the modern theologians Paul Tillich, Gabriel Marcel, and Martin Buber, while grounded in the Protestant, Catholic, and Jewish traditions, respectively, reveal strong existential influences. Other commitments may be *atheistic,* with the emphasis perhaps on the selfish "me" or on "humanity" viewed in a universal and **altruistic** way. The variety of possible commitments must not, however, be permitted to distract us from the crucial point that the existential focus is on *how* we choose and not on the specific content of our choice.

Existential awareness of total freedom and the responsibility to create our own meaning in an absurd world is frightening. Anguish and despair (even nausea) are often associated with existential freedom. But this is not necessarily the case. Existentialists may also expose themselves fully and openly to the infinite possibilities of life so that the particular commitments they affirm clearly express social concern or profound human compassion.

Because it is so radically subjective, and because it relies so fundamentally on personal affirmation, existentialism presents many different faces. The term "existentialism" itself is a loose and ill-fitting label applied to a diverse collection of philosophical writers. The passionately religious Kierkegaard, the nihilistic Nietzsche, the atheistically militant Sartre, all made unique contributions to modern philosophical thought, but they can be lumped together only insofar as each expresses a subjective posture. Each existentialist expresses a subjective posture that cannot be evaluated by the usual objective standards. For this reason it might be accurate to include **postmodernism** as the latest variation of existentialism's themes; at least it appears to be a bedfellow.

Critiques of Existentialism

1.

The metaphysical foundation of existentialism is expressed in the statement "I exist." The fundamental weakness in this metaphysical position can be traced back to Descartes. Descartes experienced a state of doubt that led him to conclude, "I think, therefore I am." From this he inferred that he existed as an isolated and independent self. But the experience of doubt and all other experiences point beyond bare existence to dimensions of reality within and outside the person. Therefore, existentialists misinterpret the human situation when they adopt as their major premise the conception of an ego cut off from the rest of the world.

2.

Carl Rogers describes the psychologically healthy, fully functioning person as moving, like the existential person, *away* from definitions of self and life meaning that are externally imposed by the culture or other persons. However, the fully functioning person does not move toward the existential trap, to make a blind, arbitrary choice of a life project in anxiety and despair. Rather, the fully functioning person comes increasingly to trust the spontaneous functioning of his or her total human organism. Unlike the existentialist, who imposes definitions on existence, the fully functioning person allows life meanings to emerge through participation in situations from moment to moment.

3.

What is the self-conscious ego that is faced with the awesome responsibility to define itself? Where did it come from? Eastern thinkers and Western psychologists alike suggest that a person's self-concept stems primarily from how other persons see and respond to that person. What an irony if my existential definition of myself is no more than a reflection from society's mirror!

6. The Antimetaphysical Posture

Alternative metaphysical theories have been presented and criticized, with the suggestion that the reader weigh the strengths and limitations of each theory and come to a reasoned conclusion. This suggestion rests on the assumption that metaphysical statements are *meaningful*. Exactly this assumption is rejected by the linguistic analysts, whose epistemological position was set forth in a preceding chapter. The linguistic analysts are skeptical of the whole metaphysical enterprise. To say that most of them are skeptical of metaphysical thinking is, indeed, a serious understatement; they reject it as a morass of confusion.

For a representation of the linguistic analysts' antimetaphysical posture, let us examine some of the arguments put forward by A. J. Ayer in *Language,*

Truth, and Logic. The first chapter of Ayer's book is entitled "The Elimination of Metaphysics." Ayer's thesis is that philosophizing, properly understood, is solely an activity concerned with the analysis and clarification of language. Philosophy in Ayer's definition is "wholly independent of metaphysics." Philosophical analysis can and should "overthrow" and "demolish" metaphysics. Ayer summarizes his position in these words:

> We may accordingly define a metaphysical sentence as a sentence which purports to express a genuine proposition, but does, in fact, express neither a tautology (one meaning stated in different terms) nor an empirical hypothesis. And as tautologies and empirical hypotheses form the entire class of significant propositions, we are justified in concluding that all metaphysical assertions are nonsensical.[2]

In other words, metaphysical statements about existence are literally meaningless because they cannot possibly be verified as true or false. Take, for example, the metaphysical statement by a theist that "God exists" or by an atheist that "God does not exist" or by an agnostic that "God does or does not exist, but there is no way of knowing which way it is." All three statements are totally nonsensical. We cannot *demonstrate* God's existence or nonexistence by *deduction,* since all deductive truth rests on premises that simply define how terms are being used. Statements about God's existence cannot claim to be empirical hypotheses either, since we cannot say, "If God exists, X would be observed." It is impossible to specify what sense observations might confirm the existence or nonexistence of a **transcendent** being. If it is argued that a certain regularity in nature provides evidence for God's existence, then the assertion "God exists" would be "equivalent to asserting that there is the requisite regularity in nature."

Ayer focuses his analytical powers on the metaphysical dispute between idealists and realists. Is the reality of an object mental (as Berkeley claimed in his formula "to be is to be perceived") or physical (as in the realists' claim that objects exist whether or not perceived by any mind, human or divine)? Ayer states that this long-standing metaphysical dispute raises "an altogether fictitious question." All that is necessary is to give a clear definition of what we mean by a "material object," and the metaphysical problem disappears completely; it was a language problem all along. Suppose we follow J. S. Mill and define a material object as "a permanent possibility of sensation"—that is, as a *potential* sensation. We then see that Berkeley was correct in holding that every *statement* about a material object is equivalent to a *statement* about sensations; he was incorrect in saying that the material object *is* the sum of someone's sensations. Applying the proper definition of "material object," it is clear that unperceived objects *can* exist, and empirical evidence supports the hypothesis that they *do* exist—for example, I awake and observe the world as

---

[2]A. J. Ayer, *Language, Truth, and Logic* (New York: Dover, 1952), p. 41.

I left it. To assert that an unperceived object exists is to *predict* what sensations would be perceived *if* an observer were present. "To be is to be perceivable." The metaphysical argument between idealists and realists dissolves when words are defined clearly; indeed, metaphysics can be completely eliminated.

Critiques of the Antimetaphysical Posture

1.

The linguistic analysts, such as A. J. Ayer, insist that their philosophizing is free from any and all metaphysical taint. Their sole commitment is to make language clear. Yet Ayer refers to himself as an empiricist; he explicitly defends phenomenalism as a theory of perception, and he obviously holds the view that the scientific method is the *only* source of reliable knowledge. Critics argue that such epistemological commitments necessarily carry with them metaphysical commitments. When Ayer says, in effect, "If X (mind, God) does not exist *to* and *for* one of my five senses, the question of its existence or nonexistence is meaningless," does he actually avoid taking a stand on the nature of what is real?

2.

It is possible to consider metaphysical theories as metaphysical hypotheses. It must be admitted that metaphysical hypotheses cannot be tested empirically as in science. However, we might evaluate alternative world views in terms of their ability to integrate and explicate the total range of human experience. A worldview with a high degree of integrating capacity would hardly be meaningless.

3.

It has been asserted that "man is an incurably metaphysical animal." The linguistic analysts prescribe a powerful medicine to cure the metaphysical disease. The danger is that a side effect might be sterility of the human imagination in confronting the vital concerns of life.

E. Conclusion

Our sketch of six worldviews is seriously incomplete. There are many variations of each one and some completely different worldviews that were not even mentioned. Moreover, as with all alternative views, you may find some combination of two or more positions most adequate. The following combination of two metaphysical positions may be suggestive of the many possibilities.

Mysticism is one aspect of theological dualism. In the mystical experience the whole of one's being feels deeply identified with the One (God) of all existence. But could not this sense of identity be experienced in relation to the universe itself—a feeling of unity with nature, the central category of critical naturalism? Are awe and reverence necessarily directed toward a supernatural being? There is much support for a negative answer to this question. The seventeenth-century rationalist and metaphysician Spinoza spoke of "natural piety," and the theologian-physician Schweitzer, of "reverence for life." The Eastern views of Buddhism, Taoism, and Zen celebrate as the deepest human experience an awareness and acceptance of what *is* and a sense of complete identity with it. They are critical of Western thought for embracing the "fallacy of opposites"—that is, for classifying what is not classifiable and arbitrarily separating what is inseparable. A similar theme runs through the work of such Western poets as Blake, Wordsworth, Whitman, and Jeffers.

A possible combination of the views we are discussing can be developed around the idea of **pantheism**, or around a less familiar position called **panentheism** (literally, "all-in-God-ism"), which lies between theism and pantheism. A. N. Whitehead and others present panentheism as a "compound individual" theory of reality. Each higher level of reality is compounded of the next lower, simpler level. The human body, for example, is made up of billions of living cells yet is experienced by each of us as one. Perhaps the universe is an individual compounded of us all and experiences itself as one.

Regardless of the metaphysical view that one adopts toward life and the world, certain criteria are helpful for evaluating the adequacy of one's position and for weighing the relative merits of alternative theories. First, is the view *consistent* and *coherent*, or are there contradictions that reflect confused thinking? (For instance, one cannot be a strict materialist and a theological dualist at the same time.) Second, how *comprehensive* is the position? That is, how much of human experience does it include and integrate? Third, does it *fit* our experience and what we know about the universe? Fourth, how *practical* is it? For example, is it a view of life and the world that gives one hope and courage in living? Fifth, does it have *"disclosure value"*? That is, does it provide insight and understanding? Does it help to unify and explain life's experiences? In the end, we must assess each metaphysical posture by asking two questions: "Can I think with it?" and "Can I live with it?"

Case Study and Discussion Questions

Case Study

Ed Fredkin, a computer scientist and physicist who once taught at the Massachusetts Institute of Technology, thinks of the universe as a computer. He argues that the most fundamental ingredient that makes up all reality is not matter or energy but *information*. Atoms, subatomic particles, and quarks ultimately consist of discrete bits—binary units of information, on-and-off switches, like those used in a personal computer. Furthermore, he argues that a "single programming rule" is "the cause and prime mover of everything," which governs the behavior of the bits and thus of the entire universe. These bits simultaneously form patterns based on rules of behavior that have governed their past interactions with neighboring bits of information. Each interacting logic unit "decides zillions of times per second whether to be off or on at the next point in time," producing information that is "the fabric of reality, the stuff of which matter and energy are made." An electron, in Fredkin's universe, is nothing more than a "pattern of information"—a pattern that keeps on changing, like football fans who flip two-sided colored cards to produce pictures in the grandstands, giving the appearance of motion even though they are sitting still.

Without making any commitments regarding the existence of God, Fredkin assumes that there is an original question, the answer to which is being generated by this computer of a universe. But we don't know what the question is or what the answer will be.[3]

1. What do you think of Fredkin's theory? Is it adequate given our criteria for assessment? Is it better than a mechanistic or an organismic picture of the universe?

2. If you do not think that "bits of information" constitute all reality, then, presuming that subatomic particles can be divided into even smaller particles, where do you think the division ultimately ends (if at all)? Could it possibly end with something "nonmaterial"?

Discussion Questions

1. Assume for the sake of argument that the theory of evolution is scientifically well grounded. Can the theory be more convincingly interpreted in mechanistic or teleological terms?

2. Many modern philosophers follow A. J. Ayer in adopting an antimetaphysical posture. Do you find this posture adequate and satisfying? Why or why not?

3. In what specific ways might an understanding of the major philosophical alternatives in the field of metaphysics help a person evaluate and compare the confusing assortment of religious beliefs that are found in the world today?

4. How might a person view society and the behavior of people if she is a strict materialist? How might she view illness if she is a strict idealist?

Suggested Readings

Ayer, A. J. *Language, Truth, and Logic.* New York: Dover, 1952.

Barnett, Lincoln. *The Universe and Dr. Einstein.* New York: New American Library (Mentor Books), 1957.

Barrett, William. *Irrational Man: A Study in Existential Philosophy.* New York: Doubleday (Anchor Book), 1962.

Campbell, Keith. *Body and Mind.* Notre Dame, IN: University of Notre Dame Press, 1970.

Capra, Fritjof. *The Tao of Physics.* Berkeley, CA: Shambhala, 1975.

Du Noüy, Lecomte. *Human Destiny.* New York: New American Library (Mentor Book), 1963.

Hawking, Stephen W. *A Brief History of Time: From the Big Bang to Black Holes.* New York: Bantam, 1988.

Pinker, Steven. *How the Mind Works.* New York: Norton, 1997.

---

[3]Robert Wright, "Did the Universe Just Happen?" *Atlantic Monthly* 261 (April 1988): 29–44.

Sprague, Elmer. *Metaphysical Thinking*. New York: Oxford University Press, 1978.

Stace, W. T. *Religion and the Modern Mind*. Philadelphia: Lippincott (Keystone Book), 1952.

Taylor, Richard. *Metaphysics*. 2d ed. Englewood Cliffs, NJ: Prentice-Hall, 1985.

Underhill, Evelyn. *Practical Mysticism*. New York: Dutton (Everyman Edition), 1960.

Walsh, W. H. "Metaphysics, Nature of." In *The Encyclopedia of Philosophy*, vol. 5, pp. 300–307.

Watts, Alan. *Nature, Man, and Woman*. New York: Pantheon (Vintage Book), 1970.

Whitehead, Alfred North. *Science and the Modern World*. New York: New American Library (Mentor Book), 1948.

CHAPTER 6
Freedom and Determinism

A. Questions to Consider

- Am I a creature of fate, of gigantic forces beyond my control?
- Am I a mysterious mixture of body and spirit, part determined and part free?
- Am I an electronic computer programmed by my environment?
- Is my feeling of being free to shape my future just an illusion?
- Is it fair to punish a boy for stealing when his parents taught him to steal?
- Does it make sense to say that a person could have chosen to act other than the way he or she actually did act?
- If every idea a person expresses is strictly determined, why philosophize?

B. Introduction

How much and what kinds of freedom do human beings possess? This question is one of the most frequently asked and hotly debated in philosophy. The issue raised is one close to the core of the average person's life. In this modern age, the intellectual, social, and personal implications of the freedom question are so vital and pervasive that only the rarest of individuals can remain unconcerned.

The freedom-determinism issue might appropriately be raised in connection with the study of **metaphysics**, for it raises questions about the ultimate nature of things. Or the freedom-determinism issue could be postponed until the problem of **axiology**, or the study of values, is considered. It is often argued that any stand on morals and ethics is tied unalterably to the position on human freedom.

However, facing the fundamental freedom-determinism issue before certain other philosophical topics has the practical advantage of making it very difficult for anyone to remain indifferent to philosophical concerns. Meeting this issue early forces each serious seeker of wisdom to grapple in an immediate and personal way with fundamental questions and thus provides a lively springboard from which more extensive philosophical explorations can be launched.

The problem of freedom and determinism stems from our attempts to reconcile two convictions that most of us have. First, most of us believe that we are responsible for our moral choices and acts because we have the freedom and the ability to make such choices and perform such acts. Second, every event—including our choices and acts—seems to be caused by something else. But if this latter idea is true, how can we still be held responsible for choices and acts that we were "caused" to make and to perform? The following alternatives attempt to emphasize and relate these convictions in different ways.

C. A Freedom-Determinism Continuum

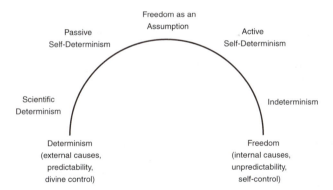

D. Alternative Views on Freedom and Determinism

1. Strict Determinism

Strict ("hard") determinists maintain that we live in the kind of universe where human choices and decisions are completely predetermined by fate, predestination, or natural causes. Let us look first at scientific determinism, the natural cause version of strict determinism.

a. *Scientific determinism.*   Our daily thoughts and communications reflect the commonsense belief that explanations are intelligible only if they are framed in terms of **causes**. If someone asks you what you did or if someone demands to know why you are behaving in such-and-such a way, your answer is typically given in a manner that describes the factors that you believe have caused your actions. Virtually all our questions about the relationships among things—and particularly those questions about how things have changed or have come to be as they are—are asked in the expectation that the answers will identify at least some of the causes.

To the advocate of scientific **determinism**, nothing happens in the universe without a natural cause. Human beings are part of the natural world; every human act or decision is simply one kind of natural event, and it, too, is caused.

One of the most stubbornly entrenched interpretations of the **scientific method** draws its strength from the basic assumption that every event can be traced back to its specific and antecedent natural causes. The argument is that the cause-effect principle operates and that its regular operation is the foundation on which the consistent concepts of science depend. The particular school of psychology that insists on limiting its study of human action to the objective observation of natural phenomena takes the scientific determinist approach and is called **behaviorism**, or stimulus-response psychology. Supported by additional evidence from other behavioral sciences like anthropology and sociology, the conclusion that there are specific and identifiable causal factors operating in human life is strengthened. The scientific determinist position holds that what we call human choices may reflect our desires and even our central ideals, but that every motive, desire, ideal, or idea is simply the result of factors in our heredity and environment. How can anyone believe that an individual human being is "free" when the evidence from psychology reinforces the conviction that every response a person makes is a product of past learning? How can it be maintained that groups of human beings are free when anthropology so clearly shows that the language, the morals, indeed the entire way of life of different human groups, are a direct result of cultural conditioning?

The case for scientific determinism appears unanswerable when we note the increasing accuracy and scope of predictions about human behavior. As the prediction and control of human behavior become more and more exact, the idea of "free will" becomes less and less tenable. **Free will** means "free from culture" and "free from past learning"—and both meanings are unsupportable.

Critiques of Scientific Determinism

1.

The behavioral sciences *do* make accurate predictions about unreflective human responses (responses that are rigidly patterned by habit, strong emotion, or unconscious motives), but they are conspicuously less successful in predicting reflective responses (responses that are carefully deliberated and reasoned). Does scientific determinism take adequate account of the process we go through when we *do* make careful, deliberative choices? The claim here is not that we subjectively *feel* free in the act of choice, but that reflective choices result from an intricate process of weighing the consequences of alternative courses of action. We have the capacity to evaluate our own attitudes and desires and thus reformulate our values and modify our behavior in the choosing process.

2.

A human being is more than a determined *process*. A human being is also, at times, an *agent* conducting an activity. For example, planning and carrying out a scientific experiment is one kind of activity that demands for its accurate description more than cause-effect terms that describe processes. What scientists do is not and cannot be adequately accounted for in the language of scientific determinism. A scientific experiment is purposive, guided by reference to criteria, and liable to error. Its results are verifiable. None of these terms applies to processes. If you stop the scientific activity at any point and ask "Why this step?" you get as an explanation a *reason*, not a *cause*. Can you stop a brain process or stimulus-response reaction and ask "Why function *that* way?" Scientific activity, then, is "purposive" and "reasoned"—yet these two terms are not in the vocabulary of the behaviorist or scientific determinist. In short, the theory of behaviorism—scientific determinism—is unscientific in the precise sense that it cannot give an account of at least one important area of human behavior: scientific activity itself.

b. *Other determinist concepts.*   Determinism is found not only in the scientific community. It is also a factor in the daily lives of those who read horoscopes or hold certain religious convictions.

(1) *Fate.* "I didn't choose my parents," we sometimes say. None of us chose the century into which we were born either. The American novelist Theodore Dreiser was acutely aware that he had not chosen his drug-addicted mother, who so deeply influenced his life. In light of such considerations, it seems only realistic to stress, as did the ancient Greeks in their idea of fate, their attitudes of **fatalism**, the limits on human freedom. Through the ages people have been haunted by the suspicion that their destiny is fixed by the stars. While many modern people reject astrology and appeal to the concept of **chance**, or accident, the idea that people cannot decide their future through free choice remains.

Our parents send us to a certain college (or to none, if that happens to be our fate), where the computer programs us into the class of Professor X, whose enthusiasm for subject Y is so contagious that we are irresistibly drawn to major in it. Yet we talk about our "freedom to choose."

The idea of fate reminds us of our limits, our relative impotence and insignificance in the vastness of the cosmos.

(2) *Providence and predestination.*   The religious concepts of providence and **predestination** contrast our smallness with the infinite greatness of God. God is all-good, but especially God is all-powerful and all-knowing. Finite human beings must not presume to understand God's plan for the world and for God's creatures. Why we were born and why we were created the way we are—male or female, smart or dull, black or white, tall or short—these are God's impenetrable mysteries; it is best to accept humbly the role we have been assigned. God asks no more than that we accept without vanity or complaint what the divine will has ordained, for God has created us, not we ourselves.

For sixteenth-century theologian John Calvin, predestination means that the final destiny of each of us, salvation or damnation, has been settled in advance by the absolute will of God. God knows this destiny, but it remains forever inscrutable to us.

Critique of Fate

Logically, people could believe in fate, or predestination, as absolutely determining their lives and still go on living them *as if* they were full of the ambiguous, choice-demanding, open-ended alternatives that they appear to be. Logically, people *could* put forth strenuous efforts to improve themselves and their society. But would they, in fact, be likely to do so? Would not the probable *psychological* effect of a belief in fate, or predestination, be a sense of resignation, an uncritical acceptance of the status quo—in a word, irresponsibility?

Critique of Providence and Predestination

James A. Pike makes the following criticism of providence and predestination:

> Were it to be supposed that . . . individuals are forever classified into one of two absolute categories—a state of complete bliss or a state of total torment, there is an inherent contradiction. Were the latter a fact, the former could not be.
>
> Presumably to qualify for heaven the candidates must have displayed some capacity for *agape* (unselfish love). So how could such loving persons be content in a heaven from which God has permanently excluded others with no chance for personal change or hope of ever receiving personal fulfillment? If these in heaven were really loving persons, their consciences would compel them, at the least, to stage a demonstration before the throne of the Most High or, more than that, to organize a "rescue party" to seek to save the lost.[1]

---

[1]James A. Pike, *What Is This Treasure?* (New York: Harper & Row, 1966), p. 84.

2. Indeterminism

a. *The theory of indeterminism.*   The theory that decisions are, at least in certain cases, independent of any prior causes, physiological or psychological, is called **indeterminism**. The human will is not determined by anything other than itself. For example, René Descartes, seventeenth-century French mathematician and philosopher, described the freedom of the will as infinite, with no limitations whatever on the mind's power of choice.

The version of indeterminism put forth by William James, late nineteenth-century American philosopher and psychologist, included the notion of pure chance events that are completely uncaused. He gave as an example his decision to walk down one street rather than another on the way home.

Charles Sanders Peirce, late nineteenth- and early twentieth-century American philosopher, physicist, and mathematician, held that the idea of universal determinism is an unwarranted scientific assumption. Precise observations constantly turn up evidence of irregular departures from scientific laws. Indeed, he argued, the occurrence of undetermined, chance events is necessary to explain the great diversity of the universe.

In the scientific realm, the claim for indeterminacy is supported by the observation that some subatomic particles behave in irregular and unpredictable ways that perplex the research physicist. The indeterminate behavior of subatomic particles is sometimes cited to support the possibility of indeterminism on the human level.

James and others espoused chance and indeterminism on the ground that they allowed one to view the future as open and subject to improvement, with the result that people can be said to be morally responsible.

A caution is in order at this point. Indeterminism does not insist that the universe is chaotic, nor does it deny that human behavior can be explained in terms of laws governing such behavior. There must be sufficient uniformity in the world to allow us to depend on certain acts yielding certain effects so that we can make predictions about the consequences of our behavior. In other words, indeterminism does not necessarily rule out *some* determinism in the universe. But, as we have seen, the indeterminist insists that human behavior is not *completely* explicable in terms of laws and that the world is open enough to permit humans to make genuinely free and responsible decisions.

Critiques of Indeterminism

1.

The theory of indeterminism asserts that human decisions cannot be traced to antecedent causes, that the human will is a cause that is not itself caused. But the whole notion of an event occurring without a cause goes against the teachings of common sense and undermines the foundations of the whole scientific enterprise. A belief in the indeterminateness of the will would render futile all attempts to understand human behavior or to improve it.

2.

If people's choices and actions are not determined by their established characters or by anything else, if they are the result of pure chance, what reason is there to believe that they would be *theirs* in any significant sense? Such choices and actions would be random, capricious, unreliable, and unexplainable. Since these are not the characteristics of most human behavior, there must be something defective in the theories of chance and indeterminism.

---

b. *Other indeterminist concepts.*   Indeterminism is basic to some conceptions of religion, morality, or the human condition itself.

(1) *Freedom as God's gift of free will.*   Some in the religious tradition of the West offer us an alternative view on the freedom-determinism issue. Humankind was created in God's image and was given the gift of **free will**. This gift is symbolized in the story of the Garden of Eden. Adam and Eve, the first human beings, were given the freedom, the free will, to disobey God's command not to eat from the tree of knowledge, and they used this freedom to perpetuate forevermore the freedom of human beings to think and to choose. Guided by instinct, every animal lives out its given nature; only human beings ask "Who am I?" and only human beings must consciously guide their lives by the knowledge of good and evil in their freedom to choose either.

It should be clearly understood that free will may be espoused by persons outside a religious framework (for example, by many existentialists), but the view now under discussion, like that of predestination, shares belief in a divine plan and in God's infinite goodness, power, and knowledge. God wants creatures who *voluntarily* choose to love and serve God. If God used divine power to coerce obedience, then human love, service, and obedience would be morally meaningless. Hence, God has freely shared power with human beings by granting them a will that is completely free. Our particular background of heredity and environment may *influence* our thinking and moral choices, but it never *determines* them. In the final accounting, our will is free, and we will be held accountable for using it to choose good or evil.

It is true that God has foreknowledge of the future. God knows exactly how we will use our free will, but this knowledge does not *determine* us in any way. How the future may be known in advance and yet not be pre-established raises a difficult question. An analogy may help to show how foreknowledge and free will are mutually compatible ideas. Suppose a person is standing on a hill, where she sees a man paddling a canoe on the river below, and at the same time she sees that a tree has fallen across the river around the next bend. The observer has *foreknowledge* that the man will decide that he cannot continue to paddle downstream, but this knowledge in no way affects the man's decision.

Critiques of Free Will

1.
What precisely does it mean to say that past learning "influences" but does not "determine" what we choose? Is there not a point at which we must say that past learning does determine? For example, do we "freely choose" to speak English rather than Greek in somehow responding to "influences" rather than strictly determining factors? Or, here is a very different example: Following the attack by Japan on Pearl Harbor, in what sense was President Roosevelt "influenced" rather than "determined" in his choice between defending the United States or not defending it?

2.
How can the free-will position adequately account for such observable facts as the following: (1) most children from families of low socioeconomic status reject middle-class values; (2) most Catholics and Protestants were raised in Catholic and Protestant environments, respectively; (3) the overwhelming majority of mainland-Chinese young people today believe in communism, and the vast majority of American young people do not believe in communism? To generalize, do not the behavioral sciences show that our values, attitudes, and beliefs are learned responses over which we have little or no conscious control? Do we not in fact choose, time after time, exactly what our past learnings have taught us to prefer?

(2) *Moral freedom.*   Moral freedom is the freedom to act in conformity with a chosen moral belief. Free will as a gift of God embraces moral freedom, but in a specific religious context. It is important to see how the human claim to free will can be defended apart from a religious framework.

Most moral-freedom theorists rest their case primarily on an appeal to inner experience. In a situation of moral temptation, for example, I sometimes feel that I am free to move freshly toward a personal ideal. In such a case, I sense myself as an *agent* with power to fashion a self that is more like my ideal self. At other times I am not aware of my moral freedom; I feel bound to the self already formed. In this case, I experience myself as an *object* rather than as a morally free agent.

Advocates of the moral-freedom position grant that a person's existence as a morally free agent cannot be known objectively; it can be known only subjectively—that is, introspectively. This knowledge is based on a direct intuition in situations of moral import. Thus, the only freedom that a person can affirm with any certainty is his or her *own* freedom. For this reason, moral freedom is sometimes referred to as "**introspective** freedom" or "intuitive freedom."

Kant put the case for moral freedom on a logical rather than a personal basis. His formula was that "ought implies can": If one rightly judges that a certain person is morally obligated to act in a certain way, then one must logically assume that he *can* act in that way, that he possesses an independent will that can exert moral control.

An example of moral freedom would be the case of hardened criminals who turn completely from their former ways of life and guide their conduct by a firm commitment to new moral ideals.

Critiques of Moral Freedom

1.

The primary evidence advanced in support of the idea of moral freedom is subjective, and subjective evidence is notoriously untrustworthy. In psychology, conclusions derived from the method of introspection are accepted only when confirmed by independent, publicly verified observations. No such evidence is put forward to support the claim that human beings possess moral freedom.

2.

The concept of a person as a "subject" who somehow chooses apart from and undetermined by self as "object" (the person's formed character) is untenable. It is no more than a rephrasing of the traditional notion of the human will as a cause that is not itself caused; this concept incorporates the unscientific idea of an uncaused event. A choice that does not reflect a person's established character would be arbitrary—and, in most cases, immoral.

(3) *Freedom as an existential framework.*   The English novelist Joyce Cary's declaration that "freedom is all our joy and all our pain" suggests an existential alternative. Proponents of **existentialism**, existentialists, insist that freedom pervades the human condition and is the central fact of human life. Science provides one perspective on the world; science sees everything as *objects*, and it is appropriate to set objects in a deterministic framework. But to claim that the scientific perspective—abstract, detached, precise, impersonal, unemotional, unconcerned with overall meaning—is the only or the most important perspective is fantastic. You and I are *subjects*. We are engaged in the project of creating meaning in our lives. We live in a *life* world, a world utterly different from the science world. The life world is concrete, here and now, stretched toward the future and the certainty of death; the science world is abstract. I am thrust into the life world and am concerned, involved, engaged; the science world is detached. I am confronted with ambiguity; the science world is precise. I am suffused with feelings of joy and dread; what I am as a person, the very meaning of my life, is at stake, but the science world is impersonal, unemotional, and unconcerned with life meaning. In this life world I *am* free, and I *am* responsible; I am free and responsible to say, authentically, who I am and what the meaning of my life shall be. It is pointless to debate the question of freedom versus determinism. I *exist* in the framework of freedom. The science world, with its determined objects, is part of my lived

world, and I take account of it, but I do not exist in such a world. In the freedom of my lived existence, I am challenged to create meaning out of all the facts: the size of the solar system, the electrochemical nature of my brain, the conflicting welter of cultures, the history of my particular past. But no matter how precisely science describes these objects and traces them to their causes, I know that their *meaning* depends on what I freely choose to affirm about them.

Critiques of Freedom as an Existential Framework

1.

Van Cleve Morris, an existentialist, writes:

> . . . We are individually confronted in every waking moment by phenomenal situations to each of which there are numberless responses we could give. But the responses must rise as possibilities in our imagination before they can play a role in genuine choosing. Moreover, no choice is possible unless the free subjectivity is aware of the act of choosing as such. This means, therefore, that the free subjectivity must be aware not only of alternatives but of the *act* of considering alternatives before one may say that choosing is actually taking place. So-called "blind choosing" is a contradiction in terms.[2]

This interpretation of existentialism, then, holds that an awareness of alternatives is necessary to a genuine choice. It would seem to be only a slight extension of Morris's view to hold that knowledge about the consequences of alternative actions is necessary before they can be "considered" as "possibilities in our imagination." But with these qualifications, doesn't the existential view lose its distinctive character?

2.

Suppose that we grant an existentialist the extreme assertion that I am always free to choose anything, that nothing at all weights the scales of my choice. Is such freedom worth having? Any meaning to my life must then be imposed through arbitrary choice. For example, the knowledge that people experience self-fulfillment when they are open to experience, accept themselves and others, and function autonomously with a sense of individual identity—such knowledge counts for nothing. Since the choice is arbitrary, I can just as well search for my life's meaning through being closed to experience, rejecting myself and disdaining others, and functioning dependently, with no sense of my own identity. The existentialist concern for freedom in a context of arbitrary choice makes all choice meaningless; how can I create existential meaning out of essential meaninglessness?

---

[2]Van Cleve Morris, *Existentialism in Education: What It Means* (New York: Harper & Row, 1966), p. 46.

3. Self-Determinism

Self-determinists accept the scientific determinists' insistence that every human act or decision is *caused*, but they put forward the claim that persons themselves are causal agents. People's knowledge and values, their hopes and fears, are dynamic factors in their choices. Unlike other animals, human beings can reflect and deliberate before they act; they can give reasons for what they do, and reasons are causes.

Two quite different versions of self-determinism have been proposed. One version conceives the self as passive, as wholly produced and defined by the past. The other version views the self as active, as self-producing and self-defining in the present.

a. *Passive self-determinism: Freedom as the absence of outside coercion.* Hobbes, Locke, and Hume argued that there is really no problem of freedom or determinism. Freedom means "to act according to the strongest impulse in the absence of external constraint," "to act according to the preferences of one's own mind," "to act according to one's own motives." Freedom in this sense is completely consistent with the scientific determinists' position that people's impulses, preferences, and motives are strictly determined by past events. For this reason, this position is sometimes called "compatibilism" or "soft determinism."

If we refer to common sense and to the everyday way in which we use the term "free," we can see that freedom means simply the absence of outside coercion and does not run counter to the arguments put forward by scientific determinists. Suppose that I ask a friend, "Did you cut your hair of your own *free* will?" He may answer, "Yes, I like it that way" or "Yes, I don't identify with the longhair crowd." Or he may respond, "No, army regulations demanded that I cut it." Notice that in neither set of circumstances does freedom or free will imply indeterminism—that is, an absence of causes for the behavior. The scientific determinist is obviously right: Every act has an identifiable set of causes and is strictly determined by them. The only meaningful distinction is whether the causes of our act stem from our personal desires or are imposed on us from outside so that we are *forced* to act in a certain way. Our language reflects this distinction quite clearly when it classifies some acts as voluntary and others as involuntary.

A person who is forced at gunpoint to participate in a crime does not fully choose to commit the crime; on the other hand, a boy who is late getting to school because he stopped to jump in puddles did freely choose to be late (and will therefore be held morally responsible for his tardiness). We can summarize the idea of passive **self-determinism** in the statement that we are free to the degree that in our choices we express our selves—what we are and what we want. We are unfree insofar as circumstances limit our self-expression or other persons force us to do what we do not want to do.

It is granted that certain situations are ambiguous in that they seem to involve a combination of inner desire and outside limitation. For instance, you can freely choose a desired goal (for example, to become a professor), but the means required to attain this goal may be set by forces over which you have no control (for example, expending effort to acquire a college degree). The ambiguity posed by such an example can be clarified by saying that your choice is free when you prefer one set of goals-means over another; your choice is unfree when you are limited to a single option.

Critiques of Passive Self-Determinism: Freedom as the Absence of Outside Coercion

1.

Aren't there all kinds and degrees of *inner* coercion that limit the free expression of our selves just as rigidly as outside forces? For example, people driven by a compulsion to wash their hands hundreds of times a day, or people with severe feelings of inferiority that restrict their ability to achieve their own goals, or people dominated by uncontrollable emotional states—are these people "free" in any meaningful sense?

2.

Certainly Mr. A, who "wants" Miss B and "chooses" to marry her because she unconsciously reminds him of his mother, is not as "free" as Mr. C, who feels a similar attraction to Miss D but becomes insightfully aware of why he is attracted and reevaluates the situation in light of this awareness.

b. *Active self-determinism: Freedom as insightful awareness.*   Advocates of freedom as insightful awareness, such as Thomas Aquinas and John Dewey, begin by agreeing with the scientific determinist at several points. They reject indeterminism and hold that all events, including human choices, are caused. They accept the view that a person is not innately endowed with a free will that enables that person to choose independently of culture and past conditioning. Finally, they agree that all human responses must be learned and that wider and wider ranges of human behavior are subject to accurate prediction. However, holders of this view claim that the scientific determinist and the passive self-determinist overlook one crucial factor in the human equation: the ability of human beings to think and reflect and thus become insightfully aware.

People are *unfree* insofar as their behaving and choosing stem from desires, habits, beliefs, or *any* aspect of themselves or their environment of which they are unconscious, unaware, or lacking in insight. People are *free* to the degree that their behaving and choosing are guided by insightful awareness of the situation within and outside themselves. People can *learn* to be free in this sense of the word "freedom."

In order to predict the outcome of insightfully aware decisions, predictors cannot stand off and add up the past interplay of hereditary and environmental factors because that is not the kind of process confronting them; a predictor would somehow have to live through, step by step, the intricate process of reflective choosing.

The scientific determinist assumes that the final word about human action is an objective description of it or a scientific prediction about it. The insightful-awareness theorist claims, on the other hand, that persons can use these descriptions and predictions to make ever more informed, reflective choices. The scientist, then, would not have the last word; the seeking person looking over the shoulder of the scientist would.

No person can be free from culture or free from the past in the literal sense of getting outside either. But reflective thinking is precisely a standing apart from and a taking account of. Such thinking is *itself* a *causal* process, the dynamic process of insightful awareness, through which people become self-directing; they become free to make new and creative responses. A person is not simply the effect of previous causes; he or she can also be an agent, an active self, and thereby a causal factor in each present situation.

Critiques of Active Self-Determinism: Freedom as Insightful Awareness

1.

This view uses the terms "free" and "freedom," but, on close inspection, leans far toward the scientific determinist position and is, in fact, no more than a refined version of determinism. Do people really have to "learn" to be free? Is human freedom so limited that it is proportional to the knowledge one acquires about oneself and the world? Doesn't every normal person, by the very possession of self-consciousness, have at least some dim awareness that he or she *can* choose and be responsible for whatever life he or she leads?

2.

Are insight, awareness, and reflection clear and definable causal factors in the decision-making process? Do they add to or change the complex elements (past learning, present feelings, and so on) that are synthesized in the brain and produce the choice? If the answer to both of these questions is no, it would be fair to conclude that insightful awareness is a vague concept, a symbol with nothing in fact to support it, that it is thus virtually impossible to understand human behavior in any systematic or practical way.

4. Freedom as an Assumption

A final alternative is one that cannot be readily placed in a discrete niche on the freedom-determinism continuum. Freedom as an assumption takes a position that cannot be resolved in terms of the arguments presented for or against the other alternatives.

Mr. Jones cannot give up the idea that somehow he is free. He tries to convince himself that one of the freedom positions can stand up against the criticisms leveled at it. One by one he considers the arguments in support of the various freedom alternatives: free will, moral freedom, existential freedom, freedom as absence of outside coercion, and freedom as insightful awareness. In each case he then considers the counterevidence and counterarguments advanced by the determinists. He reluctantly concludes that none of the freedom positions can be adequately defended. Finally, he decides that the only way to resolve the issue is to *assume* that he is free. He therefore adopts the following line of reasoning:

> I have to admit that I cannot produce evidence or arguments that are convincing to myself or anyone else that human choices are free. However, I find that many things that are important to me make sense only on the *assumption* that people are free to choose. For example, I want in several ways to become a different person from what I am now, and I feel responsible to bring about these changes in myself. If I were to adopt the scientific determinist posture, I would just resign myself to the fact that I am what I am because of what has happened to me in the past. Only when I assume that I am free to change myself (whether I *am* free or not) does my life take on meaning. And, in dealing with other persons, I don't want to feel that I am conditioning or manipulating them. If their responses to me are to be at all meaningful, I must assume that they respond voluntarily and deliberately—that is, freely.

Proponents of freedom as an assumption grant that scientists have a right to assume the principle of scientific determinism as a basis for carrying on their scientific activity. But the proponents claim that people have an equal right to assume the principle of human freedom as the most meaningful basis on which to conduct their lives. The proponents might admit that human creatures are no more than presumptuous animals who clothe themselves in the fiction of freedom, but where human responsibility and social order are concerned, the assumption of freedom becomes a necessary fiction that is satisfying and workable. Unless freedom is assumed as an operating principle, life is chaotic and futile.

Critiques of Freedom as an Assumption

1.

Ms. X says that she "wants" to become a different person and that she "feels" responsible for changing herself. These "wants" and "feelings" can best be understood as stemming from her past experiences and thus can most reasonably be interpreted in a scientifically deterministic framework.

2.

The assumption of human freedom is unnecessary even if it is granted that a sense of personal responsibility is essential to a mature, meaningful outlook on life. For example, other people may force one to accept a position of responsibility.

In speaking of her relationships with other people, Ms. X uses the loaded terms "conditioning" and "manipulating." She should simply accept the fact that she has an effect on others and that their response to this effect does not have to be "free" (whatever that means) in order to be meaningful.

E. Conclusion

Having assessed the strengths and weaknesses of the various alternative views on freedom and determinism, you may wish to test whichever position you have tentatively adopted by seeing how it applies to specific kinds of situations, especially to ethical questions. The discussion questions at the end of the chapter suggest some of the possibilities.

Since each viewpoint on freedom-determinism can be criticized, it is possible that some combination of views is most defensible. For example, might not a religiously oriented person argue that God endowed human beings with freedom of choice—not directly, by giving inborn free will, but indirectly, by giving the capacity to think and reflect and thus learn to become self-directing? Can the active self-determinist and existential positions be modified and integrated into a single, consistent position? Scientific determinism and the two versions of self-determinism all reject indeterminism and accept the idea that all human behavior is "caused"; are they, then, three distinct positions, or can they be stated as emphases within one expanded theory?

Several of the freedom-determinism alternatives revolve around the complex and controversial question of what, in the final analysis, a human being really is. When you select your preferred view of human nature from the alternatives presented in Chapter 10, therefore, you may wish to reexamine the freedom-determinism option you have tentatively selected—at least to make sure that the two positions you have chosen are consistent with each other.

The word "freedom" is constantly on our lips, and for most of us it is more than an abstract symbol or a meaningless concept. Few ideas are more significant to us or invite more careful scrutiny than that of freedom. Philosophy demands that we be explicit about every concept we use and that we become especially critical about those that are commonplace and appear obvious.

Case Study and Discussion Questions
Case Study

A young couple become disturbed at the fact that their ten-year-old son has recently become sullen, exhibits a great deal of hostility, and indulges in frequent temper tantrums. The parents consult a psychologist. The psychologist analyzes the case and recommends that the parents alter their method of dealing with the child: The advice is to cease inflicting severe punishment each time the child disobeys one of the strict rules the family has laid down. "The scientific evidence demonstrates," the psychologist concludes, "that forcing a child of this age to conform to the kind of rules that you have set up and then punishing him for breaking those rules makes him feel unworthy and rejected, and these feelings in turn lead to the symptoms that have disturbed you."

The parents follow the psychologist's advice, and their child's behavior becomes more cooperative, he shows less hostility, and there are no more temper tantrums.

1. In what sense were the actors in this situation "free" or "determined"?
2. Was the son responsible for his hostility and temper tantrums?

Discussion Questions

1. One issue frequently raised in freedom-determinism discussions concerns the treatment of criminals. Advocates of free will and moral freedom argue that punishment serves the cause of justice only if it is assumed that a person freely decided to commit an unlawful act. It does not make sense to punish someone who is completely determined by the past. Criminal law seems to be based on the idea that the violator might have chosen to behave differently from the way he or she actually did. On the other side, the scientific determinists maintain that the purpose of punishment is to rehabilitate, that is, to "redetermine" the person to make predictable changes in his or her attitudes and subsequent behavior. How would other positions on freedom-determinism approach this issue?

2. Here is a more subtle example of how our view of freedom and determinism affects our evaluation of criminal behavior. Bob and Jim together hold up a grocery store. Bob's parents abused him and taught him that taking whatever one can get away with from other people is a good thing. Jim's family is upper-middle class; his parents were intelligent, caring people who taught and modeled good behavior to their children, all of whom in turn enjoyed a close-knit family life. Are Bob and Jim equally guilty for their crime? Should they receive the same penalty? If Bob and Jim were minors, should their parents be held responsible? How similar is this situation to recent cases in which perpetrators of crimes (such as murdering a spouse) claim to be the *real* victim (e.g., of a long history of spouse abuse before the murder)?

3. You have been confronted with various views on freedom and determinism. Are you "free" to decide which view to adopt, or is this choice, like all others, simply "determined"? In what exact sense is it either one? What are some of the implications and consequences of your answer to this question? Are all the views about freedom and determinism consistent with the activity of philosophizing?

4. Suppose you are a socially concerned person trying to preserve the environment or prevent nuclear war or promote economic justice in the third world. On which freedom-determinism premise could you most consistently operate? Suppose you are a political conservative concerned about preserving the status quo. Which freedom-determinism option would you select to buttress your position?

5. A growing number of modern "counselors" are engaged in the effort to help people turn their lives around. Does this mean that human beings are really free to change or simply that others have become involved in the causal systems that determine their behavior?

Suggested Readings

Adler, Mortimer J. *Freedom: A Study of the Development of the Concept in the English and American Traditions of Philosophy*. Albany, NY: Magi Books, 1968.

Basinger, David, and Randall Basinger, eds. *Predestination and Free Will*. Downers Grove, IL: Inter-Varsity Press, 1986.

Berofsky, Bernard, ed. *Free Will and Determinism*. New York: Harper & Row, 1966.

Dray, W. H. "Determinism in History." In *The Encyclopedia of Philosophy*, vol. 2, pp. 373–378.

Enteman, Willard F. *The Problem of Free Will: Selected Readings*. New York: Scribner's, 1967.

Hollis, Martin. *Models of Man*. London: Cambridge University Press, 1977.

Hook, Sidney. *Determinism and Freedom*. New York: Macmillan, 1969.

Krutch, Joseph Wood. *The Measure of Man: On Freedom, Human Values, Survival and the Modern Temper*. New York: Grossett & Dunlap, 1953.

Lehrer, Keith, ed. *Freedom and Determinism*. New York: Random House, 1966.

Morgenbesser, Sidney, and James Walsh, eds. *Free Will*. Englewood Cliffs, NJ: Prentice-Hall, 1962.

Partridge, P. H. "Freedom." In *The Encyclopedia of Philosophy*, vol. 3, pp. 221–225.

Skinner, B. F. *Beyond Freedom and Dignity*. New York: Bantam, 1972.

Taylor, Richard. "Determinism." In *The Encyclopedia of Philosophy*, vol. 2, pp. 359–373.

Van Inwagen, Peter. *An Essay on Free Will*. Oxford: Clarendon Press, 1983.

Watson, Gary. *Free Will*. Oxford Readings in Philosophy. New York: Oxford University Press, 1982.

Williams, Clifford. *Free Will and Determinism: A Dialogue*. Indianapolis: Hackett, 1980.

CHAPTER 7
Philosophy and Religion

A. Questions to Consider

- Is religion what you feel and do or what you believe?
- Is God a supernatural Being or a part of nature?
- How can one believe in a loving God when there is so much suffering?
- Can a person be a Christian without believing in God?
- How can you decide which religion is the true one?
- Can you believe in science and religion at the same time?
- Should humanism be considered a religion?

B. Introduction

Theology today is in ferment. Not only is there tension among various theological views, but there is also tension within religions regarding what is most important: relationship to God or ethical behavior. Moreover, the religious alternatives put before us by modern thinkers are perhaps not new, but they are often couched in unfamiliar language, such as religionless Christianity, theistic naturalism, secular Christianity, panentheism, and Christian atheism.

We shall limit the discussion in this chapter to a brief description and analysis of the philosophical implications of some major religious alternatives that are currently under debate. The analysis will utilize, so far as possible, the terms and concepts that have been presented in earlier chapters.

1. The Philosophy of Religion

The proper function of the philosophy of religion is to study religious beliefs in an open-minded, impartial spirit. Its posture is neither acceptance nor rejection of the claims of any particular religion. The philosophical task is primarily one of criticism in the sense of careful analysis and evaluation.

The term **theology** has two distinct meanings. It may refer to a theoretical study of God and God's relation to the world; in this meaning it constitutes one area of the philosophy of religion. However, "theology" often refers to a systematic expression of the theories of one religion, for example, Catholic theology or Jewish theology; theology in this sense is not an aspect of the philosophy of religion but one of the objects for its study.

2. Religion Defined

Before examining diverse religious proposals, we must face the thorny problem of definition. It is widely agreed that a **religion** is a pattern of beliefs, attitudes, and practices. Religion is more than a set of intellectual beliefs, and it involves more than what is implied in Matthew Arnold's famous definition, "Religion is morality tinged with emotion." Granted that all religions are patterns of belief, feeling, and action, we can ask what distinguishes religion from science or psychoanalysis, both of which are patterns made up of these three elements. This question can be answered by presenting a few definitions of "religion." According to Royce, religion is devotion to a moral code reinforced by beliefs about the nature of things. According to Oman, religion is the recognition of the claim of ultimate reality—a reality worthy of and demanding worship. According to Bertocci, the core of religion is a personal belief that one's most important values are sponsored by or in harmony with the enduring structure of the universe. According to Barth, religion is individuals striving to make themselves righteous before that which they recognize as ultimate and decisive. According to Wieman, religion is ultimate commitment to what has power to transform human beings, because they cannot transform themselves. The common kernel of these definitions suggests that religion is what people believe, do, and feel in light of the conviction that their values are rooted in reality.

Paul Tillich's concept of religious faith as "ultimate concern" appears to enlarge the concept of religion to include such meanings as "his religion is success," "she worships her husband," and "his ultimate concern is himself." Such meanings, however useful in other contexts, far exceed the common usage of the term "religion." Tillich himself goes on to interpret "ultimate concern" to mean "a passionate concern for the ultimate."

In *Philosophical Thinking*, the Beardsleys provide a careful definition of "religion," consistent with most of those cited, which in abbreviated form can serve our purpose: "Religion" refers to any set of interrelated beliefs, together with the attitudes and practices determined by those beliefs, about human nature, the nature of the universe, how people should live, and the best methods to seek the truth about reality and values. This definition is open to criticism in that it gives priority to beliefs over attitudes and practices on the assumption that the latter are dependent on beliefs. The priority of beliefs can be defended on the ground that religious values and ceremonies, while they may be of greater personal significance to the believer than intellectual beliefs, necessarily *imply* certain beliefs and would wither unless the beliefs were accepted in some important sense as *true*. The central religious concern may be that a believer put faith *in* God and commit his or her life *to* God, in contrast to giving intellectual assent to the statement "God exists." But it is reasonable to hold that faith and commitment are meaningful only if the individual claims that the proposition "God exists" is a true one. We shall follow this line of reasoning in our discussion of religious alternatives and focus on the belief dimension.

3. Religious Language

Before we examine the alternatives we must consider the status of a statement like "God exists." Apart from whether or not it is true, philosophers in the twentieth century have asked whether or not it is *meaningful*. What does it mean to say "God exists" or "God created the world"?

This question was forcefully raised by logical positivists (see the discussion in Chapter 4, Epistemology, page 76). They argued that such religious statements are meaningless, as are any statements that are neither analytic nor empirically verifiable. In a similar fashion, Anthony Flew insisted that the claim "God exists" is vacuous because those who make it will not allow anything to falsify it; that is, any objection one may bring is met with a qualification by the believer. Flew used the story of a person who claimed a gardener was responsible for the continued existence of a garden. When asked to produce evidence of this gardener who had never been seen, the believer insisted that this gardener is such that he cannot be detected in any way. The problem is that when a religious assertion is qualified enough that nothing will count against it, it stands for everything and therefore says nothing.

R. M. Hare responded that Flew was right: unfalsifiable statements are *cognitively* meaningless. But religious statements can still be meaningful as convictions that have an impact on our conduct. This is similar to a position taken by R. B. Braithwaite who argued that religious assertions can be noncognitively meaningful because they have the practical value of supporting a "way of life," whether they are true or not. A variation on this theme was provided by Basil Mitchell: religious statements are falsifiable assertions in principle, but not in practice, because believers are not able to say what would count as a *decisive* falsification.

Those who follow Ludwig Wittgenstein insist that religious statements are meaningful, but one must attend to *how* they are meaningful. Wittgenstein argued that there are many "language games," such as those of newscasts and of mathematics. In each case the speaking of a language is part of the activity or "form of life." Meaning depends on the use of the language or which language game is being played. To understand a statement like "God exists," one must understand the context of its use and the rules embedded in the shared practices of the language-using community. That is to say, if you want to know what a person means who says "God created the world," you have to enter into the context of the religious community in which that statement is being made. A question then arises: Are we left with a kind of relativism or incommensurability in which each "form of life" is autonomous and impervious to judgments made by those outsiders who do not play a particular "language game"? Followers of Wittgenstein differ at this point. Those who answer in the negative argue that Wittgenstein insisted that the religious form of life is not necessarily separated from other linguistic practices and life activities.

These modern discussions of the meaning of religious language have their predecessors in earlier works of philosophers such as Thomas Aquinas. Aquinas argued that religious language is analogical, since language that was originally developed for finite creatures cannot literally apply to God. That is to say, words that humans use to describe God are used in a similar or related sense, not in exactly the same way (i.e., univocally) and not in a totally different way (i.e., equivocally). The analogy is based either on the fact that God is in a causal relation to humans (so that the effect is like the cause) or on the proportional difference between God and humans (so that, for example, human love gives us an idea of divine love). Our contemporaries continue to discuss the role in religious language of analogy, metaphor, and models, notably Max Black, Frederick Ferrè, and Ian Ramsey. And, as we shall see later in this chapter, theologians like David Tracy develop a symbolic use of religious language. In the end, no one has a corner on a theory of religious language. The discussion has gone on for some time and will continue.

C. Epistemological Issues

1. Introduction

The current state of religious thinking is in turmoil, and the reason for this condition is abundantly clear. Religion confronts a secular, science-oriented world, and most religious thinkers insist on engaging contemporaries in dialogue. They argue that religion must make sense to the modern mind or be dismissed as irrelevant. The present context of religious discussion is, then, a search for relevance, and the search hinges on the question of religious knowledge. The question is: How can religious beliefs be justified to the modern mind?

2. A Continuum of Religious Knowing

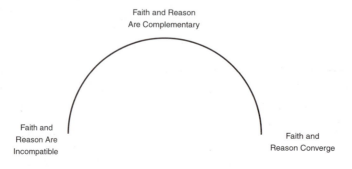

Faith and Reason
Are Complementary

Faith and
Reason Are
Incompatible

Faith and
Reason Converge

3. Ways of Religious Knowing

The tension between the modern mind and religion does not result primarily from a collision between two conflicting bodies of knowledge. The tension is sharper and deeper; it is a clash between seemingly irreconcilable ways of conceiving *what* reality is and *how* it can be known. In the philosophy of religion this tension is usually discussed in terms of the relation between faith and revelation on the one hand and reason on the other.

Undoubtedly the most common justification that people give for their religious beliefs is **faith**. What does "faith" mean in a statement such as "My belief that God (or soul or immortality) exists is based on faith"? It means very different things to different people.

"Faith" can refer to an act of complete commitment—"I am willing to bet my life on the truth of my belief." In this sense faith is often contrasted with reason because people do not give reasons or intellectual arguments to show that their beliefs are true; they simply report that they have taken "the leap of faith." It might even be argued that faith and reason are radically incompatible. On the other hand, if total commitment means commitment of a person's total, integrated self, faith will then necessarily include **reason** by being consistent with the beliefs to which that person gives intellectual assent. This consistency might be so complete that the objects of reason and faith are seen to converge; or reason might complement faith by providing rational grounds for holding a belief.

Revelation, with which faith is usually linked and which may stand allied with or opposed to reason, is interpreted in various ways. A traditional view in Western **theism** is that God revealed in the Bible a complete set of religious doctrines and truths. Within this overall view, some people hold that every biblical statement is inspired by God in word-for-word fashion and is thereby a *literal* truth. Others insist that biblical stories and descriptions must be demythologized and held as *symbolic* truth. In contrast to the traditional view, certain influential twentieth-century theologians, including Karl Barth and Emil Brunner, defend the idea that God is revealed in a *personal* way to people in all periods of history. In Brunner's words, "Scripture is only revelation when conjoined with God's spirit in the present." This view, which stresses the importance of personal religious experience, has been called a nonpropositional view of revelation. It is nonpropositional because the crucial connection is not abstract or even logical; it is fundamentally subjective.

a. *Faith and reason are incompatible.* The early Christian theologian Tertullian gave classical expression to this view with his rhetorical question "What hath Athens to do with Jerusalem?" The same orientation was expressed by Martin Luther, the Protestant reformer, who insisted that human reason could not reach God because grace is not rational and human reasoning has been distorted by sin. In his "Memorial" to his conversion to Christianity, Blaise Pascal began with the words "'The God of Abraham, the God of Isaac, the God of Jacob,' not of philosophers and scholars." Reason has its place—for instance, in science—but its place is not in religion. Thus, in

Western theism there have been those who refuse to let faith and revelation have anything to do with reason.

In modern thought this position is best expressed by religious existentialists such as Bultmann and Tillich. They are content to let science usurp the field of "knowing" reality and to ground religious faith in a personal response to reality. Faith, says Tillich emphatically, is not a dimension of knowledge and should never claim to be a type of knowledge. For him, "faith is a total and centered act of the personal self." His view is that metaphysical-theological statements are statements not about what exists but about people's experienced relation to existence. For example, the proposition "God exists" means "I experience a depth in my being when I respond to reality with ultimate concern." On the view that the term "God" refers to whatever is ultimate in a person's experience, the assertion that "God does not exist" is meaningless unless people encounter no depth in themselves at all. For Tillich, the only issue is to discover appropriate symbols for what *is* ultimate in human experience.

Kierkegaard spoke of the "infinite qualitative distinction" between God and humans. Human reason is incapable of contemplating God. Neverthless, Kierkegaard wrote that the postulate of God's existence "is so far from being arbitrary that it is precisely a life necessity. It is then not so much that God is a postulate, as that the existing individual's postulation of God is a necessity." Existentialists who follow this direction do not give logical reasons for their *belief* that God exists; instead, they give personal reasons for their *decision* to believe.

Critiques of the Incompatibility View

1.

By giving up all claims to religious knowledge and dealing solely with personal responses, the existential stand does not conflict with science but may end up as an extremely personal stance—what has been called radical subjectivity.

2.

Tillich and Bultmann assume that most human beings *are* concerned with ultimate matters, the depth in life. But modern people are not only science-minded; they are also increasingly oriented to finding satisfaction in practical, secular interests. They appear to lead full lives without probing to the depths of their existence.

3.

Tillich and Bultmann advance their ideas in defense of the Christian religion, but their epistemological stance could equally well support non-Christian beliefs or, indeed, a worldview that most people would consider nonreligious.

b. *Faith and reason converge.* One might summarize this view with the statement "All truth is God's truth." Perhaps the most outstanding proponents of this view in the Western tradition were the Christian Apologists, who defended the Christian religion against intellectual attacks in the second and third centuries. Justin Martyr and the Alexandrian school (which included Clement and Origen) identified the Greek philosophical concept of the "logos"—the rational principle that pervades the universe and gives it order—as the pre-incarnate Christ. They argued that the "seminal logos," in which all minds participate, has now been fully and clearly revealed in Jesus Christ. Thus, philosophers like Socrates knew something of the same truth that Christianity teaches. Philosophy, then, seeks the same God and the same truth as theology.

Some of these Christian theologians were influenced by Neoplatonism, found in the teachings of people like Plotinus. God is the One from whom all things emanated and to whom all things are drawn. It is understandable how such a belief would lead to the insistence that faith and reason ultimately converge.

Some would place Tillich in this category, since he believes that the theologian must be a conscious philosopher; but his existentialism qualifies his placement in this category. A better contemporary example of this position is Wolfhart Pannenberg. He insists that the scientific method is as applicable to theology as it is to other areas of academic discourse; theologians must operate under the same universally accepted methods of reasoning as does the rest of the West. Further, since theology investigates God—who, as the all-determining Reality, involves all reality—theology is the study of all reality from a certain point of view.

Critiques of the Convergence View

1.
While this view has much to commend it for its attempt to unify faith and reason, it is liable to dissolve the distinction between the religious and secular realms such that the former becomes a meaningless or needless category.

2.
Some would argue that this view illegitimately places God and other objects of intellectual inquiry on the same plane, whereas these belong on two radically incompatible levels of reality.

c. *Faith and reason are complementary.* This position argues for some overlapping between faith and reason; they neither contradict nor converge with each other but complement each other. For instance, the medieval theologian Thomas Aquinas thought that reason takes us part of the way to a true knowledge of God; for those who had the intellectual ability, reason not only confirmed what faith received from revelation but laid the foundation for truths that only revelation could provide (such as the doctrine of the trinity, which transcends reason's ability to grasp). For those who lacked the intelligence or time for philosophical reasoning, revelation would provide what reason could not grasp in the area of religious knowledge.

Though he had his predecessors, Aquinas gave classical expression to several proofs for the existence of God (such as points [1] and [3]), which are called the "Five Ways." Others have developed (or critiqued) these arguments or added to the list, (including points [2], [4], and [5]). They include the following:

(1) *The cosmological argument.*   In the **cosmological** argument everything that we observe in the world is dependent on conditions and causes that precede it in time, and these, in turn, are dependent on still other things. But there could not be an infinite regress of these dependent causes. Facing the contingency of things in the world leads us to recognize that there must exist *some* being whose existence is not contingent but necessary. The unconditioned, necessary source of the world's being is God—the First Mover and First Cause.

(2) *The ontological argument.*   First developed by Anselm and later elaborated by Descartes, this argument begins with the nature of being (refer to **ontology**). By definition, God is the most perfect being that we can conceive. A perfect being possesses all the attributes or characteristics of perfection, including the property of "existence." (That is, it is more perfect to have all the characteristics of perfection and exist than it is to have them and not exist.) Thus, the very definition or *idea* of God entails God's existence, and to say that "God does not exist" is therefore contradictory.

(3) *The design argument.*   The third of the classical arguments for God's existence is often considered the strongest because it affords a reasonable interpretation of the universe. The argument is founded on the observed orderliness of the universe. Consider the following analogy. Suppose you were wandering about in a barren desert and stumbled across a watch. Would you seriously entertain the hypothesis that the watch had been created by the purposeless swirling of the sand?

Many of the scientists of the seventeenth century were convinced by the design argument for God's existence. They found order and regularity in the universe. William Paley concluded that God was a perfect watchmaker who had created an orderly and harmonious machine that would run forever. Because God was perfect, the machine was perfect. God did not need to tinker with the creation but could leave it alone, and it would operate eternally. This view of God as a perfect and unconcerned inventor is called **deism**.

(4) *The moral argument.* Immanuel Kant, William James, and a host of others justify belief in God's existence by pointing to the desirable moral consequences that belief produces in the lives of many people—lives dedicated to noble causes and replete with meaning and peace of mind. A belief should be accepted on pragmatic grounds when empirical evidence does not support or

deny its validity. The belief in God is in this category. The belief in God not only motivates and supports our moral striving but is also necessary to explain the very existence of moral concern and the hunger for righteousness. However various the themes played by the instrument of culture, they all point toward a deeply embedded moral sense, the God-given moral nature in human beings.

(5) *The common sense of humankind argument.* The evidence is clear that every culture in every place and period of history (with the possible exception of our own) has had some form of religion and some conception of God or gods. The common sense of humankind, then, supports the supernatural worldview. No scientific worldview has ever stood up to the test of time.

Arguments like these represent classical attempts to develop a **natural theology**. Recently, developments in this area have included efforts to treat the existence of God as a hypothesis and to evaluate it in terms of its ability to integrate the full range of human experience. Peter Bertocci utilizes this approach to the discovery of religious knowledge. He labels his conception of truth "empirical coherence." He applies his concept by developing a wider design argument for God's existence. He argues that the existence of a creative cosmic Intelligence is the most reasonable hypothesis to explain the following "empirical" evidence: (1) the purposive interrelation of matter and life, (2) the relevance of thought to reality, (3) the interrelationship of moral effort and the order of nature, (4) the support in nature for human values, (5) this world as good for human beings, (6) the significance of esthetic experience, and (7) the confirmation of religious experience.

A similar line of reasoning is used by Teilhard de Chardin, who attempts "to develop a homogeneous and coherent perspective of our general extended experience of man. A whole which unfolds." He finds the God hypothesis necessary to explain the consistent movement of evolution toward the production of ever-higher levels of consciousness in what he calls an "irreversibly personalizing universe."

Critiques of the Complementarity View

1.

With regard to the rationalistic arguments for God's existence, it should be noted at this point that statements about the *nature* of God are often derived by deduction, in the tradition of rationalism. For example, it is held that God is by definition perfect. On the basis of this principle, it is then reasoned that God must exhibit in supreme degree the qualities imperfectly found in human beings: Human beings have limited knowledge—God must be omniscient; human power is finite—God must be all-powerful. This deductive kind of reasoning seems straightforward enough, but its use has led to conflicting ideas. For example, most theists reason that, since God is perfect,

God must be eternal and unchanging; other theists reason that human beings grow and develop, and, therefore, some aspect of God's nature must also change and be enhanced through time. Modern philosophers increasingly refuse to enter such disputes since it seems impossible to resolve them on either rational or empirical grounds or in terms of revealed truth.

2.

Critiques of the arguments for God's existence are presented in greater detail:

2a. *The cosmological argument.*   Many able minds find no difficulty in accepting the idea of an infinite series of causes and effects; but, even for those who insist that there must have been a First Cause, the cosmological argument provides no ground for believing that First Cause to be God rather than, say, matter-energy.

2b. *The ontological argument.*   Both formulations of the ontological argument confuse the *meaning* of a symbol with the *existence* of that to which the symbol refers. "Ghost" means a visible immaterial apparition, but the fact that someone uses the term in no way guarantees that there are such things as ghosts.

2c. *The design argument.*   The classical criticism of the design argument was made by David Hume. In *Dialogues*, Hume suggested that the universe is actually more like an animal or a vegetable than a watch; hence we might better infer an organic impulse as creator rather than a Mind or Spirit. Then, pointing to the many imperfections of the world (the blind alleys of the evolutionary process are one example), he wondered whether perhaps our world was created by a second-rate deity on one of its "off" days.

Hume's general position might be put in the form of a question: Since earthquakes, disease, idiocy, sin, death, and all manner of human suffering are not accepted as evidence of the universe's *lack* of design, what imperfection, if it *did* exist, *would* be accepted as evidence?

2d. *The moral argument.*   Every society, it is true, has a moral code, but the practical demands of associated living provide a sufficient explanation of and support for such codes without appeal to a supernatural source or sanction.

2e. *The common sense of humankind argument.*   The common sense of humankind has consistently supported beliefs in magic, the flatness of the earth, and the supernatural origin of dreams. Why trust it concerning God's existence when we do not trust it in other matters?

In light of these criticisms of such rationalistic arguments, perhaps it is better to assume the posture of Anselm and view these not as proofs leading *to* belief in God's existence but as proofs leading *from* belief. That is, at best such arguments help to confirm the faith one already has.

3.

The difficulty in the method of empirical coherence is that people do not agree on the conclusions that come from application of the method. For example, the same evidence that Bertocci uses to support the hypothesis that God exists is explained by other observers on the hypothesis that God does *not* exist or that God exists not as a being but as a dimension of reality.

We turn now to consider some of the religious beliefs that eventuate from the diverse ways of knowing and believing that we have examined.

D. Metaphysical Issues

1. Introduction

The basic religious choice confronting Western thinkers today is whether to hold on to some version of classical theism as it developed in the Greek-Judeo-Christian tradition or to pay heed to one of the myriad voices reinterpreting or rebelling against that tradition.

The mood of many recent religious thinkers is consistent with the biblical statement "we have this treasure in earthen vessels." If the treasure of religious truth cannot be conveyed in traditional idioms, let these be discarded without regret and new models constructed. Such is the atmosphere of much present-day religious discussion.

2. A Continuum of Beliefs on the Nature of God

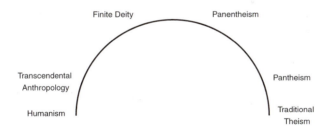

3. The Nature of God

a. *Traditional theism: God is a supernatural Being.* Theism in its traditional form was first formulated by Philo (ca. 20 B.C.E.–54 C.E.). Traditional theism lasted 1,700 years without serious challenge and remains today the most popular conception in the minds of both believers and nonbelievers. In this view, God is conceived as a supernatural Being, who is perfect in all respects. The tradition argues that human experience does not provide an adequate basis for understanding God's nature. Despite this position, God is described as *possessing* qualities that human beings prize for themselves, such as love, wisdom, and power. God is described as *lacking* those characteristics that people consider inferior in themselves, such as incompleteness, exposure to suffering, and dependence on a changing environment. In the **Thomistic** phrase, God is "pure actuality" but not pure potentiality. God is held to be supreme in Being but not supreme in Becoming. God is simple, not complex; a unity, not a multiplicity of parts. The traditional view holds that God is completely self-sufficient—in no way dependent on anything outside. God is eternal and unchanging, totally unaffected by events in time, and no aspect of God's nature ever changes. As Creator, God is omnipotent cause, never effect; wholly active, not passively affected by any event. God's knowledge is perfect (omniscient), and this includes knowledge of the future. God is wholly good, without lack or imperfection.

Critiques of Traditional Theism

1.

If God is perfectly good and all-powerful, how can we account for the excessive suffering in the world? This question poses what is known as the problem of evil. The answer that suffering is a necessary concomitant of natural laws and that therefore ours is still "the best of all possible worlds" raises further questions about God's ability to create a more harmonious order. A more frequent response to the problem is that evil results from the free will with which God endowed human beings because God wanted human love to be freely given; God wanted uncoerced obedience to the divine will. But this answer is inconsistent with the classical view that God is complete and does not want or desire anything because nothing is lacking.

2.

Is it sufficient that a God of love actively pours out love while remaining totally unaffected by the loving responses that are generated? It has been suggested that for God to experience complete (perfect) happiness, God's nature would have to change progressively in time by having added to it the joyful experiences of sentient creatures. There appears to be a tension or even a contradiction, then, between the classical view of a self-sufficient God and the conception of God as Loving Father. It is conceivable that a totally self-contained Being created the world, but in what sense could God care for creatures without directly experiencing their pains and frustrations—unless in some sense God suffers with them? The Christian would no doubt answer that God-embodied-in-Christ *does* suffer. This answer points to the central difficulty: how the timeless and unchanging can possibly become **incarnate** in our world of historical change.

3.

Other inconsistencies, or at least paradoxes, in traditional theism concern God's knowledge of the world. In the traditional view, God has an unchanging knowledge of objects that change. Furthermore, how can God have a full, perfect awareness and knowledge of the world since it is denied that the multiplicity of things are constituents of God's Being? Knowledge is incomplete unless events are directly experienced from the "inside." By analogy, I am more exactly aware of my toothache, which is inside of me and which I directly feel, than I am of your toothache.

4.

Ludwig Feuerbach and Sigmund Freud argued that the God of traditional theism is merely a projection of human minds. Religion is an illusion fed by our wishful thinking. To avoid facing up to the real world, with its stone-cold natural forces and our finite limitations, we fabricate a transcendent father figure that, if nothing else, comforts us because we know that "all is the Father's will." Freud recommended that we grow out of such an infantile response, face reality, and adopt a mature, scientific view of the world.

The religious views that will now be presented can best be understood as alternative responses to the difficulties posed by traditional theism.

b. *Pantheism: All is God.*   Pantheists put forward a double claim: First, all that exists constitutes a unity. Second, this all-inclusive unity is divine. In this view, God is not a separate being or personality; rather, all the laws, forces, and manifestations of the self-existing universe are God; God is a whole that gathers up into itself all that exists. One argument for pantheism dates from the Middle Ages: Because God alone truly *is*, all that is must in some sense be God. In Spinoza's language, there is only one substance, a single, connected system; this unlimited, all-inclusive substance is Nature/God. God is one with the incessantly active whole of Nature. Spinoza believed that by removing the traditional personal traits of mind and will from the concept of God, he opened the way for human beings to unify themselves with the divine center. The goal of Vedic pantheism in Hindu philosophy is also to unite the believer with ultimate reality, Brahma. Unlike Spinoza, however, Vedanta teaches that the imperfect, changing world of material objects and everyday experience is illusory; only Brahma, perfect, unchanging, and indefinable, is real.

Critique of Pantheism

One criticism of pantheism is that neither scientific fact nor everyday experience supports the view that all that exists is a unity, much less a divine unity. The major difficulty with pantheism for many people is that the pantheistic God is simply not a being at all.

c. *Panentheism: All is in God.*   **Panentheism** is a view of God held by a number of religious thinkers and philosophers, most notably A. N. Whitehead. The theory has been developed most systematically by Charles Hartshorne in the Process school. Panentheism claims to incorporate the strengths of both traditional theism (God transcends the world) and pantheism (God is all) while avoiding their difficulties. According to panentheists, God is the Supreme Being, who totally includes the world. Most of the polarities found in human experience, such as being-becoming and unchanging-changing, find supreme expression in God's nature. God's original (primordial) nature is eternal, unchanging, containing all possibilities. God's historical (consequent) nature is in time, constantly growing and expanding, containing all actualities. God is a unity of multiplicity. God's Being, then, contains the major contrasts: Being and Becoming; the One and the Many; sustaining activity, yet feeling receptivity; cause and effect. God's knowledge is not static, completed, outside time; rather, it is full memory of the past and full awareness of novel events as they occur in the world, which God's Being includes.

Panentheists like Whitehead present us with the picture of an organic universe made up of compound individuals. Each higher level of reality is compounded of the next lower, simpler level. A cell in the human body, for example, is a living unity of an immense number of individuals of a lower order of complexity (atoms, molecules). The human body is made up of billions of living cells, yet it is experienced by each of us as one. The universe may also be understood as an individual (God), compounded of all individuals, that experiences itself as one. This picture of the universe is captured in Alexander Pope's couplet:

> All are parts of one stupendous whole,
> Whose body nature is, and God the soul.

The metaphysical view of H. N. Wieman is a further variation of the Process position, which accords well with panentheism. People experience in their lives the challenge of ideals, possibilities for personal fulfillment, a movement forward to ever-richer value realization. The key term for Wieman is "creativity," especially the creative transformation of people in their capacity to think, control, and appreciate. God is creativity, the creative world process. Creativity is not supernatural, but it is mysterious and beyond full human understanding and control. Creativity is eternal in the sense that it functions continuously in the present; it is not "out of" or "beyond" time. Creativity is the very stuff and structure of natural reality. Creativity, says Wieman, is a power that can transform human beings, save them from evil, endow them with the greatest good—provided that they commit themselves without reservation to this transforming power.

Critique of Panentheism

While panentheists attempt to avoid the criticisms leveled against traditional theism, they are not entirely immune from them. For instance, panentheism has been criticized for having a God who is so dependent on and limited by the world (that is, who is not omnipotent) as to be incapable of bringing a final end to evil and suffering.

d. *Finite deity: God is a limited Being.* We have noted that the conception of God in traditional theology raised the problem of evil: If God is all-good and all-powerful, how can we account for the imperfections of the world and human suffering?

Some human suffering can be explained in terms of the human exercise of free will, and the suffering that leads to the perfecting of moral virtue is consistent with the idea of God's goodness. But it appears to many observers that there is an excess of both natural evils, such as destructive earthquakes and floods, and moral evils, as when temptation and suffering so far exceed people's capacity to respond creatively to them that they lead to total breakdown of the personality.

Religious thinkers typically maintain the position that God is perfectly good and cannot be conceived of as wanting or willing evil. In order to give an empirically coherent account of excess evil, some of these thinkers put forward the conception that God is a finite Being, that is, has limited power.

For example, Plato advanced the concept of chaotic matter, an environment uncreated by and external to God and recalcitrant to God's will. Plato envisioned God as a cosmic Artist, who attempts to shape the matter of the world into rational form. God is, then, not omnipotent but restricted by the receptivity involved in the original matter, which Plato called the receptacle.

W. P. Montague finds unsatisfactory Plato's dualism of two eternal principles, God and matter. Montague conceives of God's environment as "inside" rather than "outside" God. What in God is not God, God's inner environment, is the world itself, consisting of "all finite existence, energies, particles or what not." For Montague, God is an ascending force that labors to unify the relatively free and uncooperative beings and elements that compose God's inner environment. God is a kind of leaven working on chaotic elements to bring evolutionary development and greater possibilities of value realization.

E. S. Brightman has worked out yet another version of a finite God. Brightman holds that the recalcitrant factor that God struggles to harmonize and spiritualize is the Given within God's own nature. The Given is the nonrational content of God's mind, comparable to the sensations and feelings that are given as brute facts in human experience. The Given is the raw material for the expression of God's moral and esthetic purposes.

Brightman's theory differs from Montague's by maintaining that all finite beings, including human beings, are created by and dependent on God for their nature and ongoingness. Montague's and Brightman's concepts of a finite God, but not Plato's, can be fitted into the view of panentheism discussed earlier in this chapter.

Critique of the Finite Deity View

Since Montague and Brightman share panentheism's conception of God's Being, they are also susceptible to the same criticisms.

e. *Transcendental anthropology: God is a dimension of human existence.* **Transcendental anthropology** emerged as a reaction to "radical theology," which had proclaimed the death of God. Although the latter movement flared up and died quickly, it forced many religious thinkers to reformulate or reject traditional religious doctrines in order to be consistent with a scientific worldview. Proponents of this movement included Paul Tillich, Dietrich Bonhoeffer, John A. T. Robinson (*Honest to God*), Paul Van Buren, Harvey Cox, William Hamilton, and Thomas J. J. Altizer.

Bonhoeffer posed the issue most poignantly in his prison letters before he was hanged by the Nazis in 1945: "How is it possible to talk of God in a world that has shed its religious penumbra?" His answer was "religionless Christianity." He argued that modern humanity has come of age and is no longer dependent on a "God of the gaps" to explain the workings of the universe or to intrude into human lives at moments of personal crisis. People today, said Bonhoeffer, feel no need to fit the observable universe into any metaphysical framework "beyond" it. He said that "man has learned to cope with all questions of importance without recourse to God as a working hypothesis." He spoke of "God in human form" and "God as truly **immanent**."

Thus, the radical theologians totally rejected theological dualism and all ideas of a **supernatural** realm that is somehow "above" or "beyond" the natural world we inhabit. Tillich held that the protests of atheists against the existence of a Supreme Being were correct. These thinkers describe God not as creator but as "the ground of being" or "the ground of our being." They also refer to God as Being-Itself, ultimate reality, the structure of reality, and the depth of existence. Salvation is not forgiveness through the atoning death of Christ but the ontological reunion with the ground of being. Tillich, Robinson, and Bonhoeffer insisted that the supernatural God of traditional theism is no longer a living reality in contemporary minds. Thus, **secularism** is the key idea here: Any question arising in life must and can be answered in this world of space and time, without any reference to the transcendent. Classical beliefs must be "contextualized" so that the meanings of our religious terms and the language we use about God will suit the *Zeitgeist*—the modern self-understanding.

Responding to the concerns of radical theology, some "revisionist theologians," such as David Tracy, have used the method of transcendental anthropology to revise traditional theology such that the result is both appropriate to the Christian tradition and existentially adequate for the human experiences of secular people.

Tracy suggests that our everyday space-and-time experiences disclose moments or features in which dimensions of the ultimate or transcendent reality appear. Concerns are raised that cannot be answered in mere space and time categories. But traditional Christian categories can make sense of our present experience, and it is the theologian's task to give appropriate symbolic expression to the "faith of secularity." This faith involves the drive that all of us have to find life intelligible, coherent, and worthwhile. This drive implies, or is validated by, the assumption that there is an ultimate intelligible ground of being—namely, God. We express this "faith" in "limit language," a form of religious language that goes beyond the categories of secularity. For example, the awareness of our temporal existence not only opens up possibilities of advance, change, newness, and hope but also reminds us that all things decay and are transient—that we are getting older. At the limits of our temporality, facing our death, we experience a void. But we can express our confidence in that which goes beyond our experience through limit language that recalls our basic faith in the value of life (that is, "heaven" or "a new heaven and a new earth"). Or we experience evil acts, such as the Holocaust, that are so heinous that they cry out for a more-than-human judgment—for a "hell." Again, we experience a transcendental dimension to our existence that we can appropriately and adequately express only in religious language. This is how the revisionist theologians answer the question "How is it possible to talk about God in a world gone secular?" Their answer: In language that is appropriate to the Christian tradition (in Tracy's case) and adequate for modern human experience.

Critiques of Transcendental Anthropology

1.
Critics have confronted the radical theologians with a difficult question: In what sense can God as Being or the ground of being, but not *a* Being, be characterized as "gracious, personal, and loving"? It is hard to conceive how anything other than a person can have personal qualities.

2.
Is it possible that so much attention will be focused on culturally adequate expressions of religious faith that the latter loses its prophetic function and becomes a captive of the cultural milieu? This seems to have happened in Nazi Germany, when the German Lutheran Church gave religious expression and endorsement to Hitler's agenda.

3.
Does religion really end up being nothing more than an expression of lofty ideals and aspirations such that "God" is only "human in a loud voice"? (Refer to Feuerbach's critique of theism.)

f. *Humanism: God is replaced by humans.*   A modern expression of what many have called a "secular religion" is found in the philosophical perspective loosely referred to as **humanism**. Numerous definitions of humanism have been proposed, and humanists differ widely in their attitudes and activities, but there are certain common characteristics that humanists tend to exhibit.

Probably the most basic humanistic assumption is that human beings are somehow a source or center of value. Whatever else they may be, people are, in their own right, valuable or meaningful. Theistic humanists believe people to be divinely created; naturalistic humanists see people simply as natural animals; but, either way, human beings are good—simply as human beings.

Many present-day humanists echo the early Greek sophist Protagoras: "Man is the measure of all things." Humankind is the means by which the world assumes a dimension of value.

A second characteristic or emphasis among humanists is their typical opposition to supernatural and especially authoritarian types of religion. Humankind is somehow special, but this fact does not imply that it must explain its specialness or uniqueness in abstract or nonhuman terms. It is wondrous and good just to be human. It is meaningful to live here and now—without the crutch of an eternal reward or a **transcendent** existence yet to be attained. Humanism proposes a means for meeting, in a practical, secular way, some of the basic human needs traditionally met by religion. This does not require belief in the supernatural or in an abstract principle. Human beings—on this earth, in this life—can manage their most pressing affairs. As Corliss Lamont expresses it: "This life is all and enough." Those qualities referred to as "spiritual" merely reflect people at their best, fighting cooperatively, intelligently, and courageously for their own and their neighbors' welfare. Their efforts are guided by human sympathy and concern.

A third characteristic of humanists is that they view human beings as in some respect free. Human beings may live in a natural world of cause and effect, but they are not fully explained in deterministic terms. They are not *merely* material entities or machines. A human being is a special kind of complex organism that can think, objectify experience, and, within limits, rebuild his or her own environment. Furthermore, human beings are dominated by no moral imperatives beyond those they prescribe for themselves. When they obey rules or laws not of their own making, they lose their humanness and become enslaved. Human beings are answerable to each other. Humanists express the staunch conviction that human values and human potentialities must not be overwhelmed by any belief or system that does not take account of humanity's singular but fundamental humanness.

A fourth quality exhibited by most humanists is their willingness to rely on reason and intelligence to answer human questions and to solve human problems. Usually this means that in technical matters science is viewed as the most effective method for changing and improving the world. In the area of moral values human beings are credited with the capacity to reason and to apply scientific knowledge to the enlightened regulation of human affairs. No extrahuman sources of knowledge are needed or, indeed, acknowledged.

Finally, humanists typically identify themselves as **humanitarians**. This means that they show an abiding concern for the good life for themselves and their fellows. They support such causes as brotherhood and social justice in the belief that freedom, peace, and democracy are practical and attainable goals that human beings can learn about and work to create. Many humanists work toward a universal society in which people voluntarily and thoughtfully cooperate to satisfy one another's basic needs. They envision a shared life in a shared world.

Not all humanists subscribe to every one of the above points. Nevertheless, they exhibit a steadfast dedication to a person-centered morality in which humankind is viewed as a whole and in which the survival and welfare of the species *Homo sapiens* becomes a cause worthy of the time, energy, thought, and devotion of all human beings. Humanists insist that moral values be removed from the jurisdiction of theological dogma or abstract speculation. They commit themselves to the proposition that human behavior—especially relations with fellows—should be constantly reviewed and revised in the light of current human needs and changing social conditions. They prefer to accept no worldview at all rather than permit human beings to be squeezed into any categories that rob them of their integral humanness. They may even use a traditional religious imagery when they envision "a society of loved ones."

The strong **axiological** emphasis in humanism raises questions that will be addressed in the following section. (See also Chapter 8.)

Critiques of Humanism

1.

Humanism speaks of humanity's "singular and fundamental humanness." But on what basis (i.e., by the standards of which humans) is this "humanness" defined? Without some authoritative transcendent "referee," women, African-Americans, homosexuals, and "skinheads" might all question prevailing definitions. And environmentalists might even question the specialness and uniqueness of humans, arguing that the attitude that "man is the measure of all things" is precisely what has hurt our planet.

2.

Has reliance on human reason and intelligence answered our questions and solved our problems? The same reason and intelligence that has developed central air-conditioning has also unleashed atomic weapons on people—twice. It has developed a technology that keeps people alive, but cannot agree on when and how long to do so. In fact, while our reason and intelligence have informed us *about* humans, we seem to be no closer to a definition of what a "human" *essentially is*.

3.

Does experience really permit us to unqualifiedly insist that human beings are good? Isn't the problem of the Holocaust precisely the fact that *humans* killed eleven million of their own species? What other species of animal would do that?

E. Axiological Issues

1. Introduction

The particular stand a person takes on epistemological and metaphysical issues has implications for how he will think about values and moral issues.

This interrelationship also holds true in the area of religious beliefs. For example, a person who believes that God's revelation is propositional will seek a precise set of moral rules to guide his value decisions; a person who believes in God's revelation as personal rather than propositional will look for grounds other than exact rules on which to base her moral judgments. Similarly, someone who rejects belief in the existence of a supernatural order will, if she is consistent, attempt to realize her highest values during her earthly existence. In what follows, we will sample only some of the options available in the area of religious ethics.

2. A Continuum of Religious Values

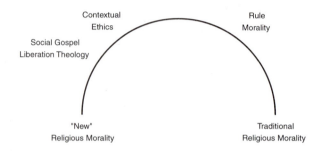

3. Traditional Religious Morality

Remembering St. Augustine's dictum "Love God, and then do what you will," we must be careful not to attribute to traditional Christian theology one uniform way of thinking about moral matters. Nonetheless, many Protestant and Catholic leaders through the centuries have located the heart of Christian **ethics** in the *content* of moral commands that are proclaimed to each succeeding generation as unchanging and eternally valid. The most vocal proponent of this view today in the United States is the Religious Right.

We will meet this view of values in Chapter 8 under the heading "Theory of Objectivism." (You may want to read that section now in order to contrast this perspective with the "new" religious morality.) This view is sometimes called rule **morality** because it is formulated into a code of specific rules of conduct.

Critiques of Traditional Religious Morality

1.

Moral rules become out of date; they cease to be relevant to changing conditions. For example, nineteenth-century codes on slavery, war, and the status of women simply do not apply to present conditions.

2.

Moral teachings, such as "love your neighbor," cannot be adequately encompassed in a set of moral dos and don'ts because moral teachings concern a person's motives and the consequences of that person's acts in specific situations, not just the behavior itself.

3.

The whole approach that arrives at what is right and wrong by a process of deduction from authoritative principles is unconvincing to people who have learned to derive guiding principles for conduct inductively from experience.

Now we can survey some alternative conceptions of religious ethics as critical reactions to the traditional moral approach.

4. "New" Religious Morality

a. *The social gospel and liberation theology.*   Following World War I, Protestant liberals reacted to what they considered the limitations of traditional formulations of morality by proclaiming that the true meaning of Christian ethics is a **social gospel**. Walter Rauschenbusch, for example, embraced God as a fellow worker in reforming society. The Christian's primary moral duty, he said, lies not in achieving personal salvation but in saving society. His obligation is to attack the social problems of disease, poverty, and social injustice and create the Kingdom of God on earth here and now.

The parallel stance of **liberation theology** was set forth in 1968 at the Catholic Bishops Conference in Medellin, Columbia: The Church must follow the gospel mandate in defending the rights of the poor, the oppressed, and the marginalized. Pope Paul VI addressed prominent citizens of Bogotá before the conference: "You, Lords of this World and Sons of the Church . . . your ears and your hearts must be sensitive to the voices crying out for bread, concern, justice, and a more active participation in the direction of society." Archbishop Romero, before his assassination in El Salvador in 1980, declared that the Church lives in a political world because it has opted for those who are oppressed and repressed. "It could not be otherwise," he said, "if the Church, like Jesus, is to turn itself toward the poor."

b. *Contextual ethics.*   Working largely from the work of Dietrich Bonhoeffer, some contemporary Protestant ethicists have developed "contextual ethics" in response to traditional moral theories that place binding rules above an empathetic assessment of the specific context in which an action is required. Bonhoeffer called for Christians to reject the idea of living in two spheres—church and world, sacred and secular. Christians are to serve Christ in the marketplace, not in a monastery. They are to get "earthy" and help the world to become truly worldly. As one contextualist, Paul Lehmann, puts it, the goal of Christian ethics is to help people become more human. In doing so, each situation will have to be assessed in order to make a free and responsible choice, which norms and rules cannot usually anticipate.

H. Richard Niebuhr was another fountainhead of this ethical position, influencing others, such as James Gustafson. Niebuhr called his theory "social existentialism" to show that the self is both shaped by social forces and radically free to act responsibly for God and others. Thus, a human being is an "answerer," in dialogue with constantly changing relationships. Believing that God is acting *in* all of these situations, we are called to respond in a way that is "fitting" to the action of such a God as Christianity conceives. Ethics, then, is response to a Person, not enslavement to rules. Ethics asks first not "What should we do?" but "What is God doing?" The answer requires knowledge of what is going on in the world *and* good theology.

As we shall see in the next chapter, contextualism shares a place in ethical theory with "situation ethics."

Critiques of "New" Religious Morality

1.

The social gospel and liberation theology have been criticized from two sides. The neo-orthodox theologian Reinhold Niebuhr argued that social evils such as war and social injustice are the inevitable by-products of our human sinfulness and that we can never perfect ourselves to the point of removing them. We must resign ourselves to the fact that we are too selfish and weak to change the power structure of society. Archbishop Romero held, on the contrary, that the essence of sin is to turn the children of God, temples of the Holy Spirit, the body of Christ in history, into victims of oppression and injustice, into slaves of economic greed, into fodder for political repression.

In the mid-1980s, Pope John Paul II and Vatican authorities expressed agreement with the liberal theologians that the Church should take a "preferential option for the poor" but severely criticized two of them, Father Gustavo Gutierrez of Peru and Friar Leonardo Boff of Brazil, for using Marxism and the concept of "class struggle" in their analyses of Latin American poverty. Father Boff stated in response that "our base is faith, religion, Christianity." Rather than being a capitulation to Marxism, liberation theology is a recovery of the prophetic biblical roots that so much of Christianity has forgotten.

2.

Christian ethicists who work from an "ethics of principles" (such as Paul Ramsey and John Bennett) criticize contextualists for relying too little on ethical principles and moral reasoning and, instead, relying too much on imagination, intuition, and free response. While the contextualists argue that they are trying to avoid relativism, they charge those who teach an ethics of principles with the removal of a *living* God and an ethic that is intellectualized.

F. Conclusion

Traditional beliefs about the nature of God, moral laws, and avenues of revealed truth have deep roots; they remain living options for many people.

But new experiences, and new interpretations of experiences both old and new, confront us with a wide variety of religious alternatives.

This wide variety was evident at the recent Parliament on World Religions held in Chicago. While it was intended to be a model of toleration, some events at the conference indicated that religious commitments are often neither tentative nor inclusive of others. In fact, to use the language that postmodernism rejects (as we saw in Chapter 4), inherent in many religious belief systems is their claim to be providing a "master narrative" that excludes (or at least supersedes) all other religions' claims to truth.

Nonetheless, religious beliefs are especially affected by science, secularism, and cultural pluralism. For instance, epistemologically those beliefs tend to be moving from authoritarianism and rationalistic positions toward empirical and experiential standpoints. This is especially evident in the narrative approach to religious beliefs, in which the stories of people who have religious experiences are more important than statements of doctrines or truths that they hold. In fact, the latter arise out of or are entailed in the former. Metaphysically, there have been movements away from traditional theism in the direction of idealist theories, such as New Age pantheism and panentheism. Axiologically, the trend is from absolutism toward contextual or liberationist positions or virtue ethics (see Chapter 8).

The student of philosophy is challenged to assess religious alternatives and trends according to philosophical criteria that have been developed in the earlier chapters. How reasonable are the assumptions underlying a particular religious viewpoint? How comprehensive and consistent is a given theological argument? What are the wider implications and consequences of adopting one or another religious belief? How adequately does a particular religious idea integrate experience and enrich understanding? A rigorous examination of alternative religious beliefs will surely increase a student's awareness of the power and the limitations—the promises and the risks—of the philosophical enterprise.

Case Study and Discussion Questions

Case Study

In the best-selling book *Embraced by the Light*, Betty J. Eadie writes about her near-death experience in which she had an encounter with Jesus. She asked him why God did not give us just one pure religion:

Each of us, I was told, is at a different level of spiritual development and understanding. Each person is therefore prepared for a different level of spiritual knowledge. All religions upon the earth are necessary because there are people who need what they teach. People in one religion may not have a complete understanding of the Lord's gospel and never will have while in that religion. But that religion is used as a stepping-stone to further knowledge. Each church fulfills spiritual needs that perhaps others cannot fill. No one church can fulfill everyone's needs at every level. As an individual raises his level of understanding about God and his own eternal progress, he might feel discontented with the teachings of his present church and seek a different philosophy or religion to fill that void. When this occurs he has reached another level of understanding and will long for further truth and knowledge, and for another opportunity to grow. And at every step of the way, these new opportunities to learn will be given.

Having received this knowledge, I knew that we have no right to criticize any church or religion in any way.[1]

1. Is the last sentence compatible with a philosophical attitude that assesses religious alternatives? Is such a sentiment compatible with other statements that Eadie makes in her book (such as, "We must never consider suicide")? Is it easier to respect all religious viewpoints while engaged in philosophical analysis than it is while holding one's own religious convictions?

2. Are there metaphysical beliefs held by a finite theist (the position that Eadie holds) that are simply incompatible with those held by a pantheist? a humanist?

3. Can the insistence that we tolerate all religions ever itself be exclusionary and intolerant? (This is sometimes referred to as a *self-referential* criticism.)

Discussion Questions

1. Assuming God exists, can we best conceive of Him/Her/It as infinite, finite, or a dimension of human existence?

2. Which is more adequate as a guide to sexual conduct: rule morality or contextual ethics?

3. Which "solution" to the "problem of evil" is most defensible?

a. God allows adversity and suffering to inspire and test human virtues.

b. Evil stems not from God but from human sinfulness, and it is morally just that sinners suffer.

c. In the final analysis, evil is unreal, an illusion.

d. Evil is real, and a finite God struggles with and through human beings to overcome it.

e. Natural and moral evils are practical realities to be faced and overcome by human efforts.

f. God created the universe with as many different entities as possible; some are on lower levels than others, but none is "evil."

4. "To be acceptable and effective as a teacher in a public elementary school in the United States today, a person must practice the philosophy of humanism." To what extent do you believe this statement to be true or false? Why?

Suggested Readings

Allen, Diogenes. *Philosophy for Understanding Theology*. Atlanta: John Knox, 1985.

Alston, William P. "Philosophy of Religion, Problems of." In *Encyclopedia of Philosophy*, vol. 6, pp. 285–289.

Altizer, Thomas J., and William Hamilton. *Radical Theology and the Death of God*. New York: Bobbs-Merrill, 1966.

---

[1]Betty J. Eadie, *Embraced by the Light* (Placerville, CA: Gold Leaf Press, 1992), pp. 45–46.

Barbour, Ian G. *Issues in Science and Religion*. New York: Harper & Row, 1966.

Berryman, Philip. *The Religious Roots of Rebellion: Christians in Central American Revolutions*. Maryknoll, NY: Orbis, 1984.

Boff, Leonardo. *Jesus Christ Liberator*. Maryknoll, NY: Orbis, 1978.

Bonhoeffer, Dietrich. *Letters and Papers from Prison*. Rev. ed. Edited by Eberhard Bethage. New York: Macmillan, 1967.

Buber, Martin. *I and Thou*. 2d ed. New York: Scribner's, 1958.

Flew, Anthony, and Alasdair MacIntyre, eds. *New Essays in Philosophical Theory*. London: SCM Press Ltd., 1955.

Freud, Sigmund. *The Future of an Illusion*. Translated by James Strachey. New York: W. W. Norton, 1961.

Gutierrez, Gustavo. *A Theology of Liberation*. 2d ed. Translated and edited by Sr. Caridad Inda and John Eagleson. Maryknoll, NY: Orbis, 1988.

Henderson, Charles P. Jr., *God and Science: The Death and Rebirth of Theism*. Atlanta: John Knox, 1986.

Hick, John H. *An Interpretation of Religion: Human Responses to the Transcendent*. London: Macmillan, 1989.

Hick, John H. *Philosophy of Religion*. 2d ed. Englewood Cliffs, NJ: Prentice Hall, 1973.

Hordern, William. *New Directions in Theology Today*. Vol. 1. Philadelphia: Westminster Press, 1966.

Huxley, Julian. *Religion without Revelation*. New York: New American Library, 1957.

James, William. *The Varieties of Religious Experience*. New York: Macmillan, 1961.

Lamont, Corliss. *The Philosophy of Humanism*. 4th ed., rev. New York: Philosophical Library, 1957.

Lehmann, Paul. *Ethics in a Christian Context*. New York: Harper & Row, 1963.

Lindbeck, George. *The Nature of Doctrine: Religion and Theology in a Postliberal Age*. Philadelphia: Westminster Press, 1984.

Mavrodes, George. *Belief in God*. New York: Random House, 1970.

Newbigin, Lesslie. *Foolishness to the Greeks: The Gospel and Western Culture*. Grand Rapids, MI: Eerdmans, 1986.

Niebuhr, H. Richard. *The Responsible Self*. New York: Harper & Row, 1978.

Owen, H. P. *Concepts of Deity*. New York: Herder & Herder, 1971.

Robinson, John A. T. *Honest to God*. Philadelphia: Westminster Press, 1963.

Ruether, Rosemary Radford. *Sexism and God-Talk: Toward a Feminist Theology*. Boston: Beacon Press, 1983.

Russell, Bertrand. *Religion and Science*. New York: Oxford University Press, 1961.

Stace, W. T. *Religion and the Modern Mind*. Philadelphia: Lippincott (Keystone Book), 1952.

Tillich, Paul. *Dynamics of Faith*. New York: Harper & Row, 1958.

Tracy, David. *Blessed Rage for Order*. New York: Seabury, 1975.

Wieman, Henry. *Man's Ultimate Commitment*. Carbondale, IL: Southern Illinois University Press, 1958.

Wittgenstein, Ludwig. *Philosophical Investigations*. 3d ed. New York: Macmillan, 1958.

CHAPTER 8
Philosophy and Ethics

A. Questions to Consider

- Is lying always wrong?
- When I *want* to do something but society says it is wrong, how can I decide which course to take?
- Why not get fun out of life without worrying about long-term consequences?
- Is it wrong to try out things—like cocaine?
- Who really has the authority to set up rules about right and wrong?
- Is conscience a reliable guide?
- Isn't every act selfish, because even martyrs do what gives them satisfaction?
- Don't we say American life is better simply because we've been brought up that way? In other words, aren't *all* values relative?

B. Introduction

Value questions can be approached in two quite different ways. Take the proposition "It is bad to lie." Why is lying bad? One answer would be, "Because it is morally wrong; it violates a moral law, and it is our duty to obey moral laws." Another answer might be, "Because lying has undesirable consequences; it destroys people's trust in one another, and such trust is an ingredient of a satisfying human life." We might label the first kind of answer a "right" or "duty" or "moral-law" (**deontological**) theory, and the second a "consequence" or "good-life" (**teleological**) theory. In the example cited, the two approaches reach the same conclusion ("It is bad to lie") but for different reasons. However, this is not always the case. We know, for example, that some people condemn the use of artificial means of birth control as morally wrong, while others approve their use because they produce desirable consequences. Therefore, it is important to decide which *kind* of reasons best justify the value judgments we make. Indeed, a closer look at the question of lying may disclose a basic difference between the two types of theories. Right theories may support the proposition "Lying is *always* wrong," while consequence theories may make a very different claim: "Lying *usually* leads to undesirable consequences but can be justified under certain circumstances."

As we consider the alternative views on the *nature* of **values**, then, we need to assess the various *methods* of justifying value judgments. In Chapter 4, Epistemology, the question raised was "How does one know?" Now, as we enter the field of **axiology**, we rephrase the question and ask, "What sorts of reasons and what kind of thinking justify a value judgment?" Such questions concern the logic of **ethics**, and, logically speaking, they come first; when you say *what* you value, you imply a prior stand on *how* you value. But psychologically speaking, the process is reversed. We make all sorts of claims about *what* is valuable (which is called **normative ethics**), and only later, if ever, do we examine the *grounds* for our value beliefs, their logical foundations (which involves us in the inquiry known as **metaethics**). Can any theory about what is valuable be valid unless the thinking leading to it is itself sound and reliable?

C. An Ethical Continuum

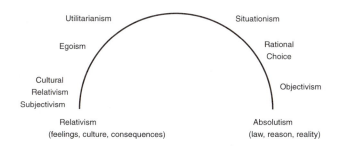

D. The Nature of Values (Alternative Theories)
   and the Justification of Value Judgments
   (Alternative Methods)

1. Theory of Subjectivism.
   Method of Justification: Feeling or Commitment

Subjectivists assert that all values are relative to the individual. According to adherents of **subjectivism**, to claim that something is good or right is simply to say "I like it" or "I approve it." The only justification for value judgments, then, is how a person feels or what he or she is committed to. Different people value different things, and each has an equal right to an opinion.

On one side, existentialists adopt a relativistic, subjectivist posture. On another side, linguistic analysts have developed subjectivism systematically in the form of the **emotive theory** of values. Although existentialists and linguistic analysts proceed from very different philosophical assumptions, they agree on the subjectivity, and thus the relativity, of values. Existentialists stress inner awareness, the "I," person as subject rather than object. They discount the scientists' description of person as object because it is incomplete and certainly inconclusive regarding value questions. Each individual, according to the existentialist, is first and foremost a free, responsible agent; values are whatever a person freely chooses to become committed to. For the existentialist there is no correct or best way to justify a value judgment. In fact, a value judgment is totally unjustifiable—it is simply *made*.

Linguistic analysts ground the emotive theory of values on a careful, systematic examination of the use of moral terms. Like existentialists, they arrive at a subjectivist conclusion: that values and value judgments reflect the attitudes and feelings of individuals and are therefore relativistic. Analytic philosophers typically recognize three kinds of statements: (1) statements that are analytically true; that is, they are logically true or true by definition, (2) statements that are empirically true or false; that is, they are testable or verifiable by scientific procedures, and (3) nonsense (non-sense) statements; that is, statements that are incapable of being either true or false because no objective or logical criteria can be applied. According to most linguistic analysts, value judgments fall in the third category; they are no more than expressions of feeling or direct commands. For example, the statement "Murder is wrong" means no more than "Murder! Yuck!" Therefore, value judgments are totally unjustifiable, just as existentialists say they are.

Existentialists and emotive theorists, then, hold that it is pointless to argue about values or to attempt to justify value judgments; you and I can only state our personal feelings. No matter how much we reason or how thoroughly we examine consequences, in the final analysis we end up with an arbitrary "I prefer."

Critiques of the Theory of Subjectivism and the Method of Feeling or Commitment

1.

The subjectivism of existentialism and the emotive theory lands us in a complete *relativism*. Hitler felt it defensible to murder eleven million Jews and political enemies; in the United States and South Africa, blacks were denied the right to vote; Jim shoots heroin. Is it really meaningless to ask whether these value judgments are morally justifiable? Can it be right for someone to drive 80 miles an hour through a school zone just because "it feels good"?

2.

Some people take the position that values are relative to each individual because they do not want to be told what to do or think and are ready to grant others a similar freedom to live their own lives. Do not such people confuse (1) their concern for conditions that promote individual fulfillment with (2) the right of individuals to value anything, including behavior that promotes neither their own nor anyone else's fulfillment?

3.

Suppose Joan says, "I want to be a doctor; a medical career is right for me." Suppose further that Joan's desire stems from an unconscious drive to please her father and that vocational tests show that her abilities are totally unsuited to medicine but would enable her to become a highly successful lawyer. Is Joan's "feeling" enough to justify her value judgment? Can she rightly say, "Whatever career I choose is 'right for me'"?

4.

If feeling is an unreliable guide to value judgments as personal as choosing a career, how much less reliable it is when we try to make decisions on social and political issues. Do we really want to live in a society where the opinions of uninformed fanatics are morally respected simply because "individuals feel that way"? The person raising this criticism might claim that we can respect the fanatic's right to hold and to express views and at the same time give reasons for these views' being immoral or leading to undesirable consequences.

5.

Subjectivism's claim that ethical judgments are merely expressions of attitudes not only forces us to accept conflicting value judgments as true but flies in the face of our experience. When discussing issues such as the Holocaust, child abuse, or apartheid, people *do* provide objective and rational justifications for the positions they hold. A person holding an ethical position usually assumes that those who impartially scrutinize the facts and assess alternative positions will arrive at the same conclusion.

---

2. Theory of Cultural Relativism.
Method of Justification: Social Authority

According to a cultural relativist, what is good and right is what a particular culture says it is. Most Americans feel deeply that free speech is a value; indeed, it *is* a value to them—but only because they happened to be brought up in American society. If these same persons had been raised in a totalitarian nation or had been born slaves in Athens at the time of Socrates, they might not value freedom. Our society says that monogamy is right, but other societies practice polygamy—it all depends on what the particular culture teaches.

Values are relative to and emerge from a group's way of life. There may be few or no values that are **universal**, or common to all cultures.

In **cultural relativism**, then, value judgments are justified by appealing to the "social authority" of a particular culture. This method of justification claims support from many experts in the behavioral sciences. A pioneer sociologist, William Graham Sumner, defined values as the **mores** of a given society; right and wrong are no more and no less than what each society sanctions.

Freud's concept of the superego seems to lead to a culturally relative conclusion: Right and wrong are ideas that we take in from society's representatives, our parents in particular.

Ruth Benedict's *Patterns of Culture* points out that the ideals of one society may be diametrically opposite to the ideals of another society. Navajos value cooperation and refuse to push themselves forward as individuals; Kwakiutls value competition and bend their efforts toward individual superiority. Each system "works"; each culture defines values in its own way, and there is no neutral standpoint from which to approve one and disapprove another. We stand *within* culture, and the culture itself is the only possible basis on which to justify the value judgments of its members.

What the modern behavioristic psychologist tells us about socialization, learning, and **conditioning** supports the view of social authority as the final arbiter of values. When we come to understand the *causes* that determine our value beliefs and *why* we believe as we do, and can predict how the values of an American child will differ from the values of a child reared in China, what more is there to say?

Other methods of justifying value judgments, such as feeling, revelation, and reason, do no more than express and rationalize, perhaps unconsciously, the cultural milieu of some time and place. When these other methods are carefully analyzed, they ultimately boil down to expressions of value dictated by the culture and perpetuated by social authority.

Critiques of the Theory of Cultural Relativism and the Method of Social Authority

1.

The central thesis of cultural relativism is "whatever a culture *believes* is good *is* good." Does it follow that whatever a culture believes to be true *is* true? For example, if one culture believes the earth to be 1,000 years old and another believes it to be billions of years old, are both cultures right? Is truth so relative that its full meaning is caught in the phrases "true for me" or "true for my society"? If believing is an insufficient ground for asserting a *truth*, is it not also insufficient for asserting a *value*?

2.

The social scientist's *descriptive* statement that cultural practices and mores differ does not entail that *prescriptive* ethical statements are therefore relative. The empirical *fact* of cultural diversity and moral disagreement does not *logically* lead to the conclusion that there is no objective moral truth. Both the objectivist and the relativist agree about the fact of diversity, but the former may argue that such is due to ignorance of moral truth, not to the absence of absolute moral standards.

3.

The central thesis of cultural relativism rests on the totally indefensible assumption that every society, at each period of its history, knows what is good for it. The stark facts of history contradict this assumption. The historian Arnold Toynbee reports the fall of more than thirty great world civilizations and cites their reliance on militarism as a major cause of their demise. Surely one goal of the leaders and peoples of these civilizations was the survival of their way of life. Yet they valued an institution (militarism) destructive of their own purpose. Was this institution, then, good for them because they *believed* in it? Is America's culturally sanctioned faith in the diplomacy of "national interest" justifiable if the predictable consequence of this faith is a nuclear holocaust?

4.

What guidance does the theory of cultural relativism provide in managing social change? For example, how would a U.S. senator and a U.S. citizen, firm believers in cultural relativism, make up their minds whether to favor or oppose national health insurance, a guaranteed annual wage, or the Peace Corps? Was racial segregation in schools morally right prior to the Supreme Court decision of 1954 and morally wrong immediately thereafter? In other words, does a culture change through some impersonal process and thus remold its members' values, or is it not more reasonable to argue that the members (at least sometimes) critically assess inherited beliefs and institutions in the light of human needs and then deliberately change culture? Furthermore, if cultural relativism is right, we cannot speak meaningfully of moral *progress*. For instance, it would make no sense to say that the status of women has *improved* in the United States. Comparison of the morality of societies and eras requires a standard that transcends place and time.

5.

To be consistent with her own principles, the cultural relativist (as well as the subjectivist) must tolerate intolerant and imperialistic cultures. The problem is this: while the *fact* of cultural relativity cannot be denied, the theory of cultural relativism is an *interpretation* of the observed differences. The theory may claim to teach the lesson of tolerance, helping us to avoid **ethnocentrism**, the practice of judging the institutions and beliefs of other societies by our own. But cultural tolerance is not a widely held value in our society or in the vast majority of the societies of the world. How, then, can a cultural relativist, in the terms of her own value theory, possibly support the value of cultural tolerance? Perhaps it is a value in the subculture of anthropologists, but on what grounds can it be recommended for a complacently intolerant society?

6.
Some criticize cultural relativists for (1) overstating the case for moral diversity and (2) not clearly defining the boundaries of the "social group."

3. Theory of Egoism.
Method of Justification: Self-Interest

Like the subjectivist and unlike the cultural relativist, the egoist bases morality on the self. But whereas subjectivism states that "right" is what the individual *approves*, **egoism** claims that "right" is what *benefits* the individual. Egoism is "I-ism" (the Greek word for "I" being *ego*), teaching that the proper concern in life is to maximize one's own welfare regardless of what happens to other people. Egoism stands opposed to **altruism**, which maintains that our proper concern should be to work unselfishly for the well-being of all humanity.

There are two forms of egoism: **psychological egoism** and ethical egoism. The former argues that every act is motivated by self-interest. It is human nature to seek one's own personal satisfaction. In fact, the psychological egoist contends that it is impossible for a human being to act unselfishly, even when doing something for another person.

If psychological egoism is right, its tenets should be acknowledged in one's moral theory. Accordingly, the ethical egoist claims that each person *ought* to pursue his own good as well as possible. Self-fulfillment becomes an imperative and the primary ethical obligation.

Thomas Hobbes argued for both forms of egoism in his great political treatise, *Leviathan*. But he argued that the egoist does not always have to act in a narcissistic or selfish manner if she believes that it is to her advantage in the long run to be self-sacrificing or respectful of others' rights. Hobbes called this kind of person an "enlightened egoist."

Critiques of the Theory of Egoism
and the Method of Self-Interest

1.
Psychological egoism is refuted if it can be shown that self-interest is not always our sole motivation or even our primary one. One counterexample would negate the egoist's universal claim. But the egoist will still argue that what *appears* to be unselfish was unconsciously done in one's own interest. This uncovers the real problem with psychological egoism: It is irrefutable because it assumes what it tries to prove. That is, the psychological egoist claims that if we cannot detect the selfish motive in someone's seemingly

altruistic action it is only because we did not look hard enough. The psychological egoist places himself beyond empirical proof or disproof.

2.

Even if we grant the claim that every motive is an interest *of* a self, it does not follow that every interest *of* a self is an interest *in* oneself. Egoism holds that people are always interested only *in* their own welfare. Altruism claims that people can be interested *in* others' welfare. In both cases people pursue their "self-interest," but what each is interested in is markedly different.

3.

The fact that a sense of satisfaction *results* from an act (or a way of life) that is intended to promote the happiness of other people does not mean that one's own satisfaction was the *motive* or *aim* of the act (or way of life). We may get satisfaction from doing an altruistic act, but that does not mean that we did the act *because* of the satisfaction we expected to receive. It may be noted that we do not label a person "selfish" who gains satisfaction, consciously or unconsciously, from helping others.

4.

The ethical egoist's claim that seeking one's own interests brings happiness or fulfillment can be refuted empirically. Many selfish people are very unhappy, and many altruistic people are very happy. This is the "hedonic paradox": the pursuit of pleasure for its own sake can be counterproductive and often results in frustration.

4. Theory of Objectivism.
Methods of Justification: Reason and/or Divine Authority

On the other side of the continuum, standing opposed to the relativism of the theories just discussed, is what some call **objectivism**, which maintains that values are grounded in a reality outside humanity. What is valuable is independent of what any individual thinks or likes, and it is independent of what any particular society happens to sanction. These **absolutists** hold that moral laws are universally *binding* for all and eternally true, whether or not any moral law is in fact universally respected or obeyed.

There are different ways of thinking about absolute values. Probably the most widely held view is the belief in moral laws established by God and interpreted in a religious tradition. The Ten Commandments are an example. These moral laws apply to everybody everywhere and are not dependent for their value on what produces human satisfaction or on the mores set up by particular societies.

The justification of moral laws such as the Ten Commandments rests directly on the authority of God, or indirectly on the authority of a church through authoritative interpretations of God's will by religious leaders, or on the personal interpretation by an individual through private faith. The Bible or the Koran may be directly appealed to as the authority. Buddha is the guide to the good life for millions of people. Divine authority as a justification of value judgments is so widely held that it needs little elaboration.

Christian theologians have developed a natural-law theory of absolute values that finds its precedent in the **Stoics** of ancient Greece. According to this view, God endowed each creature with certain intrinsic tendencies (natural laws), according to which it is supposed to act. These laws can be discovered by the use of *reason alone*, thereby enabling people to know the will of God without recourse to special revelation. It is claimed that Western civilization has been founded largely on the doctrine of **natural law**. For example, note these famous words in the Declaration of Independence: "We hold these truths to be self-evident, that all men are created equal, that they are endowed by their Creator with certain unalienable Rights, that among these are Life, Liberty and the pursuit of Happiness."

Another conception of absolute values was developed by Immanuel Kant. He based his idea of absolute values on man's rational nature. As rational beings, we cannot make exceptions for ourselves when we make moral judgments. If I claim that my act is right, I mean that it would be right for anyone and everyone who faced the same circumstances. For example, if it is right for me to break a promise when it is to my personal advantage, it must be right for anyone to do so. I must be willing to generalize my act and say that breaking a promise when it is to anyone's advantage is a universal principle. But then my reason tells me that such a universal principle is inconsistent with itself; if everyone acted in terms of it, promises would be meaningless, and the whole system of promise keeping would break down. Therefore, Kant's conclusion is that reason itself sanctions certain universal moral principles (absolute values) and that the good person is one who acts from a sense of duty to such principles. Thus, moral principles that are right have the form of the **Categorical Imperative**: So act so that you can at the same time will that your act can be raised to the level of a universal law for anyone at any time.

Kant justified his value judgments by reason alone (**rationalism**) and claimed that this method led him to the central principle of ethics, the generalization principle: Whatever you claim to be good or right must be good or right for everyone.

Still another conception of absolute values was developed by Plato. Plato expressed the view that the patterned Forms of the Good, encompassing Truth, Beauty, and Justice, are the ultimate realities. All the changing, temporal things that most of us call good are but pale shadows of the eternal Good. Only the wisest individuals, guided by the light of reason, can discover the Forms of the Good. The good society, visualized by Plato in the *Republic*, was to be founded and governed by such wise people—the philosopher kings.

Critiques of the Theory of Objectivism and the Methods of Reason and Divine Authority

1.

In their attempt to resist the moral anarchy of relativism, people have turned to divine authority, with its promise of *one* set of *changeless* values. But the conflicting interpretations of what values are absolute have left an anarchy of competing moral values. At one time God is revealed as a jealous God, a God of wrath; at another time, as a God of love and forgiveness. How can one trust a method that justifies as God-given such conflicting values?

Cultural relativism is denounced, yet for centuries religion defended the divine right of kings and explained that it is God's will that subjects obey unquestioningly the decrees of their secular rulers.

The fact that revealed values generally coincide with the social values of the time and place in which they are revealed raises the question of whether their source is God or culture.

2.

Similar difficulties beset the appeal to reason. "Rational intuitions" differ. How do you know when your rational intuition has hit the mark? For example, Plato, one of the leading exponents of this method, immortalized in the *Republic* his rational vision: **Utopia** is a society organized along totalitarian rather than democratic lines. Rational intuition has led others to insist that all people are brothers with equal political rights. Can reason alone be trusted to discover the Right and the Good? And is natural moral law really universal, or does it differ from culture to culture?

3.

Even within the *same* value system it seems impossible to frame a rule that does not admit of exceptions and that will never conflict with other rules in that system. If an absolutist tries to avoid these problems by creating a list of more specific rules and a hierarchy of principles, she seems to end up with a long list of petty rules to cover each situation.

4.

Kant believed that reason alone led him to the moral principles that he enunciated. Many observers, however, have concluded that Kant's ethical conclusions are convincing precisely because he *did* take into account empirical consequences. For example, when Kant shows that the principle of breaking a promise defeats itself, isn't he in fact taking consequences for human welfare into consideration?

5.

The postmodernist argues that the kind of Enlightenment reasoning of Kant is self-legitimizing. It mistakes a historically and culturally specific use of reason for the universal form of all Reason; thus, all competing forms of reason are unreasonable. So, a rational concept like "justice" is defined by the "victor"—the master narrator of history who has decided what rationality and justice mean for everyone. The entire cultural and social history of the "victim" is ignored, denied, or brought into line with the dominant narrative of the victor. The victim appears as a deviant or as wrong. Such victims might include dissidents, communists, women, homosexuals, or "foreigners." Enlightenment morality, then, assumes that "justice" and other such concepts are objective and discovered by reason, when in reality such moral concepts are produced or invented by the dominant group in society. What we should do is respect the different views of the Other and reject any pretense about holding "objective" or "absolute" moral truths.

5. Theory of Utilitarianism.
Method of Justification: Empirical Evidence

Justice may be a high value; breaking a promise in a selfish way may be wrong. If so, according to **utilitarianism** it is not because justice is an absolute moral principle or because promise keeping is a universal law established by reason; it is because justice and promise keeping produce better consequences and more human satisfaction than do hatred and lying. Utilitarianism leans far toward relativism on the continuum because it claims that all values depend on human satisfaction. But it also comes around part of the way toward objectivism because it insists on the test of consequences—what *in fact* produces the maximum satisfaction. (Refer to the **teleological** theory of ethics.)

The classical doctrine of utilitarianism was developed by Jeremy Bentham and modified by John Stuart Mill. It takes the position that the Good is whatever provides the greatest happiness for the greatest number of people. In "greatest happiness" Mill included not only quantitative but qualitative considerations as well. Pleasures involving mental capacities are more satisfying for human beings than those that have to do only with physical sensations. In this refined version, then, Mill advocated seeking the greatest balance of pleasure over pain, especially since the individual's happiness is wrapped up in the happiness of the greatest number of people. But is happiness the whole story? Aren't there moral rules, what W. D. Ross called "prima facie" duties? For example, "It is wrong to imprison an innocent person." Suppose a prosecuting attorney discovers incontrovertible evidence that the slum gang on trial did not commit the crime it is charged with but reasons: "I'll suppress this evidence (which no one else can possibly find out about) because the gang did commit other crimes and will predictably act unlawfully in the future. Putting the gang in prison for two years will protect the community and produce the greatest happiness for the greatest number of people." The attorney's decision may be justified in terms of *act utilitarianism* (calculating the consequences of the specific act) but wrong in terms of *rule utilitarianism* (calculating the consequences of violating the general rule or practice: Don't imprison innocent people).

The utilitarian justifies value judgments by appealing to the pragmatic theory of truth. John Dewey, an American proponent of **pragmatism**, insisted that all value claims must meet the "test of consequences" and that the consequences of an act or a moral principle are verifiable by an appeal to empirical evidence. Can we not agree that scientific medicine produces better overall results than the efforts of witch doctors? Why not consider *all* value judgments in the same light and decide their adequacy in terms of their effectiveness in producing desired results?

Scientific evidence can at least direct us to the most efficient means to achieve desired ends. If we agree on physical health as the end, the evidence favors scientific medicine over magic as the appropriate means. Furthermore, says the utilitarian, we can evaluate the worth of physical health, or any other proposed end, by finding out whether it in fact supports or undermines the achievement of the whole set of goals that we cherish. In other words, we can empirically check the desirability of each possible *end* by viewing it in its role as a *means*.

In a similar fashion, any "absolute" moral rule, whether religious, Platonic, or Kantian, can be subjected to the test of empirical consequences: What are the *results* in human life of observing the rule?

Critiques of the Theory of Utilitarianism and the Method of Empirical Evidence

1.

"Is X valuable?" "Yes," says the utilitarian, "X is valuable because empirical evidence shows that it leads to human satisfaction." It appears that the utilitarian has committed the **naturalistic fallacy**; that is, he or she has made a *value* judgment solely on the basis of a *factual* judgment. The utilitarian may clarify the reasoning in the form of a syllogism:

Whatever produces human satisfaction is valuable.
X produces human satisfaction.
Therefore, X is valuable.

The minor premise affirms the antecedent, and the conclusion is valid. But what is the status of the major premise? If it claims to be a descriptive ("reportive") definition of "value," it is still open to the charge of committing the naturalistic fallacy, because we can reasonably ask: "But is what satisfies always good or moral?" The major premise of utilitarianism, then, involves a value *assumption*; it puts forward a value *claim* that must somehow be justified over competing definitions and claims about the nature of the Good.

2.

If we accept for a moment the utilitarians' assumption that values are whatever maximize human satisfaction, we can focus more closely on the difficulty of their position. How can "empirical evidence" really give us any guidance about the ends of life? Science says, "If you do so and so, this will be the result." Suppose that scientists could tell us *all* the consequences of various value choices (a very unlikely supposition!). So what? How would we decide the value of these consequences themselves? Does this not result in an infinite regress and utter confusion? Furthermore, will our idea of satisfaction be any more than a reflection and rationalization of the values of our time and place, as claimed by the cultural relativist? In the end, the principle of "the greatest good" itself is difficult to justify on purely utilitarian grounds.

3.

There is a serious ambiguity in the term "human satisfaction." What exactly is meant? Is *my* satisfaction the goal? Or the satisfaction of the majority? Or the happiness of every human being? The theory may appeal to some people because it is interpreted in the first way (egoistically) and to others because it is read in one of the latter two ways (altruistically). As stated, the doctrine appears to be an altruistic one; every human being is to count as one, equally. But if so, has not the utilitarian smuggled in a key ethical principle—Kant's principle of impartiality or, indeed, the golden rule itself? A crucial ethical principle of this kind needs to be *justified*, not just *assumed*. Has the utilitarian adopted at least *one* absolute value without crediting its source?

4.

Sometimes "maximum benefit" for a limited number of people in a society is in conflict with just distribution of benefit to all people in a society. The principle of utility is not very helpful in resolving this conflict, especially when the calculated results of both options appear equal. Furthermore, it is possible that the "greatest good" principle could justify the majority in depriving the minority of their rights.

---

6. Theory of Situationism.
Method of Justification: Existential Context

Another view that shares with utilitarianism a location on the continuum between relativism and absolutism is situationism, or **situation ethics**. Advocates of this position, who include Christian theologians such as Joseph Fletcher and John A. T. Robinson, do not reject completely the idea of values as absolute but insist that there is only *one* absolute value, *love*. The love principle can and should replace moral rules as a guide to moral decisions. **Value judgments** depend on the unique circumstances in which individuals find themselves. That is why the "new morality" is referred to as situationism or contextualism. The crucial point is that a person who lives in the concrete situation, as either a giver or a receiver of love, has priority over any and all legal or abstract conceptions of what is right or good. While situationists claim that love is absolute, they argue that the specific demands and implications of the love principle cannot be settled in advance but must be worked out in the context of each particular situation. Each person, therefore, must make a personal decision in situations of moral importance and do the best she can with the knowledge and experience at her command to act as a concerned, loving person. The example of Jesus is given as one who expressed directly his personal loving commitment in human affairs—over and above the authoritarian claims of law, custom, or absolute principles.

Situation ethics also supports a dynamic or changing view of morality. Morals are not fixed; they evolve with the times. Changes in moral codes and practices should be welcomed rather than resisted. Situationists maintain that morality is, and must be, revolutionary—at least in the **dialectical** sense of producing something new and more relevant to the actual state of the world. This is also the position of liberation theology, which reflects Archbishop Romero's view that it is the poor who tell us what the world is and what the Church's service to the world is.

John Robinson suggests that the saying "The Sabbath is made for man, and not man for the Sabbath" can be used as a model. Thus, "Marriage is made for man, and not man for marriage." The traditional morality set down clear rules for sexual conduct outside marriage but no clear ones for sexual relations within marriage. The new morality asks that the norm of love, respect for the integrity of persons, and a deep concern for their welfare be the guiding principle of sexual relations in the myriad of complex situations that arise within and outside the bounds of marriage.

Critiques of the Theory of Situationism and the Method of Existential Context

1.

From the traditional standpoint, situation ethics undermines morality, involves a cutting loose from strict moral rules, and constitutes, therefore, an unfortunate lapse into moral **relativism**, where "anything goes." The advocates of the new morality reply that to follow the precept and example of Jesus in "living a life for others" invokes a moral standard that is more flexible, but also more demanding, than that required by rule morality. The critics are unconvinced; they continue to believe that "love" is too vague and imprecise a principle to provide adequate moral guidance.

2.

Since situationism is a form of both relativism and utilitarianism (act utilitarianism in this case), many of the criticisms we have listed already apply to situationism. One of them is particularly apropos here: The situationist cannot consistently say that legalism or objectivism is *always* wrong.

3.

Many of the moral conflicts that situationists describe to show that we cannot rely on absolute moral rules are simply conflicts of rules. Either the conflict is resolved through some sort of hierarchy of rules or unaided intuition is used, in which case the situationist is being guided by cultural and environmental influences. Neither option is wholly consistent with situationism.

7. A Possible Combination of Value Theories and Methods: The Theory of Rational Choice. Method of Justification: Free, Impartial, Informed Choosing

A particular value, such as love, or a moral rule, such as respect for the rights of others, can be justified on the grounds that it is an essential ingredient of a total way of life. The theory of **rational choice** denies the thesis of cultural relativism by contending that one way of life is clearly better than another if the preference for it is the outcome of a rational choosing process. The theory starts with the subjectivist value position, which asserts that values are relative to the individual. Individuals make the ultimate choice of what is good and right on the basis of what they "feel" or prefer. But, as reasoning, reflective beings, those same individuals must recognize that feelings are trustworthy only to the degree that they are free, impartial, and informed—in a word, rational.

A *free* choice of a way of life is free from being determined by the unconscious mind, free from strong emotion, and free from mere conditioning or indoctrination.

An *impartial* choice of a way of life incorporates the generalizing principle proposed by Kant: Right means right for everyone. It means to choose without favoritism for oneself; if I rationally approve a slave society, I must be willing to be anyone in that society, master or slave.

An *informed* choice of a way of life is made with full knowledge of alternative ways of life, including the probable effects of actually living them. To be informed thus means to rely on empirical evidence, as stressed in the theory of objective relativism; but it also includes the enlightenment of the imagination afforded by an understanding of the art, literature, philosophy, and religion of alternative ways of life. This view, then, embraces the culture concept, but it sees cultures not as mechanisms that arbitrarily define and restrict value choices but as human inventions that constantly enlarge the options for human choice.

The method of free, impartial, and informed choosing, it is claimed, describes the actual practice of reflective persons in different cultures and provides the most likely basis for reaching eventual agreement about values on a cross-cultural level.

If we are going to have confidence in any conclusions about values, we must agree on the criteria for reaching them. Let us agree, then, to accept as valuable whatever people *do* agree on when they are impartial, informed, and free from internal and external constraint.

Critiques of the Theory of Rational Choice and the Method of Free, Impartial, Informed Choosing

1.

The theory of rational choice rests on an unrealistic premise because the concept of a free choice of a way of life is contradicted by overwhelming evidence. People's choices are limited by what they have learned. Their choices reflect how they were nurtured and are never free from it. For example, Western peoples are notably blind to the values of Eastern culture. Unable to experience or understand Oriental values, Westerners cannot rationally choose to accept or reject them.

2.

The theory of rational choice claims to provide a promising basis for universal agreement about what is valuable, but it seems highly unrealistic to expect that all human beings will ever agree on their value judgments. And even if agreement were reached, it would not necessarily be reliable, for the majority could still be wrong.

3.

The recommended method cannot be practically or democratically applied to ordinary human situations. Few people ever attain the ideal of becoming free, impartial, and informed. Therefore, value decisions would have to be handed down to the masses by an elite group—an intellectual **aristocracy** similar to Plato's philosopher kings. This is a formula for totalitarianism, or rule by a partisan minority that is convinced that it alone knows what is good and right.

E. The Ethics of Virtue

Up to this point we have seen that ethics is preoccupied with questions of right *actions* and *rules*. But some contemporary ethicists are returning to an older discussion—namely, questions of good *character* and **virtues**. Whereas the focus had been on the specific choices and deeds of a person in particular circumstances, today much of the attention has shifted to the kind of person one should become. These ethicists ask: What are the traits of a good person, and how are they cultivated? Interestingly, this same emphasis is seen now in psychology and theories of education (for example, in the works of Erik Erikson, Lawrence Kohlberg, Carol Gilligan, and Parker Palmer).

The ethics of virtue has its roots in ancient and medieval sources. Plato explicated the classical or cardinal virtues of wisdom, courage, temperance, and justice. A rightly educated and intellectually well-endowed person would develop these inner dispositions in the society that Plato envisioned.

These traits would enable one to live the "good life" as a rational human being should live it.

Aristotle examined other virtues, dividing them into intellectual and moral categories. He defined a virtue as the prudent mean between two extremes—an excess and a deficiency—depending on the particular situation. Plato's pupil also wrote about the development of moral character, especially in his *Nicomachean Ethics.*

In the late Middle Ages, Thomas Aquinas added the three theological virtues of faith, hope, and love to the classical virtues. Recently, ethicists such as William Frankena have elevated the virtues of benevolence and justice, all other virtues being derived from these.

In the classical sense, virtues are those qualities that help us to function well as human beings—to become *good* or excellent men and women. Just as strong legs would be a virtue for a race horse, so, Plato taught, wisdom is a virtue for the rational creatures that human beings are. Such qualities are not just passing inclinations but settled habits. Nor are they innate; they are cultivated through example, teaching, discipline, practice, and—in theological circles—grace. Thus, these traits predispose the possessor to act in certain ways, providing the motivation to act morally and the flexibility and guidance that rigid and conflicting rules do not always provide. (But even Plato did not do away with moral rules, as is evident in his *Laws.*) One's will is strengthened to do what is right, and one's desire or love is redirected toward what is just and good.

Contemporary exponents of virtue ethics from Alasdair MacIntyre to Christina Hoff Sommers to Stanley Hauerwas emphasize the role that community plays in the development of a virtuous character, particularly since moral conceptions depend on the way that a culture shapes the moral person to view the world. As Hauerwas puts it, "We can only act within the world we can envision, and we can envision the world rightly only as we are trained to see." The primary ethical task is to train people to see reality a certain way—to share the community's vision. Thus the Enlightenment notion that there is some universal rational understanding of "right" and "good" is misguided; there is no objective impersonal stance from which to judge morality, though rules based on consensus to ensure peace and survival give that impression. Ethics always requires a qualifier—for example, Jewish, Christian, American, utilitarian. Ethics has a narrative character: "No ethic can be freed from its narrative, and thus communal, context" (Hauerwas). In other words, ethical systems are "tradition dependent" (tradition being a set of stories that creates or forms a community).

Although feminist moral philosophy is not monolithic, the contextual orientation of moral reasoning that Carol Gilligan argues is characteristic of women shares some features with the contemporary ethicists we have mentioned. Women operate from a "morality of responsibility" using the "psychological logic of relationships," while men operate with a "morality of rights" using the "formal logic of justice." Gilligan cites research that demonstrates this difference among girls and boys in their game playing. In contrast to an Enlightenment emphasis on competing rights and formal and abstract connections, females typically operate with an awareness of conflicting responsibilities and a mentality that is contextual and narrative; in contrast to Kant's universalizable morality, the "female voice" speaks of the specific situation.

Critique of the Ethics of Virtue

Some have criticized the classical notion that human beings have an essential nature and purpose or function that are universal and that, in turn, dictate what moral qualities should be pursued. Some argue that the list of virtues is culture-dependent or that it varies with the ethical system one prefers (for example, utilitarianism or ethical egoism).

F. Conclusion

In the course of making day-to-day choices involving a value dimension, we must operate in terms of a fundamental ethical decision: Shall I seek first and foremost my own happiness, or shall I give equal or greater weight to the happiness of other people? And so we face the choice between *egoism* and *altruism.* Between the poles of egoism and altruism, but on the altruism side of the continuum, lies the principle of impartiality: The good of every person is to count equally. This is the principle that Rawls has developed in his defense of "justice as fairness" in his book *A Theory of Justice* (see Chapter 11).

If we choose one of the right, duty, or moral-law (deontological) theories of value, we will in all probability find ourselves on the altruism side of the continuum, since the preference for altruism over egoism is an inherent feature of most of these value frameworks. Indeed, the most prominent element in "the moral point of view" is the principle of impartiality—that each person is to count as one. The moral point of view claims to be the only reasonable one. Suppose that egoist A holds that his welfare is more important than B's; egoist B asserts that *her* welfare is more important than A's. The two claims are mutually contradictory; an impartial observer, C, can only conclude that the egoist position is **irrational**, since it cannot function as a general principle. (See Kant's Categorical Imperative, page 162; "impartiality" in the theory of rational choice, page 168; and the love principle in situation ethics, page 166.)

The choice between egoism and altruism arises acutely for value theories of the consequence or good-life (teleological) type. In calculating the greatest happiness for the greatest number of people, for example, will the utilitarian take into account the moral principle that each person is to count as one? (See Critique 3 of utilitarianism on page 166.)

Our motives can be either egoistic or altruistic. We can choose to adopt or reject the key principle that each person is to count as one. We can be guided by an ethic of rules or by an ethic of consequences. We must make choices about the kind of people we are to become. In the final analysis, each of us must make a personal decision. But our decision concerning the nature of values and the methods for justifying value judgments need not be made in an arbitrary fashion. We can choose responsibly after a careful examination of the available options (including a check of their claims against the findings of the natural and social sciences) and after an imaginative assessment of the overall way of life within which our preferred option would find its place. Ultimately, perhaps the most precious ingredient in a way of life is not a constellation of "content" values but an open and deeply questioning *process* for making value commitments.

Case Study and Discussion Questions

Case Study

Christina Hoff Sommers, a professor of philosophy at Clark University, has argued that public education could do a far better job of moral education by de-emphasizing "dilemma ethics" (which focuses on ethical problems that students debate) and "values clarification" (in which the student is left to discover his or her own values). She advocates returning to moral education that emphasizes the cultivation of virtues by teaching Aristotle to college students, for instance, or by using tales and parables to instill moral principles in elementary and high school students. Here are excerpts of the proposal Sommers brought before the American Philosophical Association:

> It is obvious that our schools must have clear behavior codes and high expectations for their students. Civility, honesty and considerate behavior must be recognized, encouraged and rewarded. That means that moral education must have as its *explicit* aim the moral betterment of the student. If that be indoctrination, so be it. How can we hope to equip students to face the challenge of moral responsibility in their lives if we studiously avoid telling them what is right and what is wrong?
>
> Many school systems have entirely given up the task of character education. Children are left to fend for themselves. To my mind, leaving children alone to discover their own values is a little like putting them in a chemistry lab and saying, "Discover your own compounds, kids." If they blow themselves up, at least they have engaged in an authentic search for the self.
>
> To pretend we know nothing about basic decency, about human rights, about vice and virtue, is fatuous or disingenuous. Of course we know that gratuitous cruelty and political repression are wrong, that kindness and political freedom are right and good. Why should we be the first society in history that finds itself hamstrung in the vital task of passing along its moral tradition to the next generation?
>
> Some opponents of directive moral education argue that it could be a form of brainwashing. That is a pernicious confusion. To brainwash is to diminish someone's capacity for reasoned judgment. It is perversely misleading to say that helping children to develop habits of truth-telling or fair play threatens their ability to make reasoned choices. Quite the contrary: Good moral habits enhance one's capacity for rational judgments.[1]

---

[1]Christina Hoff Sommers, "Teaching the Virtues: A Blueprint for Moral Education," *Chicago Tribune Magazine* (September 12, 1993): 18.

1. Should teachers in public schools explicitly work to develop the moral character of their students as Sommers suggests? Should public schools and teachers insist on behavior that emphasizes basic decency, kindness, fairness, self-discipline, and honesty?

2. Is a basic common morality compatible with a pluralistic society?

3. Which of the alternative methods for justifying value judgments would be useful for Sommers's proposal? Which would not?

Discussion Questions

1. When visiting a foreign country, do you believe it is appropriate or inappropriate to adopt the local norms of the society during your stay there? What if the norms conflict with promises you have made or ethical obligations you have to other people "back home"?

2. *Rule utilitarianism* proposes to test a moral rule ("Lying is wrong" or "Lying is wrong except to prevent great damage to other persons") in terms of the consequences for human happiness of observing or violating the rule. Does this proposal do justice to "the moral point of view," that is, right, duty, and moral law theories?

3. Do you accept the principle of impartiality: The good of every person is to count equally? What kind of domestic and foreign policies would the richest and most powerful nation in the world adopt if it took seriously the proposition that the well-being of each person on earth is of equal importance? If policies based on the principle of impartiality are not acceptable to you, what alternative "principle of partiality" can you propose and justify?

4. Suppose that you are opposed, for whatever reason, to racial or sexual discrimination. What method of value reasoning could you effectively use to change an individual, class, or nation that practices such discrimination? In other words, can ethical reasoning bake any bread?

5. There is currently no case law stipulating what procedures should be used to treat severely premature babies (even whether to let them live). Whether the parents' wishes are honored and what doctors do when a severely disabled child is born depend largely on the policies of individual doctors and hospitals. Which method for justifying value judgments would be helpful for parents and doctors to make decisions in these circumstances? for hospitals to establish policies?

Suggested Readings

Aristotle. *The Nicomachean Ethics*. Cambridge: Harvard University Press, 1926.

Barnes, Hazel E. *An Existentialist Ethics*. New York: Knopf, 1967.

Bradley, F. H. *Ethical Studies*. 2d ed. London: Oxford University Press, 1927.

Broad, Charlie E. *Five Types of Ethical Theory*. New York: Harcourt, 1930.

Bronowski, J. *Science and Human Values*. New York: Harper & Row, 1956.

Dworkin, Ronald. *A Matter of Principle*. Cambridge, MA: Harvard University Press, 1985.

Fletcher, Joseph. *Situation Ethics: The New Morality*. Philadelphia: Westminster Press, 1966.

Frankena, William K. *Ethics*. 2d ed. Englewood Cliffs, NJ: Prentice-Hall, 1973.

French, Marilyn. *Beyond Power: On Women, Men, and Morals*. New York: Summit, 1985.

Gilligan, Carol. *In a Different Voice*. Cambridge, MA: Harvard University Press, 1982.

Hare, R. M. *Freedom and Reason*. New York: Oxford University Press, 1965.

Hauerwas, Stanley. *The Peaceable Kingdom: A Primer in Christian Ethics*. Notre Dame, IN: University of Notre Dame Press, 1983.

Kant, Immanuel. *The Moral Law; or Kant's Groundwork of the Metaphysics of Morals.* London: Hutchinson, 1948.

MacIntyre, Alasdair. *After Virtue.* 2d ed. Notre Dame, IN: University of Notre Dame Press, 1984.

Nielsen, Kai. "Ethics, Problems of." In *The Encyclopedia of Philosophy,* vol. 3, pp. 117–134.

Noddings, Nell. *Caring.* Berkeley: University of California Press, 1984.

Noonan, John T., Jr. *Bribes: Theory and Practice Throughout 4000 Years of Human Experience.* New York: Macmillan, 1984.

Palmer, Parker. *To Know as We Are Known: A Spirituality of Education.* San Francisco: Harper & Row, 1983.

Pieper, Josef. *The Four Cardinal Virtues.* Notre Dame, IN: University of Notre Dame Press, 1965.

Plato, *Euthyphro.* In *Five Dialogues.* Translated by G. M. A. Grube. Indianapolis: Hackett, 1981.

Rachels, James. *The Elements of Moral Philosophy.* New York: Random House, 1986.

Taylor, Richard. *Good and Evil: A New Direction.* New York: Macmillan, 1970.

Toulmin, Stephen. *The Place of Reason in Ethics.* New York: Cambridge University Press, 1950.

Williams, Bernard. *Ethics and the Limits of Philosophy.* Cambridge, MA: Harvard University Press, 1985.

CHAPTER 9
Philosophy and Esthetics

A. Questions to Consider

- Does beauty reside in things or in the eye of the beholder?
- Should art serve a moral purpose, or should art be for art's sake alone?
- Do esthetic objects reveal the nature of ultimate reality?
- Do works of art reflect values or create them?
- Does a poem or symphony simply express the emotions of the poet or composer?
- Can a person's life be a work of art?
- Do artistic visions alter our view of life?

B. Introduction

Esthetics (traditionally "aesthetics") is the term applied to the philosophical study concerned with the understanding of beauty and its manifestations in art and nature. The identification of the characteristics of what people call beautiful and the analysis of theories of art are major interests in this philosophical area. Because it focuses on the value dimension of certain kinds of human experience, esthetics qualifies as an aspect of axiology. In an esthetic experience, our attention is caught by something; we perceive it and become absorbed in the process of experiencing. Our posture is one of appreciation or what might be called worth-assigning awareness.

1. Is There a Distinctive "Esthetic" Experience?

There is wide agreement that the term "esthetic" does point to a distinct type of human experience; students of esthetics, however, continue their controversy regarding the most adequate language with which to talk about it and also regarding whether the distinction between esthetic and nonesthetic experience is clear-cut or a matter of degree. As we shall see, disagreements about the nature and significance of objects that arouse an esthetic experience run much deeper.

We respond to most objects in one of two ways: either cognitively (What is it? Where did it come from? How does it work?) or practically (What is it good for? How can I use it? How is it important to me?). Before me is a tree. I ask cognitive questions: What kind of tree is it? How tall is it? How does it reproduce? Is it alive or dead? I ask practical questions: Will it provide shade? How much money is it worth as lumber? If it falls, will it block access to my house? While asking such questions, my response is not esthetic. I am *looking* at the tree, but I am not *seeing* it; that is, I am not perceiving it just for the sake of the perception. I "have" the tree esthetically only if I "contemplate" it, in the sense of giving my undivided attention to its qualities.

The distinctiveness of the "esthetic" experience is more obvious if we have before us a statue or a painting. We can ask practical questions: How much does it cost? How well does it complement the interior design of our living room? But an answer to the question "What is it good for?" calls for a response that somehow indicates our appreciation for the unique, qualitative thing that the statue or painting is, in its own right. Moreover, we can employ an art object as a stimulus for thought or reverie about our personal lives, but such therapeutic "use" will divert us from the impact and excitement of esthetic experience itself. The esthetic experience remains somehow special and not wholly translatable in terms of other kinds of responses.

We may also be diverted from appreciation by cognitive responses to the art object, asking about the artist's life and other works, intentions (if any) while fashioning the object, techniques in creating certain effects, and the artistic tradition surrounding the creation of the work. Some art critics, the contextualists, argue that to have such "external" knowledge about the art object enhances one's esthetic experience. Other critics, the isolationists, claim that such knowledge is unnecessary for full esthetic appreciation or may even handicap appreciation by turning attention away from the object itself. Both agree that "having" the esthetic experience is what counts.

It has been held that the esthetic attitude is characterized by detachment, disinterestedness, or psychic distance. These terms are ambiguous. They serve to remind us that practical and personal concerns should not intrude themselves into the process of appreciation; but the terms are misleading if interpreted to mean that the appreciator should forgo intimacy, emotional participation, and identification with the esthetic object.

Consider the following: A partisan football fan watches the opposing quarterback flip a perfect touchdown pass to the enemy end. "Beautiful!" he exclaims, temporarily detached from his partisanship, disinterested in the scoreboard, and psychically distant from the effect that the perfectly executed play might have on the final outcome of the game. Consider another example. I sit listening to a moving rendition of "We Shall Overcome." I reminisce, flashing back to the 1960s, visualizing blacks and whites marching in Montgomery, batons being brandished by the police. Deep personal feelings are aroused by the refrain "We are not afraid." (I am often afraid.) I, too, want somehow to "walk hand in hand." The haunting phrases "deep in my heart I do believe" and "the whole wide world around—someday" trigger echoes of the self I am or yearn to be. The esthetic dimension of the experience is maintained as long as I remain absorbed in the song, its mood and flow of meanings, as long as I attend to *them*, and not to *my* visualizations and feelings.

A conclusion from this discussion might be that it is easier to indicate what esthetic experience is *not* than to depict exactly what it *is*.

2. The Objects of Esthetic Experience

Is there any limit to the range of things that can be appreciated esthetically? We think first of objects of fine art, whose main function is to embody an esthetic vision and elicit an esthetic response—dramas, paintings, sculptures, symphonies, poems, dances. But how can we draw a sharp line between the "fine" arts and the "useful" arts? Artists in many times and places have left their imprint on utensils, buildings, vases, clothing, furniture, ceremonial objects, and sometimes on an entire city. How do we distinguish between "fine" and "popular" arts? Is folk music, for example, a less significant art form than opera?

It has been suggested that an esthetic response is a natural accompaniment of the culminating, consummatory phase of *any* experience. A scientist, for example, finally achieves a solution to a complicated problem. At the completion of her project, she (or an observer who imaginatively reenacts the process) savors appreciatively the new pattern of meaning that has emerged and exclaims: "Lovely!" Is the case different when the outcome of effort and subsequent appreciation is a loaf of bread, a stack of firewood ready for winter, or the purr of a finely tuned engine?

Handcrafted objects, concrete expressions of the seemingly boundless human imagination, hold a unique fascination for esthetic experience. Nature, in turn, offers galaxies and glaciers, seashells and pounding surf, orchids and flamingoes, cataracts and mountain peaks, male and female bodies (yes, and sunsets); in short, intricate patterns and structures of color, light, sound, and movement—these, and many more, invite, at times compel, our appreciative awareness.

One test of any esthetic theory is its capacity to account for the wide, apparently limitless, range of objects that call forth an esthetic response.

C. An Esthetic Continuum

Esthetic experience is a focused appreciation of *something*. What is the nature of the something, art object or natural event, that calls forth the esthetic response? The continuum below points to five alternative views concerning the themes and meanings expressed in esthetic objects.

It must be emphasized that, whatever the object's theme or meaning, it is expressed through and embodied in a *concrete form*. Without form there is no esthetic object; critical opinion on this point is unanimous. But what is "form"? The term "form" refers to the *internal* relations of the esthetic object. To avoid monotony, the object must be a complex of different parts, but these parts must be interrelated to form a whole (**gestalt**)—an "organic" whole in the sense that the parts are interdependent. Thus, form is commonly interpreted to mean unity in variety. Some observers hold that esthetic form also refers to some pervasive quality that gives the whole intensity (brightness or clarity). Form in-the-large is structure; form in-the-small is texture.

The theory of **formalism** maintains that the art object is "pure form" and that its formal excellence alone determines its esthetic quality. This interpretation is particularly congenial to the proponents of abstractionism in art. The claim that formal excellence is a *sufficient* condition of esthetic quality is open to question; that it is a *necessary* condition is not debated. (See the entry for **Cause** in the Glossary.)

It may be noted that to the extent that agreement is reached on the ingredients of "formal excellence," esthetic evaluations are objective rather than subjective (see section E, this chapter).

An esthetic object expresses (embodies) in a concrete form . . .

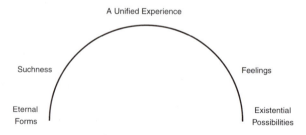

A Unified Experience

Suchness   Feelings

Eternal   Existential
Forms   Possibilities

D. The Nature and Meaning of Esthetic Objects: Alternative Views

1. Esthetic Objects Express Eternal Forms

Plato and Aristotle held that artists create an *imitation*, or *representation*, of reality. They were not advocating the naïve idea that artists strive to mirror natural objects as exactly as possible. Rather, the artist seeks to represent the essential nature (essence) of objects, the rational forms on which they are patterned (Plato) or that are inherent in them (Aristotle). For Plato, objects of art are twice removed from the Eternal Forms, since they are only images of copies of the Forms; that is, natural objects are imperfect copies of Eternal Forms, and works of art are only "imitations" of natural objects.

The idea that esthetic objects represent or symbolize an ultimate Reality that is eternal, perfect, and complete (the True, the Good, the Beautiful) recurs frequently in the history of esthetic thought. Keats and Hegel refer to beauty as truth in sensuous form. Music, says Schopenhauer, gives us an intuitive grasp of ultimate reality (timeless forms of the Will to Live). Santayana refers to beauty as an eternal, divine essence suffusing a material object. Tolstoy conceives beauty as a quality of perfect goodness. The art object, says Goethe, is a sensuous embodiment of a spiritual meaning. Clive Bell defines an esthetic object as significant form that reveals ultimate reality as a divine, all-pervading rhythm. In the Hindu tradition, esthetic objects give intuitions of the ultimate as pure being, which, in contrast to the view of the Greek philosophers, is beyond all conceptions and distinctions accessible to reason.

To summarize, the metaphysical idealist insists that art objects point beyond themselves to a realm where the True, the Good, and the Beautiful already exist in completed form. When representing a human body, for example, a painter or sculptor quite rightly creates an idealized figure whose proportions are perfectly symmetrical.

The proposition that esthetic objects express eternal forms usually carries both an epistemological and a moral implication. We can "know" or grasp the ultimate nature of things intuitively. Since ultimate reality is morally perfect, artistic productions can be judged good when they accurately depict the moral and bad when they represent the immoral. On this ground Plato and Tolstoy argued for censorship of the arts.

Critique

A number of critical questions can be raised about the position under consideration (see also the criticisms of objective idealism in the chapter on metaphysics). Is an art object—for example, a musical composition—a recollection of eternal harmonies or a unique creation of hitherto unimagined patterns? Does the artist *reflect* what is common and universal, or does the artistic activity bring into existence new, shared meanings? Does the esthetic object increase our knowledge or simply heighten our awareness? Is an abstract form or essence more significant than the qualities perceived in concrete objects?

2. Esthetic Objects Express Suchness

The most notable achievements of Western civilization are science (dealing with the cognitive, theoretical aspect of reality) and technology (a highly practical activity). The esthetic dimension of experience has been neglected in both achievements. Western religions, by and large, have also subordinated esthetic concerns to theoretical and practical ones; they have devoted themselves to the development of complex theologies and to moral improvement.

The esthetic dimension is more prominent in Eastern philosophies and religions—Hinduism, Buddhism, Taoism—where the thrust is not to understand (conceptualize) experience or to perfect it morally but to accept and celebrate it. This characterization applied emphatically to Zen Buddhism, the subject of the following discussion.

If the esthetic experience means to appreciate something as complete in itself, then *all* Zen experience is esthetic. If the Zen person travels, it is to travel, not to arrive somewhere else; he is already *there*. He does not strive for anything; he is goal-less. This is the art of artlessness. "When hungry, eat; when tired, sleep."

The priority of the esthetic element is revealed in the testament of one of Zen's most ardent and scholarly proponents. D. T. Suzuki, in trying to explain an Eastern perspective to a Western audience, says, "Zen naturally finds its readiest expression in poetry rather than philosophy because it has more affinity with feeling than with intellect; its poetic predilection is inevitable."[1] That uniquely Japanese literary form, the haiku, makes the case. A haiku poem, so brief, simply points to the thusness of things; it seems to say, "Just so, just as it is." The poem offers no commentary, no interpretation; it expresses a simple, childlike wonder.

> *Evening rain.*
> *The banana leaf*
> *Speaks of it first.*

Zen painting in its spontaneity does not represent nature but is itself natural—a work of nature. The Zen artist portrays asymmetry, disequilibrium, and imperfection because these, as well as harmony, characterize individual suchness. The famous dry garden of Ryoanji illustrates esthetic objects as the expression of suchness. Fifteen uncarved rocks are arranged in five groups in a large expanse of raked sand—just there.

Zen art is an expression of a living moment in its pure "suchness"; it is an awakening to the present instant as the only reality—but the instant is itself timeless. The favorite subjects of the Zen artist are natural, concrete, everyday things. Zen masters are portrayed as aimless, going nowhere in a timeless moment; and art echoes the moment. Zen art is a yea-saying to life as it presents itself—"empty and marvelous."

Critique

Is the esthetic attitude self-sufficient? Is it enough to accept and savor everything just as it is: cruelty, disease, war? Does Zen fail to balance appreciation of today's now with effort to secure a richer now tomorrow?

---

[1]D. T. Suzuki, *An Introduction to Zen Buddhism* (New York: Grove Press, 1964), p. 117.

3. Esthetic Objects Express a Unified Experience

John Dewey developed a theory of art as the enhancement of common experience. Experience involves a constant interaction between live creatures and their environments in a series of doings and undergoings. When we are conscious of an ordered movement of experience from a beginning to a culmination, the experience is unified, and we say that it was *an* experience. When we pay attention to the pervasive, integrated quality of *an* experience, our experience is esthetic. It may be noted that some educators, focusing exclusively on this aspect of Dewey's esthetic theory, have concluded that exposure of students to objects of fine art is unimportant, since esthetic appreciation can be sufficiently developed as students experience the ordered movement from the beginning to the conclusion of *any* problem-solving activity.

Esthetic objects and events elicit a quality of experienced wholeness, of an experience complete and unified in itself. Thus, objects of art focus and enrich qualities found in our everyday experience. Consider the earliest known examples of art: paintings of animals on the walls of caves to commemorate the success of a hunting expedition.

Objects take on *meaning* when we discover their interrelationships and interact with them in new ways. The moon is still a shining disk in the sky, but now it has the added meaning of men having walked on it and returned with fragments to decipher. Science takes objects out of isolation by showing us their causes and effects, thus providing us with instrumental meanings. Art is a direct expression of meanings that are not translatable into ordinary language. Poor landlubbers, we yet participate in Ahab's relentless search for the white whale. The artist has the imaginative capacity to see things whole, thus enlarging and unifying the quality of the perceiver's experience.

The artist does not reveal some ghostly "essence" of things but rather their essential meanings in and for experience. The religious feelings that may accompany an intense esthetic perception stem from arousal by the work of art of a sense of unity and a sense of belonging to the all-inclusive whole that is the universe.

The more an esthetic object embodies experiences common to many individuals, the more expressive it is. A work of art means not the artist's intention but the unified quality of experience that, through time, it can evoke in perception. Ideally, the art object is the vehicle of complete, unhindered communication, enabling us to share vividly and deeply in meanings to which we had been blind or insensitive. Who, for example, can live through a performance of the classic *Who's Afraid of Virginia Woolf?* without acquiring a new and poignant sense of what it means to hurt others and in turn be hurt?

People in all walks of life—the assembly-line worker, the agricultural laborer, the computer programmer—can become creatively involved in the products of the artist's imagination and emerge with a sharpened and heightened awareness.

Critique

Is the net cast by "a unified experience" ambiguously all-inclusive? A unified experience, in one context, seems no more than attending to the formal properties of any art object, while in another context it expands to a feeling of mystical oneness. How clear and adequate is the proposed criterion of good art, that which in the long run elicits esthetic experience in people? (Does the criterion imply "the greatest number of people"?)

4. Esthetic Objects Express Feelings

The theory that esthetic objects express feelings is known as **expressionism**. Expressionism can be interpreted in three quite different ways. The feelings expressed may be those of the artist, or those inherent in the art object, or the feelings aroused in the perceiver. Thus we may say (1) the *composer* is sad and communicates his personal feeling; or (2) the *music* is sad; or (3) the music makes *me* feel sad. Obviously, these are not mutually exclusive alternatives—either or both of the second and third conditions may result from the first one.

1. Croce, an Italian philosopher of history and esthetics, interpreted art as an expression (manifestation) of the artist's state of mind, giving us "intuitive knowledge" of mental states (see discussions of subjective idealism). Note the striking art sometimes produced by the uninhibited expression of so-called mentally ill persons. Plato and James Joyce suggested that the artist's feelings are a divinely inspired ecstasy.

The idea that art expresses the artist's personal emotions is exemplified most fully in the movement known as **romanticism**. The romanticists valued sincerity, spontaneity, passion. The role of the artist is to feel deeply and then communicate those emotions in order to stimulate imagination and enthusiasm in the audience.

The romanticists were intensely interested in Nature, which they interpreted as a manifestation of Spirit. Artists should immerse themselves in Nature, approaching it with longing and a sense of identification; in this way artists would relive the experiences of the creative Spirit and be able to reexpress them symbolically through their works of art. In this vein, Teilhard de Chardin interprets art as an expression of a universal life force, reminiscent of Henri Bergson's notion of an *élan vital*, the dynamic source of causation and evolution in nature.

Art may express the artist's feelings in a very different sense if it symbolizes a sublimated sexual impulse (Freud), or primordial images (archetypes) from the unconscious (Jung, Herbert Read), or a playful, make-believe escape from reality.

2. Does it make sense to say that *music* is sad? It can be argued that the music (or some other variety of art object) has a gestalt quality (perhaps a

mood) so that the perceiver *recognizes* (does not read into) the emotion as a felt quality of the object itself. Music is sad when it has the properties and features of people's sad feelings. Some music is iconic; that is, it has a structural similarity to what it symbolizes—such as the clattering of horses' hooves.

Susan Langer and Ernst Cassirer describe art as the creation of forms that symbolize (articulate) the structure of human feelings. *Who's Afraid of Virginia Woolf?* again provides an illustration. An art object does not assert any propositions about human feelings; it is a symbolic pointing toward them. A major function of art, in this view, is to clarify the inner life. Aristotle held that the portrayal of fearful and pitiable events in tragic drama provides a catharsis, a purification of the emotions.

3. The third view is that art expresses feelings in the sense of evoking them. It is undeniable that we experience sadness, joy, and other emotions while in the presence of esthetic objects. The question is whether our feelings tell us something about the artist's intentions, about the art object itself, about our emotional state at the time, or about the meanings and expectations we project onto the esthetic object. We may approach the question by posing another question: When two persons attend to a work of art, without paying attention to their own inner responses to it, will one of them experience joy and the other sadness?

The hedonistic interpretation of feelings aroused by esthetic objects is that, joyful or sad, they are pleasing. Beauty is objectified pleasure (according to Santayana).

Critique

Do not esthetic objects, for example, a play by G. B. Shaw, often express ideas and meanings rather than feelings? Is not the capacity of objects to elicit an esthetic response more important than the artist's overflow of emotions and intention to communicate them? If the source of artistic inspiration *is* the individual or racial unconscious, how does this affect our appreciation or evaluation of the work of art? Do romanticists fall into sentimentality when they project human emotions onto natural objects? If arousal of feeling is the main function of esthetic objects, do we then agree that Dickens's *Christmas Carol* is a supreme achievement of art? Is "pleasure" an apt description of our response to *Guernica, Hamlet,* and *Tristan und Isolde?*

5. Esthetic Objects Express Existential Possibilities

We have reached the opposite end of the continuum from Eternal Forms. The existential view is that an art object is a sheer (pure) possibility. The art object is a *presentation* of a possibility felt and imagined by its author; it is not a *representation* of a form or an essence—given, complete, timeless.

The art object is more than an imagined possibility; it is itself the *presence* of the possibility.

The work of art, like the existing individual, is not an expression of fullness; it is a thrust of spontaneity from lack of being. The art object is a spontaneous utterance, an enactment, of what an individual feels and imagines existence to be. The utterance, if authentic, is novel and original. It is "truthful" in the sense of being sincere and of revealing the vision to which the person is committed. This is not an abstract kind of truth and is not subject to any empirical test.

The artist creates by willing into existence some value in an inherently valueless existence.

The only test of a work of art is the originality and sincerity that mark its creation. Genuine art merges authentic feeling and imagination into an object whose meaning is completely clear. This authenticity and clarity sensitize us to cowardice and fakery of every kind. On the positive side, art helps us to taste the infinite variety of ways in which it is possible to be human. Such tasting is an incipient time bomb to explode the status quo.

There is no single style of "existential" art. For Nietzsche, art is **Dionysian**, celebrating human passions that overflow all civilized restraints. On the other hand, a painting in which human figures are conspicuously absent may symbolize the impersonality and dehumanization of modern existence.

Critique

The existential posture can be questioned from the viewpoint of Zen. Both positions abhor abstractions and pretense; both value simplicity, individuality, and especially spontaneity. A Zen believer might query the existentialist as follows: "How is it that you find yourself so completely cut off from nature? Why do your feelings and imagination have to spring from a void rather than from the fullness of the given? Why not let your art flow freely from the suchness within and around you? Instead of will, why not be willing? For example, if you feel dissatisfied with yourself, there is no need to summon willpower to force a change; the seed of change *is you*."

E. Three Controversial Issues

1. Subjectivism versus Objectivism

The issue here raises a methodological question. Are esthetic judgments and evaluations subjective or objective or a mixture of both elements? The alternative answers closely parallel the positions set out in Chapter 8, on ethics.

In **subjectivism** the claim is put forth that there are no esthetic-inducing properties of an artwork as such, and certainly there is no one characteristic of an object that guarantees its value. People can only report a subjective impression of what they perceive. No meaningful disagreement is possible when impressions or intuitions differ, as they often do. This brings us to an "emotive theory" of esthetics.

Advocates of **cultural relativism** in esthetics can point out that music and art in a cultural tradition very different from our own often elicit nonesthetic reactions—a sense of monotony, indifference, rejection, or sheer curiosity.

Art in contemporary **postmodernism** rejects any unified frame of reference, emphasizing diversity. Furthermore, the artist's presence in the artwork is often downplayed, and greater emphasis is placed on the audience and its interpretation. In fact, the audience's response often becomes part of the artwork or the performance (as in the comedy improvisations of *Second City*), or the reader's response is required to construct the meaning of a literary piece that is intentionally so obscure that it forces the reader's active involvement. Derrida has said that the primary form of postmodern discourse is the collage. One can see this in postmodern architecture where various styles and time periods are combined. All is in the present moment. Finally, objective reference points disappear as the boundary between fact and fiction disappears, sometimes with the intention of making a political statement about power and oppression (as cleverly portrayed in the movie *Wag the Dog*).

Objectivism as a basis for esthetic judgment takes three major forms:

a. The **absolutist** position is that we have knowledge of the ideal order of reality, either through divine illumination or through reason. This knowledge, it is held, constitutes a secure base for objective judgments of works of art. Kant contended that there is a harmony of the imagination and the understanding that is common to all people, and therefore judgments of taste are universal.

b. In **pragmatism**, an esthetic object is evaluated in terms of its capacity to produce an esthetic response. Esthetic judgment is thus an estimation of the possibilities of an object for providing esthetic experience. Granted that there are no set rules for assessing the response capacity of works of art, we can point to some properties that are likely to confer that capacity; for example, unity, complexity, and intensity. In this sense, the judgment "I do not like it" is not equivalent to the statement "It has no esthetic properties." The final test, however, is pragmatic: Does the object, through time, in fact arouse esthetic appreciation?

c. The **rational-choice** position is set forth by David Hume: Good art has those characteristics that please a qualified observer; a qualified observer is one who is experienced, calm, and unprejudiced. This position must cope with the difficulty that trained, sensitive art critics do not always agree and that later critics often *do* agree in rejecting the judgments of their predecessors. Could we agree on which critics are "qualified"? We often seem to be reduced to the circular argument that the qualified critics are the ones who have "good taste."

It may be suggested that the function of the art critic is not to pass judgment, as in a court of law, but to enlarge and deepen esthetic perception, which is the function of esthetic objects themselves. In this context, the argument between subjectivist and objectivist is of no more than secondary concern.

2. Art and Knowledge

The fundamental question here is whether art is a knowledge-producing process. What is the relation between art and epistemology?

Intuition plays a role in esthetic perception in the sense that the qualities of the art object are grasped in immediate awareness. Intuitionism, however, claims much more: that the perceiver not only has direct awareness of the esthetic object but also learns about the nature of things from the intuitive knowledge conveyed by the artist. Literature, for example, states or implies propositions about love, death, good and evil, and especially human nature; if you want to understand the human condition, we are told, go to the novelist, poet, and dramatist in preference to the academic psychologist.

Langer, as we have seen, argues that the arts express truths about human emotions, but she explicitly states that these truths are not translatable into propositions subject to empirical test. No knowledge claim is put forward in her view that art clarifies human emotions. The latter statement coincides with the view that art provides not knowledge but a sense of disclosure, insight, and heightened intelligibility.

A person skeptical of intuitionism might seek to clarify the situation by proposing that artists furnish a vivid *acquaintance with* human realities and possibilities but no *knowledge about* them. This proposal would hardly satisfy romanticists, who assert that artistic imagination furnishes immediate insight into truths about the ultimate nature of reality. The difficulty here is the contradictory character of the reported truths and the absence of criteria by which to choose among them.

The existentialist's insistence that art expressions are "true" when they spring from sincere, authentic feelings does not imply that they produce any knowledge.

Most of those who deny that artistic expression is a form of knowing do not thereby disparage its importance in human life. They hold that art's function is to give form to new meanings and distinctive visions that will expand and enrich awareness.

3. Art and Morality

We have just considered whether art is a knowledge-producing process. We now raise an axiological question: Is art, or should it be, a morality-producing enterprise?

Metaphysical idealists, convinced that they know what is right and proper, quite naturally judge the artist's work in light of their moral conceptions. The obligation of art, said Tolstoy, is to communicate the highest moral and religious truths. **Materialism**, in its Marxist version, adopts the same stance; artistic conceptions that deviate from officially established values are condemned and, if possible, suppressed. In the interests of internal harmony and political stability, censorship of the arts is deemed necessary in Plato's *Republic*, and in communist and fascist states.

Should the artist's imagination and vision be confined within the narrow limits set by a reigning moral orthodoxy? The record of censorship is not a pretty one; too often it has meant repression on behalf of a narrow **dogmatism** that is soon seen to be arbitrary and unenduring. Censorship confines the artist and at the same time deprives everyone else of the opportunity to make a free, moral choice. On the other hand, some advocate that artistic freedom and individual choice must take a back seat to the majority's preferences or the well-being of the state.

It has been argued that esthetic judgment is distinct from moral judgment in light of the fact that we can appreciate the portrayal of contradictory ways of life.

If we reject censorship and the moral absolutism in which it is typically rooted, do we automatically commit ourselves to **estheticism**, the view that moral and practical concerns should always be subordinated to esthetic enjoyment? Estheticism appears to make two claims: Art is for art's sake alone, and esthetic appreciation is the supreme or only intrinsic value. The advocate of estheticism can be confronted with a haunting test case: Mussolini's nephew returned from a bombing mission over Ethiopia and exulted over the beauty of a bomb exploding among unarmed civilians. The raw but seductively popular movie *Pulp Fiction* raised the suspicion that an inhumane way of life was portrayed as a lifestyle beyond the reach of moral assessment.

A third position, differing from both moralism and estheticism, argues that art serves morality not by promoting established standards but by expanding human sympathies and imagination and revealing a common human nature, thus uniting humankind. The moral function of art, in this accounting, is not to extol the tried and true but to give imaginative life to *new* values, to deliver us from old moralities to new ones of wider scope. A movie such as *Philadelphia* might fit this category.

F. Conclusion

There remain conflicting interpretations of the nature and meaning of esthetic objects. This fact should not blind us to the possibility of enriching our lives in ways proposed by each of the alternative views. Esthetic objects may arouse in us a sense of abiding values, an awareness of the suchness of things, an appreciation for the continuities and meanings that unify experience, a more profound recognition of the flow of feelings in ourselves and others, and a sensitivity to hitherto unimagined possibilities of existence.

However wide we spread the net of intellectual analysis in order to capture the message of the artist, the artist is vocation-bound to elude us. "Stop! Look! Listen!" cries the artist. "When imagination's train comes by and shakes the earth, reverberate!" It may be true that few esthetic events embody a vision distinct and powerful enough to shatter our complacency and alter our view of life; still, we can seek out and celebrate these few.

Esthetic experience can become a significant dimension of life, even in an overdeveloped society. A large number of people can play and compose music, paint, sculpt, tend gardens, and engage in handicrafts. There are two other, quite different, possibilities.

One possibility is that people might try to create a society as a work of art. More and more people, reacting against the impersonality and competitiveness of huge bureaucratic organizations (in business, education, welfare) yearn for an "organic" community. Thus, a small group may start from scratch and form a commune. Communes in which each person "does his own thing" are marked by variety but not unity. Other communes, where cooperation is the keynote, have qualities characteristic of a work of art; the parts (individuals) are harmoniously interrelated to form an organic whole. But in fashioning a society as a work of art, the interests and autonomy of individuals may be sacrificed to the requirements of the overall pattern. Indeed, "organic harmony" is precisely the organizing principle of Plato's *Republic* and of **totalitarian** regimes. A more appealing version of an "esthetic society" might be a society that cherished and promoted esthetic experiences in the lives of the people composing it.

A second possibility is that we all function as artists in creating our individual lives as works of art. It is true that a single art object is something finished, complete. But might not each life be fashioned into a unique form, a constantly emerging unity-in-variety with a pervasive quality of intensity? A person forming his or her own life as a work of art would never go hungry for esthetic experience, and many others would find nourishment from the bread thus cast upon the waters.

Case Study and Discussion Questions

Case Study

Two art exhibits funded by government grants caused major debates—even in the U.S. Congress. One was an exhibition of photography by Robert Mapplethorpe that included depictions of homosexuals in various poses with each other, the most controversial of which may have been one picturing a man urinating into the mouth of another. The second exhibit was Andres Serano's display of a plastic crucifix suspended in his own urine. The public rallied on both sides of questions about censorship and the definition of art.

Since 1990 the grants from the National Endowment for the Arts that had funded Mapplethorpe and Serano carry a legally stipulated restriction: "No funded work can involve obscenity 'including, but not limited to, depictions of sadomasochism, homoeroticism, the exploitation of children, or individuals engaged in sex acts.'"

1. Should artistic productions ever be censored? If so, by whom and for what reasons?

2. Are the works of Mapplethorpe and Serano "art"? Why or why not?

Discussion Questions

1. Do those who say, "I don't know anything about art, but I know what I like," have a defensible or an indefensible esthetic stand?

2. On what basis can a professional movie critic claim to be an *expert* in judging whether a movie is "good"? What determines a good or bad movie?

3. Can you name some recent movies that illustrate the different positions on the continuum?

4. When making a moral point about a historical event, should an author or a film-maker have the freedom to exaggerate, downplay, or alter certain "facts"?

5. Is a skilled carpenter or a gourmet cook an acceptable example of a real artist? Why or why not?

6. Comment on the following statement: "In contrast to Eastern philosophies, Western science and religion focus on the theoretical and practical and neglect the esthetic appreciation of 'now' and 'suchness.'"

Suggested Readings

Anderson, Walter Truett. *Reality Isn't What It Used to Be: Theatrical Politics, Ready-to-Wear Religion, Global Myths, Primitive Chic, and Other Wonders of the Postmodern World.* San Francisco: Harper & Row, 1990.

Beardsley, Monroe C. *Aesthetics from Classical Greece to the Present: A Short History.* Atlanta: University of Atlanta Press, 1975.

Connor, Steven. *Postmodernist Culture: An Introduction to the Contemporary.* Oxford: Basil Blackwell, 1989.

Dewey, John. *Art as Experience.* New York: Putnam's (Capricorn Book), 1958.

Edman, Irwin. *Arts and the Man: A Short Introduction to Aesthetics.* New York: W. W. Norton, 1960.

Fallico, Arturo B. *Art and Existentialism.* Englewood Cliffs, NJ: Prentice-Hall, 1962.

Hook, Sidney, ed. *Art and Philosophy: A Symposium.* Washington Square, NY: New York University Press, 1966.

Hospers, John. "Aesthetics, Problems of." In *The Encyclopedia of Philosophy*, vol. 1, pp. 35–56.

Jencks, Charles. *The Language of Post-Modern Architecture.* London: Academy Editions, 1984.

Langer, Susanne K. *Feeling and Form: A Theory of Art.* New York: Scribner's, 1953.

Margolis, J., ed. *Philosophy Looks at the Arts.* Rev. ed. Philadelphia: Temple University Press, 1978.

Santayana, George. *The Sense of Beauty: Being the Outlines of Aesthetic Theory.* New York: Modern Library, 1955.

Suzuki, D. T. *An Introduction to Zen Buddhism.* New York: Grove Press, 1964.

Tolstoy, Leo. *What Is Art?* Translated by Louise and Aylmer Maude. New York: Bobbs-Merrill, 1960.

Weitzel, Morris, ed. *Problems in Aesthetics.* London: Collier-Macmillan, 1970.

CHAPTER 10

Philosophy and Human Nature

A. Questions to Consider

- Is it true that "you can't change human nature"?
- In the final analysis, is a person no more than a "naked ape"?
- Are human beings endowed with creative potentials that seek to unfold themselves naturally?
- Is war inevitable because of human beings' inborn aggressive drives?
- Is human nature so plastic and indeterminate that it can be molded in an endless variety of ways?
- Does the inherent selfishness of people require constant inner discipline and outside control?
- Can we trust the statement that "our original nature *is* Buddha," so that "the self-awakened will spontaneously avoid all evil and pursue all good"?

B. Introduction

At the outset we should recognize that in the ongoing discussion of important issues the question of human nature is often raised, not in its own right but simply to distract attention from the main topic. For example, two people are arguing about whether the federal government should subsidize child-care centers. Instead of confronting the pros and cons of *that* issue, one of the disputants may sidetrack the discussion by proposing that people are by nature lazy and refuse to put forth any effort to take care of themselves. It is noteworthy that the same disputant may justify pessimism about efforts to achieve world peace by appealing to an exactly opposite view of human nature, namely, that people are inevitably aggressive in defense of their own interests. In each case, the original issue becomes lost in claims and counter-claims about human nature.

The fact that statements about human nature are used as diversionary tactics in political discussion does not mean that they are inappropriate top-ics for philosophical analysis. Such statements are not always, or even usu-ally, mere rationalizations. On the contrary, they function as the ground-work on which social, political, and educational policies are fashioned. To illustrate, we can cite the Puritan view, dominant in much of America's colonial period, that child nature is inherently evil, therefore requiring an authoritarian education, one that will instill in children fear, discipline, and unquestioning obedience to law—human as well as divine. Since one's beliefs about human nature have such important practical implications, it is the philosopher's obligation to examine them critically—that is, to evaluate the empirical evidence alleged in their behalf, to identify the theoretical assumptions on which they rest, and to trace the consequences to which they lead.

But why is the question "What is human nature?" a *philosophical* issue? Why not turn to the sciences for a straightforward, unambiguous answer? The reader, recalling from Chapter 6 the unresolved arguments among free willists, strict determinists, advocates of freedom as insightful awareness, and existentialists and from Chapter 5 the differing metaphysical views of humankind, will be convinced already of the futility of a simple "appeal to science." Furthermore, the conflicting views of human nature that we are about to examine highlight the fact that the sciences do not speak with a sin-gle voice. The biologically oriented perspective of an **ethologist** gives a very different picture of a human being from the learning-oriented approach of a behavioral scientist. Behavioral scientists, in turn, disagree among them-selves about the fundamental characteristics of human nature. Depending on which theoretical approach is adopted (behaviorist, psychoanalytic, humanistic), human beings are seen as reactive, as goaded by inner drives, or as goal-seeking.

While you carry through the intellectual analysis of alternative views of human nature (assessing the evidence, identifying assumptions, tracing con-sequences, evaluating the critiques of each position), you may find it worth-while to try on each one to feel how well it fits you and the people you know best. In response to Konrad Lorenz's view, for example, do you discover within yourself and your close acquaintances a constantly replenished well-spring of hostility and aggression seeking release in direct or sublimated form?

C. A Human Nature Continuum

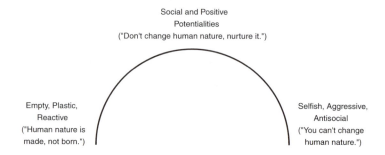

Social and Positive
Potentialities
("Don't change human nature, nurture it.")

Empty, Plastic,
Reactive
("Human nature is
made, not born.")

Selfish, Aggressive,
Antisocial
("You can't change
human nature.")

D. Alternative Views of Human Nature

1. Human Nature Is Selfish, Aggressive, and Antisocial

Pessimism about human nature—beliefs that human beings cannot trust their deepest desires and inner promptings and that if and when they do they will find themselves in conflict with their fellows—is a viewpoint widely held in past times and at present. It finds varied expression in four major modes of thought: religious, philosophical, scientific, and literary.

Traditional Judeo-Christian doctrines have stressed the idea of original sin and the human propensity to evil. St. Augustine, for example, described men and women in their natural state as seeking to realize egoistic and carnal desires, thus freely choosing to disobey God's commands. Aquinas found human nature to be weak, ignorant, and malicious; in particular, it was "concupiscent," that is, full of inordinate appetites and desires that thwarted a "natural inclination to virtue." Probably the strongest and at the same time most influential statement of our fallen nature is found in the religious orthodoxy of Calvinism. In the 1640s, John Cotton wrote a catechism read by generations of children as part of the *New England Primer*. In this book children learned that they were conceived in sin and born in iniquity and that their corrupt nature bent them to defy God's commandments, for which the punishment was eternal damnation. Indeed, Cotton viewed human nature as so intractable that he proposed the death penalty for rebellious children.

We need not harken back to olden times, however, to hear the message that all people are inherently imperfect or, in harsher terms, malicious, perverse, and full of pride and sin. Such is the constant theme of modern-day Christians such as Protestant theologian Reinhold Niebuhr and Catholic philosopher Jacques Maritain, as well as a legion of popular evangelists. Today, as through the centuries, the words of Jeremiah reverberate: "Cursed is the man who has faith in man."

While underlining the dark side of human nature, all forms of Judeo-

Christian religion offer the fallen a remedy: to exercise their God-given free will and turn from self-pride and self-reliance toward God's ever-present mercy and forgiveness, thus to be saved and regenerated. Among the requirements for salvation are individual **faith**, membership in the church where God's grace is active, and strict obedience to divine laws. This means that, strictly speaking, "you can't change human nature" but that God's grace and power make possible a change in the human condition; by transforming the "natural person" into the "spiritual person," there *is* a remedy for sin.

To discover a comparable view of human nature among the philosophers, one turns to Thomas Hobbes. Hobbes was convinced that people in a state of nature were antisocial to the core. The natural state was a war of all against all. This conclusion followed from Hobbes's view of people as inherently and thoroughly self-centered, seeking their own pleasure either through sensuality or personal glory if not simply to have a good opinion of themselves. Thus, he found in people a "natural proclivity" to hurt one another. Hobbes offered no hope of religious regeneration. His remedy was an appeal to practical reason to demonstrate that self-preservation and self-interest of each individual required the organization of a society of law and order and unquestioning obedience to a strong ruler. Only such a "social contract" would rescue people from a state of nature.

Centuries earlier Plato had expressed his reservations about the trustworthiness of human nature. Although Plato did not picture human nature in the unmitigated dark hues that Hobbes did, he did see the soul as divided into three parts; two parts, the spirit and the appetites, were like wild horses needing to be brought under control by the third part, Reason. Since this control must be exercised socially as well as individually, Plato's remedy for human nature involved, as did Hobbes's, obedience by all citizens to authoritarian political rule.

In a similar vein, Immanuel Kant referred to natural human desires as instinctive efforts at lawless, egoistic domination over others, leading to conflicts among individuals. Like the others, he prescribed regulation of selfish desires through strict obedience to laws—but in his case these were *moral* laws established by reason, rather than state regulations.

Hobbes, Plato, Kant, and the religionists concurred that although "you can't change human nature," you can *control* it—through strict political, moral, or spiritual discipline.

We can only sample the many literary and scientific viewpoints alleging that human nature is evil and basically unalterable. We will cite a few examples from literature, psychoanalytic theory, and the recently popular ethological studies of animal-human behavior.

Anaïs Nin, novelist and sensitive observer of the human condition, speaks in her diary of a "demon of destruction" inside of her—a source of energy "like some gnawing animal" that must find expression either in self-destruction or in the destruction of others. She goes on to describe her pessimism about improving the world because nothing changes human nature, and a revolution simply puts another set of people in power while the evil remains in the form of the guilt, fear, greed, and impotence that make people cruel and that no system will eliminate.

Anaïs Nin reports that Otto Rank, noted psychoanalyst, after a day with his patients jotted in his notes that human nature is evil; to be human is to be cruel, cheap, mean, jealous, possessive, lazy, exploitative; love and seeming sacrifice for others are really forms of domination, pretenses that one is good. It is Freud, in his later writings, who stated the case most succinctly. He posited two basic instincts in man: love (Eros) and death (Thanatos). The death instinct turns against the outside world in the form of aggression and destructiveness. Freud adopted the standpoint that "the tendency to aggression is an innate, independent, instinctual disposition in man . . . the hostility of each one against all and all against one."

Freud's theme that aggressiveness is a powerful human instinct has been given prominence in recent years in the writings of Robert Ardrey, Konrad Lorenz, Desmond Morris, and others. Their thesis is that war, crime, sadism, and other forms of destructive behavior are manifestations of a built-in mechanism inherited from our anthropoid ancestors. The physiological mechanism of aggression is instinctive, not only in the sense that it is an automatic response that is easily triggered but also in the sense that it is, like sex, a drive that spontaneously seeks expression. Ethologists, using their studies of animal behavior as bases, point out that aggressive impulses and behavior have played an indispensable role in the evolutionary process. Territorial aggression against members of the same species leads to the spacing out of members of the species over the available habitat; aggressive competition among males leads to the selection of the stronger ones to carry out the reproductive function; pecking-order aggression guarantees leadership of the group by the stronger, more capable members. Among nonhuman animals, these positive functions of aggression within a species were kept from becoming counterproductive by the development of elaborate rituals. Excessive killing in combat was avoided by means of these rituals, which permitted victory to be awarded to the stronger without the physical destruction of the loser. Human beings have inherited a full measure of animal aggressiveness but have not developed appropriate combat rituals. In any case, such rituals would not work under modern conditions, where elaborate weaponry has replaced face-to-face conflict.

Observers taking the psychoanalytic or ethological stance, while often pessimistic about the chances for human survival, do offer some hope that human aggressiveness will not prove fatal. First, they say, we must recognize our biological limitations and face up to the fact that we are, and will always be, aggressive animals; we must accept the fact that "warrior virtues" have been bred into us in the long process of natural selection. Second, we must acknowledge that appeals to reason and morality have proven ineffective in controlling our hostile instincts. Third, acknowledging that our belligerent drives must have *some* outlet, we can consciously seek to redirect them from destruction and mutual slaughter to less lethal undertakings. Competition in international sports, for example, could serve to vent aggressive energies, just as ritualized combat does among other animals.

More influential in Western thought has been Adam Smith's confident assertion of an acquisitive instinct in all people. His idea was buttressed in the past century by the theory of **social Darwinism**, with its claim that human competitiveness is an innate trait adapted to the inevitable struggle for existence in which only the strongest and "fittest" survive. This claim is the kernel of the capitalist theory of humankind, in which no "remedy" for selfishness or competitiveness is needed or sought. The good society that emerges is **laissez-faire**, encouraging each individual to pursue his or her own economic self-interest, without interference from the government. The inequality and social stratification that result are simply natural outcomes of the process.

Critiques of Human Nature as Selfish, Aggressive, and Antisocial

1.

From the viewpoint of modern psychology (except the psychoanalytic branch), it is highly questionable that competition and aggressiveness are innate drives. Most psychologists would consider both aggressive and competitive behavior as ways in which individuals learn to respond under specified conditions. Aggressive behavior is often a response to threat or frustration. If this is in fact the case, human aggression can be markedly reduced by eliminating as far as possible threatening and frustrating situations. For example, earlier child-raising practices—punishing any deviation from adult-imposed standards and frustrating the normal demands of the growing child—undoubtedly produced hostile, aggressive reactions, thus confirming the pessimistic premise about child nature on which the practices were based. On the other hand, if children surrounded by warmth and acceptance turn out to be warm, loving creatures, can we not conclude that aggressiveness is learned rather than inborn?

2.

Erich Fromm raises the objection that Konrad Lorenz fails to distinguish between two very different forms of aggression. On one side there is "benign aggression," which is a defense reaction to threats against vital interests. Benign aggression is biologically adaptive and instinctive in animals and people. On the other side there is "malignant aggression," which involves destructiveness and cruelty unrelated to defense or to removing a threat. Malignant aggression is biologically nonadaptive; it is *not* instinctive, and its occurrence must be explained psychologically rather than biologically. This distinction between benign and malignant aggression undermines Lorenz's (and Freud's) "hydraulic" picture of aggressive energy expanding like heated gas in a closed container until the pressure builds up to a spontaneous explosion.

Fromm points out that, neurologically and behaviorally, "flight" and "fight" are equally important defense reactions of animals under threat. Why don't ethologists elaborate on the "flight instinct" as a basic feature of animal and human nature?

3.

Anthropological studies point to the wide diversity of human cultures; they do not support the thesis that human aggressiveness or even competitiveness is a universal human trait. Benedict's *Patterns of Culture* shows that hostility, competitiveness, and mutual distrust do, in fact, characterize life in some societies but by no means all. She describes how the Zuni Indians, for example, are scornful of individuals who seek power or commit acts of violence—or even of those who compete too successfully.

Some anthropologists contend that the trend of human evolution has been toward cooperation rather than conflict. Perhaps the main lesson of anthropology is that human nature is not innately aggressive or cooperative but highly plastic.

2. Human Nature Is Social with Positive Potentialities

Let us now examine the idea that our social inclinations and our positive, life-affirming potentialities are more deeply grounded in our nature than our negative, destructive impulses. This idea has been formulated in different ways by a diverse group of thinkers in Eastern as well as Western traditions.

In this view of humankind, the core of human nature is seen as actively pressing toward self-realization, self-actualization, self-fulfillment.

In the West, the theme that self-realization is the natural goal of human nature can be traced as far back as Aristotle, who spoke of a human "movement toward fulfillment." Later, we find Rousseau and Froebel expounding educational doctrines based on the theory that our inner powers are so benign that they simply need to be "unfolded." In a similar vein, Bergson posited an **immanent** life-force, an *élan vital,* working through nature and humanity toward affirmative ends. Green, Bradley, and their fellow idealists toward the end of the nineteenth century gave a central place to self-realization as the natural and proper aim of human life.

In the East, the ancient posture of Taoism reflects a view of human nature that might be called creative quietism. In this view, human nature is at its very source identical with all that is. This "original nature" encompasses good and evil, flesh and spirit. Each is a necessary aspect of the other. At birth one's original nature is untarnished, but it soon becomes contaminated by society and superficial activity. The path by which a person awakes from delusion and becomes whole again and at one with pristine innocence is quiet contemplation and a life of spontaneous simplicity in which there is a return to "fewness of desires." Such a person discards the desire for money, power, and status and even moves beyond the demands of law, duty, and morality. Such enlightened mystics claim to be beyond contrived and artificial ideas of good and evil and to be in harmony with themselves and the world. They do not do violence to others; and they do not suffer violence to be done to them—even in God's name. They live in a world of conventions and laws but are not of that world with its fragmentary and arbitrary standards. They are not do-gooders, but what they do is life-affirming when they are in harmony with their true universal selves. Their lives echo the words of the sage Lao Tzu: "The way to do is to be."

At the heart of Mahayana (Northern) Buddhism is the doctrine that there is no separate human nature; there is only Buddha nature. What the West identifies as human nature is but the false and compulsive grasping of an illusion that has no substance or reality. Buddhists teach that the self is not synonymous with the ego; the self is subsumed in a bottomless unknown that is at the same time no-self. When the conscious self transcends ego and realizes its own infinite aspect, the self can no longer be accepted as a quality possessed by individuals that gives them a categorical identity or that holds them apart from or against other individuals. The self dissolves into and becomes one with the universal totality of being. This is the Buddha nature with which everyone and everything is endowed. In this view, the self-nature of human beings (indeed, of *all* beings) is so great that it contains all things. So, rather than concerning themselves with "human nature," which they regard as an objective distortion, Buddhists discern instead the mystical yearning for Buddha nature that is prescribed in the sacred texts and reveals itself in the wisdom of the sages. Mencius, the venerated Chinese Confucian sage, also charted the same path to enlightenment and self-realization: "All things are complete within us, and there is no greater joy than to turn our look inwards and to find ourselves true to our nature." To redefine human nature in this way means that it can have no objective structure, it cannot be named as a distinct and separate entity, and everything is possible. Human beings are one with each other and ripe with endless potential.

Modern psychiatrists, psychoanalysts, and psychologists such as Goldstein, Rank, Jung, Horney, Fromm, G. Allport, May, Rogers, Maslow, and Buhler have found it necessary to postulate a positive growth or self-actualization tendency within the human organism, in addition to the tendencies toward homeostasis and responsiveness to external stimuli. Buhler identifies a "drive toward self-fulfillment." Rogers claims to find a "forward-moving directional tendency" in every human being; he bases his claim on the observation that when external and internal restrictions are removed and the person feels free to move in *any* direction, the person moves in fact toward "full functioning." According to Maslow, human beings are so constructed that they press toward fuller and fuller being, that is, toward "self-actualization." In a recent philosophical treatise, *Man and His Values,* Werkmeister describes human beings as self-directed, self-regulated beings whose growth is basically a spontaneous process unfolding potentialities with which the human organism is endowed. This process is primarily positive and constructive; defense mechanisms and destructiveness are secondary developments that manifest themselves only under abnormal or pathogenic conditions. Fromm spells out human potentials in terms of certain basic needs, which, in addition to those held in common with other animals, stem from the very conditions of human existence.

What specific qualities of human nature are pointed to in theories of full functioning, self-actualization, and basic needs? Fully functioning, self-actualizing people are not selfish, aggressive, or antisocial. They accept and relate positively to other people and have a sense of identification with them regardless of racial, class, or other differences. Since these people are not ego-centered or defensive, their destructive impulses are weak and typically sub-ordinate to their felt need for relatedness and affiliation. Rogers speaks of the "basic trustworthiness of human nature," so that the only control of impulses that is necessary comes from the natural, internal balancing of one need against another. Such balancing leads to behavior that is appropriate to the survival and enhancement of a highly social animal.

One of our five basic needs, according to Fromm, is to go beyond self as passive and toward creativity; if a person cannot find a way beyond passivity by creating life, the person will turn and destroy life. Fully functioning and self-actualizing persons move toward self-direction, trust of their inner responses, and behavior that is spontaneous and expressive of the self in unique and imaginative ways.

If positive potentialities in the form of dynamic needs and capacities are at the core of human nature, the appropriate prescription is: "Don't try to *change* human nature—nurture it." This means to remove the hindrances to its nat-ural growth and to establish the inner (psychological) and outer (political and social) conditions that will allow it to flourish. This was Plato's agenda in the *Republic*. Another apt illustration is provided by Ruth Benedict, who tried in her last years to go beyond the doctrine of **cultural relativity** with which her name is usually associated. She selected for study eight cultures. In four of these cultures people were anxious, hateful, aggressive, and with "low morale." In the other four, people were secure, affectionate, unaggressive, and with "high morale." She compared the cultures to find a factor common to the four aggressive cultures but absent in the nonaggressive ones; she could find no such common factor in race, geography, climate, size, wealth, complexity, or kinship system. She finally discovered that the aggressive cul-tures had low **synergy** (gain for one meant loss for another) and the nonag-gressive cultures had high synergy (work for oneself helped others). The high-synergy societies provided institutions that ensured mutual advantage to everyone participating in their undertakings; the low-synergy societies were so arranged that the advantage of one individual became a victory over another. Benedict concluded that a cooperative, high-synergy social structure nurtured people's positive potentialities, while a competitive, low-synergy social structure encouraged negative traits.

From a similar standpoint, Marx envisioned a classless society within which "new" men and women would emerge to exercise their natural pro-ductive powers in harmony with their fellows.

Critiques of Human Nature as Social with Positive Potentialities

1.

Let us grant that human nature has positive potentialities and that cooper-ative (synergistic) social forms are possible. If the positive side of human nature is stronger than the negative side, how do we explain the fact that *Homo sapiens* is the *only* species known to kill its own members with systematic violence? If blame for this situation is not laid on human nature but on the organization of society (for example, the war system), how does it happen that *in fact* humankind *has* created, and still supports, social systems in which war and interpersonal violence threaten to overwhelm it?

2.

The historical record concerning political and social revolutions shows that human nature is neither as benign and trustworthy as Taoists, Buddhists, and the humanistic psychologists suggest nor as plastic as environmental **determinists** claim.

Leaders of the French and Russian revolutions promised a new order in which man's age-old inhumanity to man would be forever eradicated. But it turned out that the human greed and violence of the new regimes equaled or exceeded the old. The "new" person who was supposed to emerge "naturally" within the reformed social and economic structures established by the Chinese and Cuban revolutions either has failed to appear or exists in a framework of brainwashing and political coercion.

Selfish impulses are stronger than social, other-regarding inclinations and will subvert any attempts to improve the human situation through reforming or overthrowing the social system.

3.

The claim that *all* people by nature strive to be creative, to realize their capacities to the full, to find the "way," and to pursue long-range purposes is a romantic exaggeration. When Tillich states that to be human means to affirm oneself as a free, unique, self-actualizing individual as part of a community of similar individuals, is he *describing* human nature or setting a distant, probably unrealizable, ideal? Doubts about these optimistic views of human nature are aroused less by reference to human selfishness and aggressiveness than by simple observation that most people acquiesce in a life of passive pleasures with a minimum of discomforts. Skinner suggests in *Walden Two* that the majority of people want merely some assurance that they will be decently provided for. The rest is a day-to-day enjoyment of life.

3. Human Nature Is Empty, Plastic, Reactive

Turning now to a third alternative, that human beings are born with no given, definable nature at all and are therefore infinitely malleable, we find that its supporters include such incompatible fellow travelers as philosophers in the Age of the Enlightenment, physical and social scientists, existentialists and postmodernists.

Physical determinists from at least the time of Thomas Hobbes have interpreted human nature as an extension of the basic laws of physics. Human behavior is viewed simply as the behavior of matter and can be understood according to the same general principles that are applied to matter. Whatever happens, whether in the realm of human behavior, human thought, or voluntary action, is caused by changes of material particles. Scientists today drawing on the newer discoveries in the fields of biophysics, biochemistry, neurophysiology, and computer science take a similar stand on the human nature question. Intelligence, consciousness, and the physical and behavioral properties of human organisms are seen in all respects as the consequence of the normal operation of the laws of physics in inanimate chemical matter. A person is at best an intricate machine programmed by the forces of nature. Here we are presented with the idea of a "mechanical" human being.

In a somewhat similar fashion John Locke viewed a human being as a natural creature whose nature could be explained causally in terms of impressions coming from the environment. Locke could find no evidence for either innate ideas or original sin and rejected both concepts. Followers of Locke in the eighteenth century held that original human nature is empty and passive and therefore completely malleable. This outlook on human nature served to loosen the heavy hand of tradition and to assert the power of education to shape human society anew. In the nineteenth century, a similar perspective on human nature and the shaping power of education, but without the social-reformist impulse, was developed by Johann Herbart and became influential in the United States in the early 1900s. Out of Herbart's association psychology came the conception of instruction as a systematic presentation of "ideas"; through this procedure a teacher would literally "construct" people and provide them with all the materials of their personalities.

The mental leap from Locke and Herbart to John Watson's behaviorism and B. F. Skinner's "science of man" is not great. Watson proclaimed confidently: Give me a baby and I will shape it to whatever personality and career you care to specify—because there are no innate capacities to be developed. Skinner, likewise, proposes to develop a science of humanity and a "technology of behavior" with no reference whatever to "inner categories" or "internal states." Skinner denounces the prescientific practice of attributing human behavior to intentions, purposes, aims, and goals. "Behavior," he complains, "is still attributed to human nature." Feelings and inner states, such as plans and purposes, are by-products, not causes, Skinner insists; therefore, we should forget them and explain all behavior by reference to antecedent events in the environment. Since the environment makes us what we are, Skinner concludes (as did some of the utopian Enlightenment thinkers) that we need a society carefully designed to bring forth and reinforce responses leading to human survival.

Skinner's theory that human nature is plastic and strictly determined by environmental influences is shared by many, perhaps most, anthropologists. Anthropologists grant that human beings have certain common needs and face similar problems of survival, but they point to the exuberant variety of responses and solutions that have been devised and then transmitted to each new generation as time-tested ways of believing, feeling, and reacting.

Among contemporary sociologists there are some who lean strongly toward the view that human nature is completely shaped by culture or society. These social scientists contend that the environmental conditions under which human personality and behavior develop are crucial to an understanding of what human beings are and what they do. And other human beings, because they are the most relevant and immediate parts of one's environment, are seen as the most important determiners of attitudes and behaviors—even of one's own sense of self.

The sociologist Peter Berger, for example, believes that society is possible only if most of its members agree most of the time on the definitions of the situations that confront them. This agreement implies that powerful pressures are at work to ensure the appropriate responses. To be a participating member of the group each person must conform to specific demands and expectations. Human beings are social animals, and the culture as it is transmitted to them ensures that they will play their roles adequately and consistently. Berger challenges us with some very strong generalizations: A person becomes what he or she plays at; individual identity is bestowed in acts of social recognition; human dignity is a matter of social permission; each society produces the people it needs. The implication is that even if a human "organism" could survive without others, it would not become a human "being." Society makes us persons in the first place and then molds us to certain types of behaviors, attitudes, and beliefs. "Human nature" is thereby translated as "social nature."

The inevitability of determinism by the environment leads Skinner to advocate conscious control over the relevant factors, but most social scientists are content to accept the fact of cultural diversity and the seeming relativity of all values.

While totally rejecting all versions of cultural-environmental determinism, existentialists also adamantly insist that each individual is empty, plastic, and open to all possibilities. Human nature does not exist, asserts Kierkegaard, only each individual in his or her subjectivity. Sartre contends that there is no fixed set of characteristics defining human essence or nature. This lack of a definite, definable nature is what sets human beings apart from everything else that exists. Every creature except the human one is a "being-in-itself"—with a given nature, enclosed, completed, determined. Only the human creature is a "being-for-itself," that is, self-conscious. And consciousness, according to Sartre, is precisely "nothingness." Individuals, then, must define themselves; "human nature" is constantly being invented and redefined through the choices of each individual. Authentic individuals are aware of their total emptiness—that they are "condemned to be free"—free to accept the full responsibility to define themselves and the meaning of their lives. As the Renaissance writer Giovanni Pico advised: "Mold and fashion yourself into that form you yourself shall have chosen."

The postmodernist is a bedfellow of the existentialist. If there are no absolutes, meaning and truth are relative, and reality is socially constructed, then it follows for the postmodernist that the Self (or Subject) is free-floating and lacks any fixed "identity." In fact, ephemerality, fragmentation, and discontinuity are embraced. The autonomous Self (conscious, unconscious, and subconscious) is the source of truth and reality, creating a world with words and images. (Contemporary politics' stress on style over substance fits in nicely here.) Society becomes a network of many individuals, each with his or her own sources of truth and power (surfing on the Internet, perhaps, or programming the VCR to fit individual tastes and schedules). Each Self should create a world (a "virtual reality") that manipulates a sense of well-being. Managerial techniques and therapy become prime assets. In addition, the Other must be respected; all selves are to have an equal voice, especially the marginalized and disenfranchised. The result is a fragmented, chaotic, somewhat arbitrary amalgamation of multiple selves, none with the Enlightenment's claim to universality. In fact, François Lyotard would insist that social relations can become masks for power; the concept of a "universal humanity" or consensus has to be deconstructed so that hidden political power agendas can be uncovered.

Human nature, then, is open and plastic. The only question is what or who will shape the individual into identifiable form: the random impact of experience, the arbitrary **conditioning** of culture, some Promethean educator or behavioral engineer, or perhaps each lonely Self.

Critiques of Human Nature as Empty, Plastic, Reactive

1.

Behaviorists' conclusions about human beings, like those of the ethological instinctivists, are drawn in large part from observation of and experiments on nonhuman animals—in Skinner's case, rats and pigeons. The dubious assumption is made that human behavior is simply more complex than the behavior of other animals, not different in kind. This assumption *appears* reasonable because human subjects in laboratory situations are dependent on and under the strict control of the experimenter. If they *did* have "freedom and dignity," it would not be observable under such conditions. Skinner's claims for a "technology of behavioral control" are placed beyond question when the technology itself is built into the experimental situation.

The whole approach of Skinner and other behaviorists rests on a **reductionist** and therefore inadequate idea of science. There is no place in scientific psychology, Skinner says, for concepts referring to purpose or other inner states because physics and biology have rejected them. In other words, since **anthropomorphic** categories, such as "purposes," shouldn't be applied to electrons or cells, they shouldn't be applied to people! The emptiness of human nature is thus established by fiat before anyone even enters the laboratory.

2.

The existentialist focus on human beings as free agents, responsible for making authentic life choices, can be accepted. When this focus is combined, as in Sartre, with an absolute distinction between the For-itself and the In-itself, however, an individual's choices become rootless, arbitrary, and cut off from life forces—and quite possibly destructive of these forces in oneself and others. This isolation of the "I" is strikingly seen in Sartre's assertion that the other person is *always* "object" and that therefore a genuine sense of I-Thou or "we" is impossible. Human beings may indeed have "to make themselves," but surely they can do so more meaningfully when they let go their ego controls and permit the natural forces within and outside them to flow freely. This is the way of creative artists and scientists, and it is the "way" of Tao and Zen. In Carl Rogers's terms, healthy persons place increasing trust in their total being and allow what they are to emerge from the ongoing process of experiencing. This fully functioning, Taoist way is as alien to the behaviorist as it is to the existentialist. Of course, the postmodernist version of doing this is called into question by the seeming contradiction involved in relying on highly sophisticated scientific and technological givens (such as computer hardware and software) to create one's own "virtual reality."

3.
The truth that "culture makes us human" must be balanced with the truth that "human beings make culture." As David Bidney insists in *Theoretical Anthropology,* individuals are not merely passive carriers of social culture; they are also active agents in originating and modifying culture. In a similar vein, Robert Redfield presents the view that culture is a product of human creativeness in which we find people creating, expressing themselves, and representing their inner states, not merely submitting to the constraints of custom or adapting and adjusting to others.

Human beings do not create culture in a purely arbitrary fashion either. Cross-cultural investigations by Clyde Kluckhohn and others show that there are limits to the variety and relativity of values. There are universal values that point to a common human nature. No culture approves suffering as a good in itself; none condones rape, murder, incest, or indiscriminate lying and stealing; all cultures value moral obligations between parents and children.

Our awareness of life alternatives is becoming greater. Contacts between cultures are increasing in number and intensity. Anthropology is providing more knowledge of human goals and the means devised to achieve them. People are more alert to the operation of conditioning influences within their own society. In light of these developments, we will more and more "make culture" as active, reflective agents rather than be made by it as empty, reactive puppets. In the final analysis, culture exists for people, not people for culture.

E. Conclusion

The alternative views of human nature and the accompanying critiques have been drawn from a perspective substantially different from that of "philosophical anthropology" as developed in the European tradition. Philosophical anthropology has focused on the question of exactly which characteristics—

self-consciousness, reason, intentionality, imagination—distinguish human beings from all other animals. Naturally, many of the viewpoints presented in this chapter, for example, that "people make culture," imply or assume that the human animal possesses some of these unique capacities. Indeed, philosophical examination of alternative views of human nature is itself a meaningless activity unless we assume that the participants exercise the rational capacities identified by the philosophical anthropologists.

No matter how people decide about unique human qualities, however, they must still confront the question of whether human nature is basically aggressive and antisocial, or social with positive potentialities, or empty and plastic. They "must," because so much hinges on which alternative they choose.

If you believe that you and your fellow human beings are by nature selfish, hostile, and in conflict with one another, you will no doubt acquiesce to the claims of **conservative**, often authoritarian, social, political, and religious institutions to guide and discipline people's thoughts and actions. "Reason" will then be exercised legitimately by the few to control the many.

If you believe that people have natural tendencies to realize their positive, life-affirming capacities in cooperation with other persons, you will try to find out which social arrangements (economic, political, educational) hinder and which promote the growth of fully functioning, self-actualizing persons—and "reason" will be put to the practical task of removing the obstacles and bringing into being the favorable conditions.

If you believe that people have no given nature at all, you can live out whatever values and manner of life your culture has taught you—or what a benevolent (or not so benevolent) behavioral engineer has conditioned you to. As for "reason," there will be no limits to the inventions it fashions to fill the empty organism. Or, finally, you may stand firmly on the ground of your emptiness and (perhaps like God in the beginning) create yourself out of nothingness.

A majority of people in a recent survey indicated that they believed that human nature is such that future wars are inevitable. True or not, this belief could well be a self-fulfilling prophecy. That possibility suggests that we examine alternative beliefs about human nature with utmost care—remaining suspicious of all pronouncements about human nature.

Case Study and Discussion Questions

Case Study

Two Classroom Models

Teacher as Authority (traditional classroom)	Teacher as Facilitator (democratic classroom)
Students are passive recipients of a standardized curriculum, which is the same for all	Students choose individual learning goals and explore their own interests

Teacher lectures	Teacher provides stimulation and learning resources on an individual basis
External discipline (New teachers are advised: "Make sure you get control of your students on the very first day.")	Self-discipline (New teachers are advised: "Show respect and positive regard for each student and try to understand [empathize with] each one as a whole, feeling person.")
Classroom climate: mutual suspicion and competition	Classroom climate: mutual trust and cooperation
Evaluation by standardized tests and teacher authority	Self-evaluation in consultation with teacher
Decision making: from the top down	Decision making: equal participation
Overall focus: absorption of prescribed subject matter	Overall focus: the process of learning how to learn
View of human nature_____	View of human nature_____

Carl Rogers reports that David Aspy and his colleagues in the National Consortium for Humanizing Education tape-recorded and assessed 3,700 hours of classroom instruction from 550 elementary and secondary teachers, involving African-American, Caucasian, and Mexican-American teachers and students.[1] They found a clear positive correlation between facilitative conditions provided by the teacher and academic achievement of the students. In facilitative classrooms, students were more adept in problem solving and in one study showed an increase in IQ. They also showed more self-confidence and initiative, exhibited fewer discipline problems, and had a lower rate of absence from school.

1. In light of these findings, why do the vast majority of classrooms continue to be traditional and teacher-centered?

2. What is the view of human nature in each model?

3. Why is the concept of human nature underlying the democratic classroom often rejected?

4. Is sharing power and decision making with students politically unacceptable to teachers, administrators, and school boards—even if it is more democratic and "works" academically?

Discussion Questions

1. From what angle can the frequently heard pronouncement "You can't change human nature!" be challenged?

2. Identify and compare the philosophical assumptions in the current psychological and psychotherapeutic theories about human behavior (for example, Freudian psychology, behaviorism, humanistic psychology, existential psychology).

---

[1]Carl Rogers, *A Way of Being* (Boston: Houghton Mifflin, 1980), pp. 307–310.

3. Defend or criticize the following statement: Human nature is such that future world wars are inevitable. Is your position based on scientific or historical evidence? an arbitrary assumption? some theoretical approach? Or is it a kind of working hypothesis?

4. What are the social and political consequences of adopting each of the alternative views of human nature? If you judge that the consequences of adopting a particular view are undesirable, is that a sufficient reason to reject it?

Suggested Readings

Becker, Ernest. *Angel in Armor: A Post-Freudian Perspective on the Nature of Man.* New York: Free Press, 1969.

Berger, Peter L., and Thomas Luckman. *The Social Construct of Reality: A Treatise of the Sociology of Knowledge.* Garden City, NY: Doubleday, 1966.

Ferguson, Marilyn. *The Aquarian Conspiracy: Personal and Social Transformation in the 1980's.* Los Angeles: J. P. Tarcher, 1980.

Fromm, Erich. *The Anatomy of Human Destructiveness.* New York: Fawcett, 1973.

Hollis, Martin. *Models of Man.* New York: Cambridge University Press, 1977.

Isbister, J. N. *Freud: An Introduction to His Life and Work.* Cambridge: Harvard University Press, 1985.

Krutch, Joseph Wood. *The Measure of Man: On Freedom, Human Values, Survival, and the Modern Temper.* New York: Grosset & Dunlap, 1953.

Lorenz, Konrad. *On Aggression.* New York: Bantam, 1966.

Maslow, Abraham H. *The Farther Reaches of Human Nature.* New York: Viking, 1972.

Nott, Kathleen. *Philosophy and Human Nature.* New York: Dell, 1971.

Rogers, Carl. *A Way of Being.* Boston: Houghton Mifflin, 1980.

Sartre, Jean-Paul. *Existentialism and Human Emotions.* New York: Philosophical Library, 1957.

Skinner, B. F. *Beyond Freedom and Dignity.* New York: Knopf, 1971.

Stevenson, Leslie. *Seven Theories of Human Nature.* 2d ed. New York: Oxford University Press, 1987.

Taylor, Charles. *Sources of the Self: The Making of the Modern Identity.* Cambridge: Harvard University Press, 1989.

Venable, V. *Human Nature: The Marxian View.* New York: World, 1966.

Watts, Alan. *The Book: On the Taboo against Knowing Who You Are.* New York: Random House, 1972.

CHAPTER 11

Philosophy and Politics

A. Questions to Consider

- Should political power be concentrated in the hands of a few leaders, or should it be widely dispersed among the members of a society?
- To what ends should organized government be directed?
- What moral principles underlie the distribution of power among human beings?
- When does a person or a group have the right to exercise authority over other human beings?
- Under what conditions is it legitimate to replace those who rule?
- Are freedom, equality, and security mutually compatible, or are they irreconcilable goals?
- Over what specific areas of their own activities should individuals retain absolute control?
- What does it mean to take a "liberal" or a "conservative" stand on political issues?

B. Introduction

"Man is a political animal." Aristotle made this observation many centuries ago, but his words take on fresh significance in the light of recent world events. The exercise and distribution of power in human affairs is a long-established interest of philosophers.

Political philosophers study the basis of social authority; they examine the grounds on which the exercise of power is justified; and they analyze the criteria by which power is distributed among human beings. Political philosophy is

STUDY OR THE BASIS OF HUMAN AUTHORITY
HOW? WHY?

thus seen to be related to, but at the same time distinct from, political science. Political science is a comparative study of the forms and functions of power systems, whereas political philosophy directs much of its attention to the basic assumptions about human nature, reality, and value that are claimed to justify the patterns and practices by which human beings govern themselves and exert authority over one another.

A great deal of philosophical discussion has centered on the question of how to justify the imposition of social or political authority over an individual human being. Many of the arguments are based on the assumption that the best and most effective political system is one that recognizes the basic conditions of human nature. For this reason the previous chapter, on human nature, is an appropriate introduction to the field of political philosophy.

Political philosophies are deeply rooted in axiological theory, where the emphasis falls on value assumptions and value judgments. Typically, political philosophers propose answers to such questions as the following: What is the good society? What is the best way to achieve the good life? What is the proper relationship between those who rule and those who are ruled?

But the philosophical issues that emerge in the study of politics do not restrict themselves to the domain of **axiology**. Every political philosophy rests on explicit or implicit assumptions about human nature and the extent of human freedom. Furthermore, any philosophy of power takes a basic stand on what is ultimately real and thus involves, in part at least, a **metaphysical** assumption. A parallel case can be made with respect to **epistemology**, for political structures and decisions are proposed and defended by appealing to the distinctive ways human beings are believed to obtain reliable knowledge. Finally, political philosophies tend to rely heavily on some view of how human societies have come to be what they are over a period of time, and this leads into that special field of philosophy called the philosophy of history. These philosophical connections will be examined in the pages that follow.

The discussion will pose some significant questions, place the problems of power and order in a philosophical context, and examine briefly some of the alternatives. At the very least, the initial exposure to political philosophy should enable students to deepen their understanding of political and social life. But even more, it should provide a chance to apply the techniques of analysis, comparison, and evaluation to a timely and vital area of human concern.

C. A Political Continuum

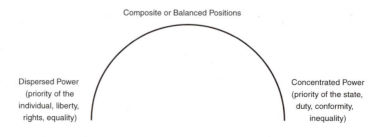

Composite or Balanced Positions

Dispersed Power
(priority of the
individual, liberty,
rights, equality)

Concentrated Power
(priority of the state,
duty, conformity,
inequality)

D. Political Alternatives

1. Concentrated Power

There have been many examples of concentrated political power in human history. Virtually all major civilizations have been based on systems of organization and control that have stressed centralized power in the belief that the quality and continuity of society had to be established and maintained through a strong government. The classical dynasties of China, Egypt, Rome, and pre-Columbian America were founded on the forceful integration of economic, religious, and political power. The attempt was to create and ensure a stable, orderly, and impregnable way of life. As society evolved, the defenders of concentrated power developed theories and proposed systems to underscore the need for centralized authority and to justify its existence. The **totalitarian** regimes of the twentieth century that emerged in Germany, Italy, Argentina, and Russia are recent examples of political systems committed to highly concentrated power.

Concentrated political power is often defended and justified on the philosophical grounds that human affairs must be guided by ideas or principles that are somehow superhuman. In the fifth century B.C.E. the Greek philosopher Plato proposed such a political philosophy, outlined in his famous work the *Republic*. Plato held that the fundamental purpose of the state is to create order in human affairs. The ideal or perfect state would reflect the natural harmony of the real world, which for Plato was the world of absolute and unchanging ideas, or **Forms**. These absolute and universal truths are discovered through the exercise of **reason**, and the logical conclusion of the reasoning process is a social order in which the state is supreme, absolute, and totalitarian.

Plato's metaphysics is that of the objective idealist. Ideas are the ultimate reality, and the perfect state will reflect the basic character of this reality. The capacity to know this reality is found in those who are able to reason about ultimate things—the philosophers. A state or society can be judged good or right only if it is so ordered and governed that it faithfully reflects or becomes congruent with the objective structure of universal reality. The ideal state is not just a collection of individuals; it is an organic whole made up of human beings but superior to them. It has no necessary relation to what human beings happen to prefer or think they want. What is good is neither subjective nor relative.

Plato's republic is not democratic. Human beings are not born with equal capacities. Individuals should assume their natural stations in life and play their assigned roles in society. Leadership is vested in the philosopher kings, who exercise absolute sovereignty over all members of the state. These rulers, or "guardians," hold their supreme power not because they possess individual rights but because they perform a vital service required by the state. Since some individuals have the talent or art to govern wisely, the entire society is better off if these individuals do in fact direct affairs. No trust is placed in the average human being. Everyday individuals are emotional, **irrational**, and capricious; they do not understand what is in their own best interests. They must be guided or compelled by an elite that acts in the best interests of the whole.

Obviously, for Plato, there is no tolerance for dissent or rebellion. As citizens, people have duties, not rights. Their freedom is to serve the state, which completely supervises their lives. Individual human beings are born and die, but the state, which gives meaning and purpose to their lives, continues to exist in its own right over and beyond the separate existences of its members. Political power is concentrated so it will promote security and stability and ensure the good life for members of the city-state.

The seventeenth-century Englishman Thomas Hobbes argued the case for a powerful state from radically different premises. Hobbes said that in the original state of nature human beings are selfish but rational animals living in a material cause-effect world. Each human being struggles to survive and to maximize his or her own pleasure and gain. Individuals are roughly equal in strength and cunning, so their selfish actions result in a war of all against all. But because they are also rational animals, people see the advantage of entering into an agreement, a "social contract," with others to establish a power that will regulate their behavior in the interest of long-range felicity and survival. Unless human beings contract with one another, life is destined to be "solitary, poor, nasty, brutish, and short."

For Hobbes, the contract once made cannot be revoked. The protection human beings seek by agreeing to submit to authority is ensured only if that authority becomes permanent. Power once granted becomes irrevocable. Those to whom power is given have the right to back up their claim with physical force. This brings the state into being, and the original contract remains legitimate as long as the state shows itself capable of exercising power—even to the extent of compelling its citizens to do many things they might dislike under the threat of consequences they would dislike even more.

In Hobbes's view, every citizen owes total allegiance to the government—whatever type it is—as long as that government is able to rule. Human beings contract for society, but society then becomes superior to its members and necessarily imposes restrictions on the behavior of individuals. Resistance to authority is never justified. Justification can come only from authority—and it would be logically contradictory for authority to destroy itself.

Hobbes contends that in the state of nature human beings are free and roughly equal, but they are also terribly vulnerable. They need—and rationally decide to accept—a power that will provide order and security. Power is thus highly concentrated (as long as the leaders can hold it, by whatever means), and individual rights or liberties are enjoyed only at the sufferance of the state.

A less extreme stand on concentrated power is taken by those who trace their political heritage to the eighteenth-century English statesman Edmund Burke. The chief concern of these conservatively oriented statesmen is the preservation of social order and stability in the face of the terrible threat of **anarchy**.

For Burkeian **conservatives**, society is seen as an organic but also mystic unity linking past, present, and future in a continuous and necessary relationship. The state is an *organic partnership* between the living, the dead, and the yet unborn. The state is nurtured by religious passion, loyalty, and faith. This means that traditions must be conserved, respect for religion and property must be promoted, and reverence must be encouraged for those things that have proved their worth by continuing to exist over a period of time. Radical change is seen as a prelude to disaster. Change for the better comes as an extension of the past; it should be slow and evolutionary; it should not jeopardize the stable social organism.

Burke held that there are no rights without duties. Individuals have only residual rights and freedoms. They exercise personal choice and control only in those areas where the state shows no interest or claim or jurisdiction. The rights or liberties that do exist are the products of the political organization of society, and political organization is charged with *prescribing* behavior that will meet the test of established or evolving tradition. Burke thoroughly distrusted the masses. People are not equal, and popular sovereignty leads only to chaos, cruelty, injustice, and folly. Burke advocates an ideal state governed by a landed **aristocracy** capable of enforcing law, protecting property, and maintaining respect for an established church. The rulers are to be the natural sovereigns, marked by birth, educated in the manner of the reigning elite, and sanctified by tradition. There is no right of revolution. It is the duty of every citizen to love, worship, and defend the society at any cost.

A widely supported stand on the historical need for concentrated power is found in the writings of Karl Marx, a nineteenth-century German political philosopher. His is the position popularly labeled "communism." Marxist Communists stress the need—at least the temporary need—for power so highly concentrated and applied to so many aspects of life that it is usually called totalitarian.

Marxist political philosophy cannot be understood apart from its metaphysics (dialectical materialism) or its economic theory (economic determinism). Metaphysically, communism takes a **materialistic** view of reality. The real world is the world of matter and motion where objects exist and events take place. Human beings and their societies are part of the natural, material, changing reality.

The theory of economic determinism is a logical extension of the materialistic interpretation of history. Marx identified two social classes: one made up of those who own or control the means of production (capitalists) and the other, of those who work and thus become simply tools of production (proletariat). These two social classes Marx found to be in natural and inevitable conflict with each other, and the struggle for advantage—the power struggle—makes history and brings about social evolution. The determining factor in history is the economic conflict.

The existence of two social classes in mortal and inevitable conflict over property rights and economic advantages sets up a natural dialectic that produces a new social arrangement. The **dialectic** is of crucial philosophical importance in Marx's philosophy. The term labels a dynamic process that occurs in three phases: the thesis, the antithesis, and the synthesis. The thesis represents an established state—or condition, in Marxist theory—that is the system of production controlled by the owners, or capitalists. Inevitably, this condition generates by its excesses the development of its own opposite, the antithesis. The antithesis is the ever-growing class of workers—the proletariat. The conflict between thesis and antithesis continues to the point of explosion (revolution), and from the ashes of revolution arises a new social order—the synthesis. The synthesis then becomes the new thesis, and the process begins anew. Marx reasoned that because capitalism had proceeded to such an extreme of consolidated power in Western Europe through increased investments and mergers, the time was at hand for a successful revolution by the proletariat. The call went out for the workers of the world to unite. They had nothing to lose but their chains.

There is a strong element of **humanism** in Marx. Basically, people are good. Human beings possess the potential for growth, but this potential is realized in collective activity with other social beings. Human life and fulfillment depend on the natural and social realities in which they flourish.

But for all his harsh and inexorable determinism, Marx was also a utopian. He looked forward to the day when the dialectic would cease because the conditions that prompted it would no longer exist. When natural circumstances no longer demanded the class struggle, the classless society would emerge, and human beings would realize their true values and relate harmoniously to the natural world. During the intermediate stages, however, society demands of its members total allegiance to a powerful, unified, and efficient state. The state is viewed as a necessary structure through which human behavior is brought into proper relationship with the historical forces at work in the real world. The state has a vital role to play until objective circumstances render it unnecessary. Then, its historical mission accomplished, the state is expected to wither away, and the communistic **utopia**, in the form of the classless society, becomes a reality. Human endowments are merely held in trust and protected until such time as all class systems in the world are eliminated and state power is no longer needed. In the meantime, individuals sacrifice their immediate interests and pool their collective hopes in a monolithic political system that protects their gains and withstands their enemies.

Critiques of Concentrated Power

1.

Concentrated power is often justified in the name of the good results it produces, but what actually comes about is a system that serves the ends of a few privileged individuals. The pessimistic view of human nature is used simply to justify the subjugation of many human beings. Concentrated power violates the democratic ideal of human association so that even the majority is usually disenfranchised or oppressed. The denial of human rights and the extermination of whole categories of people in Hitler's Germany and Stalin's

Russia are illustrations of the dangerous and destructive aspects of absolute authority.

2.

Plato and Hobbes emphasize the critical importance of human rationality. But if the ability to reason is a human characteristic, why must so many people be patronized or coerced by a few who insist that they know best what is good and right? Is it not contradictory to support the premise that human beings are, on the one hand, rational and, on the other hand, shortsighted or untrustworthy?

3.

The Marxist idea that power is a *temporary* necessity, that it is merely held in trust for people until a later time when it will be reduced or dispersed, is not acceptable. Power once concentrated is seldom relinquished. Power tends to maintain itself and feed its own need—even to the detriment of the initial values it is designed to promote. Lord Acton, an astute student of political life, warned: "Power tends to corrupt and absolute power corrupts absolutely."

2. Dispersed Power

Most of the alternatives presented in this section do not qualify as political philosophies in the same way as the more formal and systematic theories already considered. They are, perhaps, more accurately described as "postures." Extreme individualists typically insist that they are *free from* political control, political obligation, and political definition. So, in the pure philosophical context, they may think of themselves as apolitical or nonpolitical. Nevertheless, even an aloof, neutral, or negative stance is still a stance. In the world of human activity, involving as it does issues of personal obligation, group effort, and political participation, even the most self-sufficient individuals exert, either intentionally or simply by accident, an undeniable influence on the attitudes and actions of others and thus become involved in the exercise and distribution of power. In short, they become political—whether or not they want to.

On the side of those who favor dispersed power are the proponents of passive, or nonviolent, resistance. Mohandas K. Gandhi, twentieth-century spiritual and political leader in India, attracted world attention by demonstrating the effectiveness of organized *noncooperation* in political affairs. Gandhi stressed the cultivation of spiritual resources as an antidote to materialism and the tactics of force. He categorically opposed violence of any sort, and, even though he believed in the necessity of establishing a new social order, he took the moral stand that indefinite bondage is better than violent revolution. When political negotiation for human rights does not succeed, Gandhi advocated the tactic of refusing to cooperate with the forces of oppression. Evil cannot be overcome by evil. But through the cumulative example of lives personally lived in consecration to spiritual truth and channeled when necessary into a mass movement, Gandhi believed it is possible to redeem a world dominated by the false doctrine of force. Power is to be disseminated to its broadly human and spiritual roots.

A century before Gandhi, Henry David Thoreau, nineteenth-century American **transcendentalist**, launched a one-man crusade against organized authority. Invoking the doctrine of individual nullification, Thoreau preached and practiced a program of civil disobedience. It was his conviction that individual conscience stands above all law and government and that there is a personal *obligation* to disobey any rule or statute that conscience cannot affirm. Thoreau maintained that a single individual standing for the right is more worthy than the largest of majorities standing for the wrong. He held that good governments are those that govern least, and the best government is one that governs not at all.

Gandhi and Thoreau share the conviction that moral obligation derives from a principle that transcends the sphere of power relationships in worldly affairs. They insist that **morality** is not established by political authority and does not reside in human law. Moral ends can never be achieved by force. The only justifiable tactic for righting a moral wrong is passive, or nonviolent, resistance. In the final analysis, what is good and right is not validated by the political power of the state. The ultimate criterion is individual conscience. These ideas of Gandhi and Thoreau had a profound influence on the political philosophy and activities of Martin Luther King, Jr.

A similar position is taken by the libertarians, who insist that human beings instinctively or intuitively know themselves to be morally responsible creatures. Moral responsibility implies some degree of choice in which *free will* can be truly exercised. Since we know ourselves to be morally responsible, the universe must be the sort of place in which moral responsibility is possible. In situations where actual alternatives confront us, we must choose on the basis of some inherent sense of "duty" that may have little or nothing to do with the practical political realities of a particular time or place. What is socially approved or politically expedient is not the major issue. There is a "higher politics" that can be known and expressed only by individuals who think and act as responsible agents with free will. The rights to political power and the values of political systems are matters decided by rational human beings. For the libertarians, legitimate political power, like all power, resides ultimately with the rational chooser in response to moral imperatives. Power is thus dispersed and is not the legitimate right of either arbitrary legal systems or organized groups.

Anarchists are also on the side of reduced or dispersed power. There is a popular stereotype that portrays the anarchist as a wild-eyed demolition expert bent on creating havoc and confusion. This picture does not do justice to the position of **anarchism**. It is true that some anarchists categorically deny the right of any government to exercise power, but most anarchists simply oppose government based on coercion. They may regard some types of public organization as necessary to provide basic services, such as schools and sewers, but they believe that such agencies should be purely functional, with no authority to employ force or inflict punishment on individuals.

Anarchists direct their principal attack at the political state, which they regard as having usurped the right to use force. They condemn the state as an agency of human coercion that employs armies, police, and prisons to maintain its position of power. The anarchist solution to antisocial behavior is to bring community opinion to bear on the deviant or, as a last resort, to invite the nonconformist to leave the group.

The philosophy of anarchism is not highly unified or consistently developed. However, most anarchists assume that human nature is inherently good. They assert that people possess a fundamental sense of decency that impels them to cooperate voluntarily in programs that are practical and reasonable. The anarchists believe that institutionalized systems of power pervert or inhibit what are basically noble human impulses. In any case, authoritarian systems are incompatible with moral **autonomy**.

Among the communes that have sprung up in recent years, some have committed themselves to the total rejection of any sort of group coercion and to the fundamental right of all persons to "do their own thing." Although as individuals they try to live together and freely engage in spontaneous relationships, they make no demands, establish no schedules, acknowledge no official leaders, and institute no formal controls. They respect one another's moral and practical decisions, and they insist on the inherent right of each person to be free and **self-determined**. Unique individuals join voluntarily to create "intentional communities" in which power is reflected only in personal abilities, personal feelings, and personal consciences. Arbitrary force and organized control are viewed as totally illegitimate. While these anarchistic forms of human association characterize perhaps only a minority of the experimental communes functioning today, they attract the interest and scrutiny of those concerned with alternative lifestyles in a world that often appears to be moving in catastrophic directions.

Modern existentialists often reflect a similar stance on power. Theoretically, an existentialist might freely choose to affirm any political philosophy or system, but one of the most visible characteristics of those who adopt the existentialist posture is indifference or opposition to established political principles or organized political systems. This **nihilistic** leaning tends to make existentialists an enigma and a threat to those who believe that structured political arrangements and permanent political principles are essential to human life. Postmodernists would largely share the existentialist's perspective, as long as the Other is respected; no person's or group's narrative is to be marginalized by the violence of a master narrative.

Frequently in human history the search for true and basic "freedom" has led to passionate statements about the oppressive nature of society or the coercive effects of established authority. The question of what it means to be fully human is often answered in a way that points up the undesirable effects of concentrated power and underscores the necessity of diffusing power widely and limiting it to the exercise of personal decisions. Rousseau's declaration echoes still: "Man is born free but is everywhere in chains."

Critiques of Dispersed Power

1.

The appeal to higher moral laws or individual conscience is naïve and unrealistic. It becomes a romantic view that does not face up to the practical realities of human existence. Furthermore, because there is disagreement on what the basic moral principles are, it is unworkable. Libertarians and other "moralists" fail to propose a livable social matrix in which everyday human beings are nurtured and sustained. The special rational powers demanded by the free willists are outside the experience and beyond the capacity of ordinary mortals. The position turns out to be highly arbitrary and, in its own way, authoritarian.

2.

The optimistic view of human nature incorporated in some of the dispersed-power arguments does not come to grips with the daily occurrence of interpersonal hostility and aggression. There is little recourse for the weak or the vulnerable. Moreover, systems of dispersed power have no practical way of maintaining themselves when confronted by an organized external force. Human history is full of examples of the subjugation of "gentle" and poorly organized peoples.

3.

The existentialist insistence on the right—or necessity—of all persons to create their own lives freely is nothing but a license for people to behave any way they please. A sadist could argue that he or she was simply expressing the free and spontaneous self. It is one thing to hold that people are perfectible; it is quite another thing to hold that they will always do what is life-affirming for someone else.

3. Composite or Balanced Positions on Power

A composite position on the exercise and justification of power is reflected in the political philosophy of Confucianism. It proposes a paternalistic and humanistic view of government and its legitimacy that influenced public affairs in China for over 2,000 years and affected the lives of millions of people in the non-Western world. In Confucianism, the state is justified under a mandate from Heaven. This places the governance of society under celestial or supernatural sanction. It becomes the moral obligation of government to produce the same natural and hierarchical harmony that characterizes the well-ordered family. Respect for those in authority, virtue on the part of leaders, and a benevolent concern for the common welfare are key elements in the structure. The political power of the state is charged with the responsibility to give ethical direction to members of society in the name of peace, security, protection, and human well-being.

What might be interpreted as a forceful and unyielding form of concentrated power in Confucian political philosophy is mitigated by the underlying premise that ordinary people are ultimately more important than either rulers or territory. Education for leadership is open to all, and the most learned and the most virtuous can aspire to positions of status, trust, and responsibility. Leadership is to be earned and not inherited. Competitive examinations are recommended to search out among the populace those best qualified to serve. A ruler who fails to honor and implement the heavenly mandate is expected to abdicate in favor of a more able and virtuous person. If the ruler refuses to step aside, people retain the right to overthrow and replace him or her—by revolution, if necessary. Power is softly dispersed in the Confucian view of political affairs, with the ideals of harmony, virtue, and filial piety providing a stable foundation for the continuous ordering of social life through the generations.

Democratic political systems of the West also lie somewhere along the middle of the continuum between concentrated power and completely dispersed power. In a democracy individuals recognize that it is necessary for them to grant certain powers to the state, but they insist that these powers be exercised only with their consent. Power resides ultimately in the hands of the people, not in the hands of political leaders. Although this stance clearly distinguishes all democratic political systems from totalitarian or anarchic ones, it is far from clear how best to define and interrelate the concepts commonly associated with "democracy"—individualism, liberalism, freedom, equality, rights of individuals and minorities, and government by the people. The claims put forward in the name of liberty or democracy are often strikingly different, and sometimes they contradict each other. It is important, therefore, to probe into the concepts and claims related to the term "democracy" in order to discover what they mean, what assumptions underlie them, and what consequences are likely to stem from adopting them.

a. *Traditional liberalism.*   The tenets of **liberalism** have played a major role in the development of democratic political philosophy (political leaders in the West frequently refer to "the liberal democracies"). The traditional notion of a "liberal," however, has been sharply challenged in this century, and new meanings have been assigned to it. The result is that the term "liberal" today is ambiguous, and anyone applying the label must specify exactly what is meant.

Traditional liberals emphasize individual rights, especially the right to private property. The basic liberty, they hold, is freedom *from* the power of the state. Government is an evil—but a lesser evil than anarchy; in Adam Smith's phrase, government is a *necessary* evil. Government should be minimal and interfere as little as possible in private and business affairs. Political power should be limited to the function of maintaining public order and safety, the mutual security of citizens, and protection against foreign enemies. Political liberalism thus quite naturally weds itself to the doctrine of economic **laissez-faire** and rugged individualism. These views are summed up in the key belief: The government that governs best is the one that governs least.

Traditional liberalism traces its roots back to the seventeenth century, when many of its central affirmations were clearly expressed in the political writings of John Locke. Locke built his liberal theory on the assumption that human beings are by nature moral beings and that there are natural moral rules that they ought to obey. People are born free and equal, with the capacity to make rational choices. They are morally obligated to respect the freedom and self-determination of other people and deal with them on the basis of equality. On these premises Locke fashioned his central principle of the natural rights of every individual. To maintain their natural rights, people voluntarily give up some of their freedom and enter into a "social contract" to create a political authority capable of preserving these rights and restraining transgressors. It was Locke's view, then, that people by majority consent draw up a contract for the establishment of a government and obligate themselves to abide by the decisions of the majority. Government authority stems from the act of making a contract, and the power thus formed is limited by the terms of the contract and is subject to continuous review by the citizens involved. The contract is specific and strictly limited, and the power given up to the government is not absolute or final.

According to Locke, the basic rights that people seek to preserve by political means are the rights to life, liberty, and property. The individual's right to private property is one of the most important guarantees made by government. And one of the fundamental moral rights retained by the individual is the right to challenge and resist authority. Locke favored a constitutional, representative government and denied the legitimacy of any permanent or absolute ruler. Locke's ideas had a profound impact on the framing of the American Declaration of Independence and later the Constitution.

Departing sharply from Locke's emphasis on natural rights, Jeremy Bentham, a late eighteenth- and early nineteenth-century English philosopher, founded **utilitarianism**. He insisted that there is only one test of a good government: Does it promote the maximum amount of pleasure and least amount of pain for its citizens? The question is expressed in the familiar phrase "the greatest happiness for the greatest number of people."

John Stuart Mill, a nineteenth-century English philosopher and economist, while a staunch defender of utilitarianism, did not accept Bentham's view that all pleasures are of equal worth. He asserted that "it is better to be a human being dissatisfied than a pig satisfied; better to be Socrates dissatisfied than a fool satisfied." Mill's ringing defense of individual liberty in the realms of thought, speech, and action places him in the mainstream of the liberal tradition. In his essay *On Liberty* in 1859, he warned that the chief danger in a democracy is the suppression of individual differences and expressions of minority opinion.

The utilitarian conviction that the main purpose of the state is to promote the welfare and happiness of its members would seem to sanction a government policy of active intervention in economic and social affairs. In line with the liberal tradition, however, neither Bentham nor Mill adopted such a view. Bentham held that any restriction imposed by law was painful and was justified only to prevent a greater pain to others. Mill believed that political control should be restricted to those matters in which the needs of society cannot be met in any other way. Individuals should be free to pursue their own goals in their own way so long as other individuals are not deprived of *their* freedom.

The themes of traditional liberalism exert a wide appeal today, perhaps as often for "conservatives" as for "liberals." The central concern of traditional liberalism for limitation on the powers of the state (such as what was espoused by James Madison in the *Federalist Papers*) has been developed by Robert A. Dahl and others into a full-fledged political alternative known as "democratic pluralism." The fundamental thesis of democratic pluralism is that power should be dispersed as widely as possible. Power can be tamed, civilized, and controlled only when there are multiple centers of power and competing interests, no one of which is in a position to dominate the others. The only legitimate sovereign is the people, and even they should not exercise absolute power, either as a whole or through majorities. The democratic pluralists remind us that a cardinal principle of the American Constitution is the division and balancing of powers among legislative, executive, and judicial organs and between federal and state levels of government. In a pluralistic democracy, politics takes the shape of negotiations, compromises, coalitions, and consensus. Such procedures provide the best hope that the inevitable conflicts of power and interests can be resolved peacefully and without the use or threat of force. And these processes are necessary in American political life, because any group of people sharing the same political goals and identity is certain to be a minority; that is, any collection of citizens large enough to form a majority of voters will contain individuals and groups who agree on some issues and disagree on others. Such groups must therefore negotiate and bargain to reach compromises and maintain the coalition. Under these conditions, economic and social changes will take place slowly and in a piecemeal fashion.

Democratic pluralism offers itself as a democratic alternative in the liberal tradition. At the same time, it purports to give an accurate description of the political process at work in the United States today.

b. *Contemporary liberalism.* Traditional liberals and the utilitarian Mill stressed personal freedom and feared that broad state power would destroy individual liberty. Contemporary liberals take the position that human equality, individual freedom, and effective self-fulfillment are more certain to be achieved when people feel a strong sense of community and when the state is actively involved in planning for the general welfare. Modern liberals take to heart the ideals of the French Revolution—liberty, equality, and fraternity. They conceive liberty as the positive freedom to realize human potentialities and stress the point that liberty in this sense can be achieved only if a society

GOV SHOULD BE INVOLVED IN PLANNING

can produce the circumstances in which equality and brotherhood are also present. Contemporary liberals typically advocate government initiative to create and maintain the conditions under which the pursuit of happiness can succeed.

In recent times, the pragmatic philosopher John Dewey made a significant contribution to liberal thought. Dewey contended that the free enterprise doctrine had proved inadequate to modern circumstances and that capitalism in its present form could no longer serve the best interests of people. As an alternative Dewey proposed that the collective intelligence of all persons be enlisted to produce a social order capable of satisfying basic human needs. He believed that human intelligence is distributed widely enough so that each person can contribute to a cooperative solution to life's problems. Dewey believed that individuals are free as long as they contribute to the shared freedom of all. Freedom encompasses those acts of creative intelligence and service that help people to realize their potentialities and at the same time contribute to the welfare of the group.

Cooperative planning to produce practical results for the improvement of society is an important part of Dewey's political philosophy, but he was careful to distinguish between a planned society and a continuously planning society. A *planned* society is rigid and authoritarian; a *planning* society is open and democratic.

Political democracy is fully consistent with Dewey's philosophy, and he reasoned that democratic ends can be achieved only through democratic means. He stressed the close parallel between democratic procedures in politics and scientific procedures in the search for knowledge. Both involve principles supporting cooperative effort, the spirit of experimentation, and the demand that results be verified in the world of practice. These principles, which provide an ethical basis for relationships among scientists, need also to be applied in the realm of law and politics.

Dewey's **pragmatic** philosophy reflects a concern for human equality in which each person is uniquely valuable. Human nature is assumed to be plastic and perfectible. Only democracy, Dewey contended, has a working faith in the possibilities of human nature and a concern for creating the conditions to realize human potentialities.

In a quite different key, John Rawls, in *A Theory of Justice* (1971), maintains that a well-ordered democratic society would be based on two moral principles of "justice as fairness": (1) each person is to have an equal right to basic liberties, compatible with such liberties for all; (2) opportunity, income, wealth, and the bases of self-respect are to be distributed equally, unless an unequal distribution is to the advantage of the least favored. For example, a prospective doctor might receive a special subsidy to cover the cost of medical training, in anticipation of the benefits that would later accrue to the entire community.

Rawls seeks to show that his theory of justice provides a firm foundation for these two indispensible principles of Right, whereas the doctrines of utilitarianism, with their exclusive concern for the Good, do not do so. The greatest good for the greatest number may involve the sacrifice of the liberties or opportunities of *some* individuals in order that the sum total of satisfaction be greater; and this, Rawls claims, violates our sense of justice as fairness.

Rawls gives priority to his first principle, an equal right to basic liberties, and thus raises a warning signal to contemporary liberals that their pursuit of equality and the general welfare should not lead them to limit individual liberties.

Rawls's second principle upholds the right to equality of opportunity and to the equal enjoyment of the "primary goods" of income, wealth, and the bases of self-respect. He thus places himself in direct opposition to conservatives and traditional liberals whose exclusive preoccupation with individual rights encourages them to downgrade the equality dimension of justice as fairness.

Rawls explicitly rejects the position of democratic pluralism that the political process is simply a means of adjusting and reconciling the conflicting claims of competing interest groups. In the name of justice, we must ask whether the claims put forward are reasonable and make a moral judgment on how the interests of everyone are affected, not just the interests of the pressure groups involved.

"Justice as fairness" thus offers a standpoint wherein the strengths of liberalism, traditional and contemporary, might be accommodated and their respective limitations overcome.

In the sections that follow we will investigate the welfare state and democratic socialism. While these are distinct from each other in certain crucial respects (such as the *means* for promoting the general welfare), each one embodies in its own way some of the fundamental principles of the political philosophy of contemporary liberalism (such as the *goals* that constitute the general welfare).

(1) *The welfare state.*   The doctrine of the welfare state emphasizes human equality, the common good, economic planning, and political involvement in social affairs. Boldly characterized, this doctrine advocates the use of the political power of the state in whatever way is necessary to equalize opportunity and enhance the general welfare of society. The state is viewed as an integral part of the social order, which exists to promote the good of all its members. But the partisans of the welfare state, unlike socialists, do not advocate the overthrow of capitalism. Rather they believe that the government should strengthen the existing economic system and make it work efficiently for the good of all. They are also firmly committed to a program of reform. Although they may mount a vigorous attack on particular policies and programs of the capitalist society, their enduring aim is to eliminate gradually from society those conditions that produce human inequality and insecurity.

(2) *Democratic socialism.*   Socialism is an economic doctrine sharply opposed to capitalism. Socialists advocate collective ownership and control of

the principal means of production, distribution, and exchange. Socialists believe that the general welfare of society can be promoted by granting to the government the exclusive right to provide capital for all major social projects. The return, or profit, from government-sponsored enterprises is used to increase the wages of labor and raise the standard of living in the society.

The political philosophy of democratic socialism adds at least two important elements to the underlying economic doctrine. Those who support democratic socialism insist on preserving the right of the people to choose their government. A further stipulation is that genuine choice must exist if people are to exercise political power. This requires a multiple-party system and denotes the right of citizens to criticize their government.

Democratic socialism proposes to extend democracy by applying the principles of democratic politics to the nonpolitical areas of the social order. The aim is to reconstruct society on a basis of cooperation rather than competition and the pursuit of individual advantage. This aim helps to explain why democratic socialists typically press for government ownership and control of industry; their goal is to reorganize the economy to benefit the entire society. The platform also advocates the following goals, most of which would also be sought in a welfare state: full employment; elimination of inequalities based on birth rather than service; elimination of discrimination on the basis of race, sex, social class, or religion; guaranteed social security for the sick, the aged, and the unemployed; medical services for all; enlarged opportunities for the underprivileged; and universal public education.

The fundamental contrast between a traditional liberal and a contemporary liberal is highlighted by noting their differing interpretations of two basic concepts: individualism and freedom. For the traditional liberal, individualism means a system where individuals are so important that they remain autonomous and ruggedly independent—free to get ahead or to fall behind with no outside assistance or interference. Above all, individuals are *free from* state control; they have *liberty*. For the contemporary liberal, individualism means a system where individuals are so important that political and social institutions are deliberately arranged to enrich their lives. Above all, individuals are *free to* achieve their aims and purposes; they have *rights*. Contemporary liberals strive to bring about equality of opportunity and reward. Traditional liberals play down claims to equality on the ground that efforts to satisfy such claims inevitably infringe on individual freedom. When individualism is interpreted as "rugged," with freedom *from* any restraint and freedom to become as unequal as one's competitive strength permits, then indeed freedom and equality are opposed values, and one must be chosen at the expense of the other. On the other hand, when freedom is interpreted as respect for the worth of each individual and a concern that he or she become free *to* enjoy equal opportunities and privileges, then equality and freedom are mutually supportive values. Maximum freedom *from* social restraint is an enemy of equality. Maximum freedom *to* prosper embraces equality.

Critiques of Composite or Balanced Positions on Power

1.

Is a truly democratic form of government workable in our complex modern world? The democratic theory is that power resides in the hands of the people. They choose their representatives, judge their performance, and participate with them in making political decisions that affect their lives. It is assumed that most people have the interest, capacity, and wide-ranging knowledge to carry out these functions effectively. This assumption appears highly unrealistic for the emerging nations of the third world faced with overwhelming problems of sheer survival. And it may not be realistic in the United States today. Is it ever reasonable to expect a large percentage of a population to devote time and energy in an attempt to understand and do something about complicated political matters when their interests lie elsewhere?

2.

In traditional liberalism, particularly as set forth in Dahl's theory of democratic pluralism, the image of power and decision making is the image of a balancing society in which no one group or set of interests predominates. This image probably fit the early American society, in which 70 percent of the citizens were independent farmers and in which, in Dahl's own terms, "democracy was able to flourish because political equality was sustained by an extraordinary degree of social and economic equality." The image of a balancing society simply does not fit current realities, where we find a heavy concentration of political and economic power in a relatively few private corporations, which join with government to form an "industrial state" and a "military-industrial complex."

3.

In *Anarchy, State, and Utopia*, Robert Nozick mounts a systematic attack on the claims of Rawls and welfare-state liberals that justice demands a redistribution of wealth and that it is a legitimate function of the state to bring about this redistribution. In opposition to these claims, Nozick develops an "entitlement theory of justice," which holds that individuals have a right to own, and dispose of as they please, as much wealth and property as they can amass, providing only that they have acquired them legitimately in the first place. Legitimate "holdings" are those that were acquired historically without fraud, force, or violation of the rights of others. Once so acquired, the owners are *entitled* to their holdings, however unequal they may be, and the state has no right to interfere with them through coercive means, such as progressive income taxes.

In short, Nozick defends the classical liberal doctrines on property, a free market, and a minimal state with strictly limited powers—the *right* to be rich (or poor).

E. Conclusion

A brief and tightly condensed discussion of alternative schemes of political philosophy can do no more than expose some of the controversial issues. Nevertheless, the examination of one range of alternatives suggests the importance of taking a broad view of politics. It also points out one of the reasons that philosophers show an abiding interest in the world of practical affairs.

Active and intelligent citizenship in a modern democracy is a difficult achievement. The citizen is expected to make decisions about a confusing array of political issues and personalities. But here is where philosophy may have a very practical application. A careful examination of the major philosophical positions can help people to identify their own assumptions, to clarify their thinking, and then to participate more effectively in the arena of competing political alternatives.

In the initial effort to understand the complexities of contemporary political life, a concerned person may ask, "What is the difference between a conservative and a liberal position?" A simple conceptual approach to the question might help to clarify the difference. The idea of *change* is basic. A continuum that identifies several of the major alternatives suggests the importance of differentiating among political philosophies on the basis of the assumptions they make about change. Political terms are notoriously unstable, but there is sufficient consensus to permit rough definitions. But one should be aware that the labels used at any particular time may vary and be misleading.

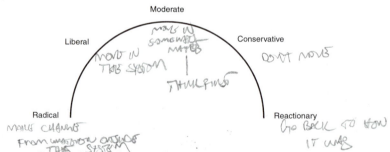

Reactionary. One who believes that things have changed too much already and recommends a return to a way of life characteristic of an earlier historical era. **Reactionaries** often express the view that recent social changes have carried society beyond the best conditions for human happiness. They typically identify change with deterioration. They maintain that political power should be exerted to bring back "the good old days." A reactionary is sometimes called ultraconservative or an extreme right-winger.

Conservative. One who defends the status quo. A conservative aggressively opposes rapid or dramatic social changes and typically insists that government should proceed slowly and with all due caution along a path that is tried and true. Conservatives believe their society to have a good thing going, and they believe that political authority should preserve and defend the existing way of life against interference from outside or subversion from within.

Moderate.   One who takes a position somewhere between the conservatives and liberals. A moderate may combine elements from both the right and the left or may take a position of suspended judgment on political matters. "Moderates" may label themselves as such to hide their true political stance or to enhance their political strength. But a moderate may also hold the unshakable conviction that the balanced middle affords the only firm and reasonable ground for practical politics.

Liberal.   One who believes that change in human affairs is either necessary or desirable. The liberal often points out that conditions *do* change and that social patterns must adapt or they stagnate. Contemporary liberals are inclined to approve of social and political experimentation. They frequently support **collectivism** and thus argue that social welfare and social planning are among the primary functions of government. The liberal exhibits tolerance for a reasonable amount of nonconformity.

Radical.   One who proposes or supports rapid and fundamental social changes. The political radical may believe that an existing power structure is intolerable and must be replaced or may, like the anarchist, oppose all authority. The radical is characterized by social nonconformity and a commitment to direct action. The view that the main function of politics is to bring about drastic change is typical.

Another critical issue in modern politics concerns the relative distribution of power between the individual and the state. Two important questions may be asked. Does the extension of political authority into wider areas of social behavior serve to drown individuals in the mass, dominate their lives, and restrict their freedom? Or, on the other hand, does a strong and comprehensive government institution serve to increase and protect the actual freedom and ultimate fulfillment of human beings? A philosophical assessment of the answers given to these momentous questions leads directly to the heart of political controversy in our time.

Case Study and Discussion Questions

Case Study

"Democracy." Greek, power of the people, term originating in Greece to designate a government where people share in directing distinct activities of the state as well as participate in its rewards, as distinct from governments controlled by a class, select group, or single dictator. Democracy has outgrown its purely political connotation, however, and in modern life such phrases as economic democracy, industrial democracy, and social democracy are familiar. In this larger sense democracy is essentially a philosophy that insists on the right and, in the long run, the capacity of a people, acting either directly or through representatives, to control their institutions for their best ends. Such a philosophy of necessity exalts the individual and would free him as far as possible from restraints not self-imposed.[1]

1. To what extent is democracy "in the larger sense" practiced in the United States, in Kuwait or Israel, and in African nations such as the Democratic Republic of Congo?

2. Is respect for the views and interests of various groups (ethnic, sexual, economic, etc.) compatible with democracy in either sense? For example, can multiculturalism and democracy coexist peacefully?

3. Liberty is perhaps the distinguishing characteristic of democracy—at least Plato thought so. He also believed that democracy was only a step away from tyranny, because democratic people will come to love liberty so much that they will eventually lose it. Plato believed that when a people feels that its freedoms are threatened, an individual will be authorized to safeguard those freedoms. This individual will eventually assume so much power that he or she will become a dictator. Do you think Plato's scenario is plausible? Do you agree that an excessive love of liberty can lead to the loss of liberty?

Discussion Questions

1. What are the arguments for and against those who maintain that the only hope of humankind is the destruction of all existing systems of power?

2. Imagine that you and your fellow citizens-to-be have the opportunity to draw up a new social contract for a democratic society. Assume that each of you is a free, rational person; equal in status; and concerned to protect your own interests, but you don't know what your particular circumstances in life will be, and, therefore, where your interests will lie. For example, if you decide that human slavery will be part of your society, you will have to face the possibility that you will be a slave in the system, not a master. What basic principles of organizing a democratic society will you and your fellows be likely to agree on in this situation? You might then ask: Does American society now operate on the principles you have agreed on? If your answer is that it does not, what, if anything, do you as a philosopher citizen propose to do about it?

3. In your personal opinion when and why would it be legitimate for U.S. citizens to actively oppose the established government?

4. Based on your view of human nature, what kinds of persons should be encouraged or allowed to lead a modern nation like our own?

Suggested Readings

Barker, Ernest. *Social Contract: Essays by Locke, Hume, and Rousseau*. New York: Oxford University Press, 1962.

Bellah, Robert H., Richard Madsen, William M. Sullivan, Ann Swidler, and Steven M. Tipton. *Habits of the Heart: Individualism and Commitment in American Life*. Berkeley: University of California Press, 1985.

---

[1]*Columbia Encyclopedia*, 2d ed. (New York: Columbia University Press, 1950), pp. 526–527.

Dahl, Robert A. *After the Revolution? Authority in a Good Society.* New Haven, CT: Yale University Press, 1970.

Gewirth, Alan. *Political Philosophy.* New York: Macmillan, 1965.

Gutierrez, Gustavo. *The Power of the Poor in History.* Maryknoll, NY: Orbis, 1983.

Harrington, Michael. *Socialism.* New York: Bantam, 1972.

Jaggar, Alison. *Feminist Politics and Human Nature.* Totowa, NJ: Rowman and Allenheld, 1983.

King, Martin Luther, Jr., *A Testament of Hope: The Essential Writings of Martin Luther King, Jr.* Edited by James M. Washington. San Francisco: Harper & Row, 1986.

MacIntyre, Alasdair. *Whose Justice? Which Rationality?* Notre Dame, IN: University of Notre Dame Press, 1988.

Marcuse, Herbert. *An Essay on Liberation.* Boston: Beacon, 1969.

Marx, Karl. *The Communist Manifesto.* (Any edition.)

Mill, John Stuart. *On Liberty.* Indianapolis, IN: Hackett, 1978.

Nozick, Robert. *Anarchy, State, and Utopia.* New York: Basic Books, 1974.

Parenti, Michael. *Democracy for the Few.* 4th ed. New York: St. Martin's Press, 1983.

Plato. *The Republic.* New York: Basic Books, 1968.

Rawls, John. *A Theory of Justice.* Cambridge, MA: Harvard University Press, 1971.

Thoreau, Henry David. *Walden and Civil Disobedience.* New York: New American Library, 1973.

Wolff, Robert Paul. *In Defense of Anarchism.* New York: Harper & Row, 1970.

Epilogue
Toward a Personal Philosophy of Life

Now that an introductory overview of the issues and options of philosophy has been completed, a personal opportunity presents itself to digest more fully what has been ingested. At this first plateau in what Plato referred to as "the ascent from below" you are challenged to put some of the pieces together in an individualized synthesis of ideas. You are invited to organize your thoughts and feelings into a tentative posture—one you undoubtedly will want to expand or revise as new knowledge or experience is brought to bear on it. What follows in this epilogue is a recommended procedure for developing and defending a personal life stance.

At the outset, you should review the personal alternatives in the prologue of this book. Are you drawn to one of the ten options presented? Is it the same one that attracted you the first time you read it? Because it is unlikely that any one of the choices reflects exactly the way you look at things, it is time for you to model a personal statement of your own either by modifying or combining elements already proposed or, better still, composing a new statement of your very own. Try it out! When you have fashioned a statement that seems reasonable and sensible to you, subject that statement to the rigorous scrutiny suggested by the following eight-point procedure:

1. Does it say what you really want to say? Have you used the right words? Are the sentences clear? Does the language enhance communication?

2. Are you truly exposing your basic assumptions or presuppositions? Have you revealed or implied your fundamental stand on how you know (epistemology), what is real (metaphysics), and what is good or right or

beautiful (axiology)? Have you expressed your belief on basic human nature?

3. Is your reasoning sound? Have you been consistent, and, if not, are you committed to the inconsistencies? Are there elements in your professed posture that contradict one another?

4. Is your stand compatible with the position already taken by a particular philosopher you have heard or read? Which one, and for what major reasons? Does your statement take into account the options and critiques presented in this book?

5. What are the wider implications or consequences of adopting your point of view? Does it suggest a course of action or a style of life that you already *have* or conceivably *could* put into actual practice?

6. What do you acknowledge to be the most serious or telling criticisms that could be brought against your stand? How would you answer those criticisms?

7. What final adjustments or important modifications are you compelled to make in your initial proposal in light of the foregoing critical analysis?

8. Finally, are you prepared to try out your statement as a public expression of your philosophy of life? Or, more modestly, are you willing to share your statement as a private confidence with a concerned friend?

If you respond to the invitation to analyze, compare, and evaluate your carefully expressed, defended, and revised philosophy of life, you should find yourself more firmly established on a philosophical plateau from which—with a certain amount of emotional and intellectual "second wind"—you can with refreshed readiness contemplate the next ascent to higher levels of understanding, awareness, or wonder. At the very least, facing the challenge to put yourself on record and enter the arena of concerned dialogue should convince you that you are, indeed, philosophizing.

Glossary

Absolutism. The doctrine that reality, truth, and values are established in the eternal nature of things; they are not made and cannot be changed by human beings; unchanging, objective, universal. Opposite of **relativism**. *See* **Objectivism**.

Aesthetics. *See* **Esthetics**.

Agnostic. One who professes ignorance and a state of suspended judgment on ultimate issues, such as God and religious or philosophical principles; "I do not know, nor do I believe it is possible to know." Often confused with **atheism**. *See* **Skepticism**.

Allegory. The setting forth of a subject or the telling of a story in figurative, or symbolic, language requiring interpretation; especially a narrative veiling a moral lesson by symbolic devices. Example: the parable of the prodigal son.

Altruism. The pursuit of ends that aid the interest and welfare of other people; benevolence; love and devotion directed toward humanity rather than narrowly toward oneself.

Amoral. Neither moral (right) nor immoral (wrong) but outside the moral realm; ethically neutral. Example: the claim that science takes no stand on values and is therefore amoral.

Analytic philosophy. Also called philosophical analysis; refers to a relatively recent emphasis in philosophical method in which activity is focused on linguistic study and the logical analysis of symbols, terms, concepts, and propositions. *See* **Linguistic analysis**.

Anarchy. Absence or utter disregard of government. In its negative sense, the word is used to denote a state of social chaos. In its positive sense, anarchy springs from the philosophical concept of the inherent goodness of human nature and contends that government is the greatest enemy of the people.

Animism. The belief in the existence of spirits or souls as distinct from matter. In anthropology, the view that spirits or souls reside in things as either an inner principle or a separate characteristic.

Antecedent. The "if" part of a hypothetical or conditional statement; the part between "if" and "then," usually appearing as the first major term in a statement.

Anthropomorphic. Having human form or human characteristics; the ascription of human attributes, feelings, conduct, or qualities to God or any spiritual being or to the powers of nature. Example: The Greek gods were believed to take human form and exhibit human feelings.

A posteriori. Following after; knowledge or reasoning that follows from experience. In logic, a type of reasoning that begins with observed facts, from which are inferred general conclusions. Opposed to **a priori.** *See* **Induction; Empiricism.**

A priori. Antecedent; that which exists before. A priori knowledge refers to knowledge that is independent of experience (specifically, sense experience) or reasoning that is based on such knowledge; hence, knowledge that is innate as contrasted with that derived from sense experience. Nonempirical. Opposed to **a posteriori.**

Argument. A group of two or more propositions or statements, one of which is claimed to follow from the evidence supplied by the others. Important in the philosophical activity called **logic.**

Aristocracy. Government or rule by the best; hence, government by a small, privileged group.

Atheism. Disbelief in or denial of the existence of a supreme being. Distinct from **agnosticism.**

Authoritarianism. The theory that the truth of an idea is to be accepted uncritically on the sole ground that it is asserted by some source that is beyond question. In politics, *see* **Autocracy.**

Autocracy. A form of government in which one individual possesses supreme, uncontrolled power and authority.

Autonomy. The power, right, or condition of self-determination; self-governing; freedom from external control.

Axiology. The subdivision of philosophy that studies value (the right, the good, the beautiful, the approved); an inquiry into the nature, criteria, and application of value judgments. *See* **Ethics.**

Behaviorism. A school of psychology that restricts study to the objective observation of behavior rather than to the study of states of consciousness. When carried to the point of denying the existence of conscious functions, this principle becomes a philosophy of metaphysical materialism.

Categorical Imperative. The supreme, absolute moral law of rational, self-determining beings. It is distinguished from relative or hypothetical imperatives as it is unconditional and admits of no exception. It is in no way relative to some further end. Kant's formula is "Act only on that maxim (general rule) through which you can at the same time will that it should become a universal law"; that is, what is right or wrong for one person must be right or wrong for anyone in similar circumstances.

Cause. That which is responsible for or leads to a condition, a change, or a motion. Aristotle identified four different causes: (1) the material cause (what something is made of or out of which something arises); (2) the efficient cause (the prior force or stimulus that produces an effect); (3) the formal cause (the concept or idea that must exist to initiate an action); and (4) the final cause (the ultimate goal or purpose toward which an action must proceed).

Chance. An uncaused event; or an event whose cause is unknown; or the coming together of two independent causal chains; or an event predictable according to the laws of **probability.**

Charisma. A dynamic quality reportedly possessed by a limited number of human beings that enables them to inspire, influence, or exercise authority over others; a powerful but intangible force within a personality capable of eliciting deep emotional commitment from a body of followers.

Cognitive. Refers to the act of knowing. Knowledge in its widest sense, including perception, memory, and introspection as well as judgments expressive of these.

Coherence theory. The view that the truth of any statement, proposition, or judgment is determined by whether it fits with the rest of our judgments. Logical consistency; agreement. Widely held by idealists. Opposed to **correspondence theory**.

Collectivism. A term referring to those social and political philosophies that focus on group and community duties rather than on individual rights. Opposed to **laissez-faire**.

Concept. A thought or idea (generalized and abstract) of any class of objects as distinct from a percept or image (specific and concrete); an awareness of some aspect of the nature of something that can be identified and grasped in thought. Hence, I have a concept of humanity, but I have a percept when I see a particular person.

Conclusion. In an argument, the proposition that follows from the premises.

Conditioning. A psychological term used to describe a particular type of learning process in which an organism comes to associate one thing with another. A pattern of behavior (reflex, response, emotion) can thus be produced when a person "learns" to substitute one stimulus (cause) for another because of its repeated association with a particular effect. Example: A child learns to repress or inhibit certain behavior when he or she comes to associate it with punishment.

Consequent. The "then" part of a hypothetical or conditional statement; the part coming after "then," usually appearing as the following major term in the statement.

Conservatism. A term that applies to those who strive to preserve what is established and who therefore oppose change. Opposed to **liberalism**.

Continuum (continua). A range of possible alternatives between two logical extremes, or polar opposites.

Correspondence theory. A theory of the test of truth that stresses fidelity to objective reality; the view that truth is that which conforms to fact or agrees with the actual situation. Opposed to **coherence theory**.

Cosmology. The study of the origin, nature, and development of the universe as an orderly system. An area of metaphysics distinct from ontology; often confused with cosmogony, which is a pictorial view of the creation of the universe. *See* **Metaphysics**.

Criterion. A standard, basis, or ground by which something is measured or judged; a test, principle, or means of determining or judging qualities in anything.

Critical naturalism. *See* **Naturalism**.

Critical philosophy. The view that the scope and function of philosophy should be restricted to the general areas of semantics and logic. Critical philosophers see their task as the special one of clarifying concepts and carefully analyzing the reasoning process. They emphasize the precise use of language and insist that philosophy should not concern itself with nonsense statements or with unverifiable speculations regarding significance, purpose, values, and the like.

Cultural relativism. A doctrine that asserts that the validity or value of any idea or pattern of behavior can be judged only in terms of that particular culture (society) in which it occurs. Since all criteria are themselves reflections of some culture, there is no impartial criterion by which any way of life can be evaluated. Human nature in one culture is thus considered to be different from human nature in another; that is, there is no universal human nature.

Cynicism. A negative attitude toward all or nearly all values; a lack of faith in unselfish motives; a pervasive doubt about either the validity or the effectiveness of human ideals.

Data (datum). That which is presented directly or is immediately available as objective evidence. In logic, facts from which inferences may be drawn. In psychology, the content of sensation.

Deconstruction. A term that describes the strategy of reexamining the presuppositions of a text, whereby one uncovers the contradictions and confusions inherent in the text.

Deduction. A form of reasoning in which the premises claim to provide conclusive evidence for the truth of the conclusion. Deduction is concerned with necessity. A conclusion derived from true premises by valid deductive reasoning is *necessarily* true. Typically, deductive reasoning begins with generalizations and ends with particulars derived from those generalizations. To be distinguished from **induction**.

Deism. The doctrine of an impersonal, indifferent God as the original cause of the world, the lawgiver of the universe, but nothing more. God cannot be described as a moral being and has no direct relation with the world or humanity. Hence, there can be no communication (prayer or revelation) between God and human beings. Example: God as a perfect watchmaker.

Deontological ethics. Any ethical theory that holds that certain actions are right or morally binding apart from any consideration of their good or bad consequences. Also known as **formalism** or **intuitionism**.

Determinism. The view that every event in the universe is completely dependent on and conditioned by its cause or causes; specifically, the doctrine that human behavior (including human will in the exercise of all judgments and choices) is determined by physical or psychological antecedents that are its causes. Distinct from **fatalism**. Opposed to **free will** and indeterminism. *See* **Self-determinism**.

Dialectic. The art of reasoning and argument that, through questions and answers, brings out contradictions and opposites in an effort to form a new synthesis or arrive at reliable or definitive knowledge.

Dialectical materialism. A philosophy developed by Marx and Engels to account for historical evolution; it involves the proposition that naturally opposing material forces act on one another over time to produce change.

Dialogue. Literally, a conversation between two or more persons. In philosophy, a form of conversation in which communicants strive for reciprocal understanding. Distinguished from a debate.

Dichotomy. In logic, the division of any class into two contradictory and mutually exclusive subclasses, such as the division of objects into animate and inanimate classes; any fundamental division, usually implying that the separation represents a permanent aspect of the nature of things.

Dionysian. Expressing a dynamic, passionate will to live. Active, adventuresome, emotional; characterized by the bursting of restraints.

Dogmatism. A view or opinion held as an established truth, along with an unwillingness to examine evidence or to admit that it is open to discussion.

Dualism. The view that reality is composed of two different substances, neither one of which can be reduced to the other. Spirit and matter, mind and body, good and evil are often designated as the opposing realities.

Egoism. Self-love; ethical egoism holds that each person should seek only his or her own welfare. Psychological egoism claims that every act is motivated by an interest in one's own welfare. Opposed to **altruism**. *See* **Hedonism**.

Emotive theory. The emotive theory asserts that ethical and esthetic judgments are not factual and essentially express only emotions and attitudes; these judgments are emotive rather than cognitive and hence incapable of being true or false. Example: Saying "stealing is wrong" really only expresses the speaker's feelings of disapproval and as a proposition is incapable of being proved true or false.

Empiricism. The doctrine that knowledge has its source and derives all its content from experience. Nothing is regarded as true except what is given by sense experience or by inductive reasoning from sense experience. *See* **Induction; Scientific method**.

Epicureanism. A refined form of hedonism or pleasurable living proposed by Epicurus in the fourth century B.C.E. Earthly peace and happiness are the goals to be attained through rational thinking, ethical behavior, and esthetic enjoyment. The greatest good is tempered wisdom, "peace of mind," or serenity rather than sensual gratification.

Epiphenomenon. The appearance or reflection of what is real but not the reality itself; a by-product.

Epistemology. The subdivision of philosophy that studies the nature, the sources, the possibilities, the limitations, and the validity of knowledge.

Estheticism. The conviction that the enjoyment of beauty is *the* fundamental value. In this view moral or practical standards are secondary or irrelevant.

Esthetics. The branch of philosophy that concerns itself with the study of beauty, especially in art; includes the study of the nature of beauty, taste, and standards of esthetic judgment.

Ethical relativism. *See* **Relativism**.

Ethics. The branch of philosophy that attempts to determine what is good for people and what is right for them to do; examination of human behavior, the proper relation of one person to another, and the ultimate ends of human life; explores the nature and limits of obligation. *See* **Axiology**.

Ethnocentrism. Perceiving and judging all other groups or societies through and by the values, attitudes, and customs of one's own society; using one's own way of life as the central or valid basis for judging all other social systems. *See* **Cultural relativism.**

Ethology. Literally, the science of behavior. Used to refer to the study of animal behavior (including human behavior).

Euphemism. A mild or indirect word or expression that is used as a substitute for an unpleasant or offensive though more accurate one. Example: to call one who lies a "creative interpreter of the truth."

Evolution. An interpretation of the process by which change takes place through time. Darwin's theory of organic evolution is an explanation of how the development of living forms has taken place from simpler to more complex types.

Existentialism. The contemporary philosophy that holds that there is no essential human nature. Instead, each individual creates his or her own essence, or character, throughout life by free, responsible choice of interests and actions. Thus, existence precedes essence since the latter is not completed until life and its endless series of choices is terminated by death.

Expressionism. The esthetic theory that art activities and objects express or evoke feelings.

Faith. An attitude of trust or belief in the reality, truth, or worth of something that cannot be demonstrated or proved.

Fallacy. An argument that is logically incorrect or in which the reasoning process is unsound. More specifically, an argument that persuades for psychological or emotional reasons rather than logical ones.

Fatalism. The belief that events are irrevocably fixed in advance so that human effort cannot alter them: "What is to be will be."

Formalism. A theory that stresses the form or ideational quality of a thing. In ethics, it is often identified with **intuitionism**. In art, it places emphasis not on content but on form for its own sake.

Forms (Platonic). The concept that the world of ordinary experience is an illusory, transitory, unimportant sequence of events; the real, stable, permanent part of the world is ideas, or Forms, which are absolute, universal, and true for all time. They exist whether perceived by human beings or not and are responsible for what occurs in the material world. The fact that people can conceive of them (for example, circularity, brownness, and so on) is proof that the Forms exist.

Foundationalism. A view of knowledge that holds there are universally accessible certitudes upon which we can build our knowledge.

Free will. Freedom of choice; the doctrine that an individual has some degree of self-determination, some power of choice between alternatives; more specifically, the doctrine that human beings are endowed with a God-given capacity to make voluntary decisions about their own actions or beliefs. Opposed to **determinism**.

Gestalt. Having to do with pattern or configuration. The term identifies a school of psychology that stresses the idea that the whole person or the total organism is not merely the sum of its parts but that the character of interconnectedness is itself an aspect of what a thing is.

Golden mean. A wise moderation; the avoidance of extremes. This is a central concept in Aristotle's philosophy.

Hedonic calculus. The view of Jeremy Bentham that we can establish the goals of conduct by weighing the pleasure that will result against the pain involved. If there is a preponderance of pleasure, the act is good; if pain outweighs pleasure, the act is bad.

Hedonism. Psychological hedonism is the doctrine that we always seek our own pleasure and that all our behavior is motivated by the pursuit of pleasure and the avoidance of pain. Ethical hedonism is the doctrine that we always *ought* to seek our own pleasure and that the highest good for us is the most pleasure together with the least pain. The criterion of ultimate good and all value is pleasure. *See* **Utilitarianism**.

Humanism. The philosophical view that accepts human beings as the ultimate source of meaning and value; a doctrine that places emphasis on human beings and focuses on human well-being, particularly in terms of life here and now. Religious and philosophical humanism is person-centered, recognizing no need for belief in a deity and abandoning all concepts of the supernatural.

Humanitarianism. A nontechnical term identifying a concern for human welfare through such activities as philanthropy or social reform. *See* **Altruism**.

Hypothesis. In general, an assumption, proposition, or tentative theory of explanation the truth of which is under inquiry; a premise for possible or probable explanation; a working guess about the possible relationship between things. Example: Bombardment by huge meteors is one hypothetical explanation for the presence of the moon's craters.

Idealism. The theory that asserts that reality is ideas, thought, mind, or selves rather than material forces. There may be a single or absolute Mind or a plurality of minds. Idealism stresses the mental or spiritual aspects of experience. Opposed to **materialism**.

Immanent. Indwelling, or operating within the process; a God who is immanent pervades the structure of the universe. Opposed to **transcendent**.

Incarnate. To take on bodily or especially human form; literally, to become flesh. Many Christians believe that Jesus was God incarnate, or God in human form.

Indeterminism. The theory that at least some acts or events are entirely independent of any prior causes.

Induction. A form of reasoning in which the premises provide *some* evidence for the truth of the conclusion. Induction involves the claim that there is some degree of probability that the conclusion is true. Typically, inductive reasoning starts with particulars and ends with generalizations regarding those particulars. To be distinguished from **deduction**.

Inference. The psychological process by which conclusions are drawn from evidence or premises; the mental process of arriving at certain opinions or beliefs on the basis of other opinions or beliefs. Not synonymous with **logic**.

Insight. The act or fact of apprehending the inner nature of things or of seeing intuitively; clear and immediate understanding or learning that takes place without reliance on overt or prior experience.

Instrumentalism. A term referring to John Dewey's version of **pragmatism**. Thoughts are instruments to resolve problematic situations through inquiry and experimental determination of future consequences.

Interactionism. A dualistic theory advanced by Descartes that asserts a two-way causal influence between mind and body.

Introspection. The act of looking within, especially the observation or examination of one's own mental states or processes.

Intuition. A direct or immediate awareness not a product of any other awareness; insight. Intuitionism: the theory that direct awareness is the most valid source of knowledge. Ethical intuitionism: the theory that human beings have a special faculty (for example, conscience) that is able to make valid moral judgments or somehow just "knows" what is true or right.

Invalid. The property of a conclusion that has not been correctly inferred; characteristic of a conclusion arrived at through illogical or faulty reasoning.

Irrational. Not constrained or dominated by reason and logic. Irrationalists emphasize the importance of intuition, feeling, spontaneity, or unrestricted freedom as a basis for belief or behavior. Existentialists are frequently characterized as being irrational.

Laissez-faire. A phrase meaning "let alone" that is used in economics, politics, and social philosophy; the doctrine that the government should not interfere.

Language. The forms, pronunciations, and methods of combining the words or symbols used and understood by a group over an extended period of time.

Liberalism. A term that applies especially in the field of politics to those who advocate change as a fundamental goal in human affairs. Opposed to **conservatism**.

Liberation theology. A theological stance within the Christian faith that originated in Latin America in the 1960s. Largely centered on the Exodus motif in the Bible, it stresses God's deliverance of oppressed people in history.

Linguistic analysis. A contemporary form of analytic philosophy in which it is claimed that all philosophical problems are at least in part language problems and in which the primary function of philosophy becomes the rigorous analysis and clarification of concepts and statements. *See* **Logical empiricism; Ordinary-language philosophy**.

Logic. The study of the correct rules of reasoning; more specifically, the study of the formal and objective correctness of the completed structure of arguments; the study of the strength of the evidential link between the premises and conclusions of arguments. *See* **Argument; Induction; Deduction**.

Logical empiricism. The view that the determination of meaning is the crucial problem of philosophical discourse. This school acknowledges only two kinds of meaning: factual and formal. Factual statements are established by sensory verification and science, formal statements by rules of logic and syntax. Statements that cannot be verified in one of these two ways are meaningless, or nonsense. *See* **Positivism**.

Logical positivism. The epistemological view that knowledge is limited either to matters verifiable by sense experience or to an analysis of definitions and relations between terms.

Materialism. The view that everything in the universe, including life and mind, can be reduced to, and explained in terms of, matter and motion. Thus, conscious events are reduced to the transformation, or spatial rearrangement, of material atoms in the brain. The substitution of "energy" for "matter" does not alter the basic theory.

Mechanism. The view that everything, including living organisms, can be entirely explained in terms of mechanical laws. Opposed to **teleology** and **vitalism**.

Mentalism. *See* **Subjective idealism**.

Metaethics. The area of ethical inquiry that investigates the meaning and justification of moral judgments.

Metaphysics. Literally, after or beyond physics. The subdivision of philosophy that involves a critical study of the nature of reality. Metaphysics is divided into ontology, the theory of the nature of being or existence, and cosmology, the study of the development of the universe as an orderly system. Metaphysics is often interpreted as synonymous with overall worldviews. *See* **Ontology; Cosmology**.

Mind. That which performs conscious and intellectual functions; that which perceives, remembers, imagines, conceives, judges, reasons, feels, wills, and so on. One category of experience used in general opposition to matter. The term is defined differently in each metaphysical system (idealism, materialism, naturalism, and so forth).

Monism. The theory that there is one fundamental reality, that there is no spirit-matter or mind-body distinction. *See* **Idealism** and **Materialism**. In epistemology, the view that an object and the percept of that object are one and the same. *See* **Naïve realism**. Opposed to **dualism** and **pluralism**.

Monotheism. The belief that there is only one God.

Morality. A term used to designate the generally accepted codes of conduct of individuals or groups. "Moral judgments" refer to the voluntary actions of human beings insofar as those actions are considered right or wrong. Violation of a moral code arouses judgments of disapproval and condemnation. *See* **Ethics**.

Mores. Practices and attitudes common to the members of a society or social group. Patterns of behavior relating to the important values held by a group of people; values often associated with some fundamental belief about the true nature of reality, for example, incest mores. Mores, as distinct from folkways, imply society's demand for conformity.

Mysticism. The experience of a more inclusive reality; the philosophy or aspect of religion that holds that reality is truly known only by relinquishing one's separate individuality and experiencing a union with the divine ground of all existence. While the context of the mystical experience varies widely, it usually involves an intense awareness of God's presence or a direct communication with Him, although this Being is likely to be the ineffable One rather than the personal deity of most theists. Mystics are found in most of the major religions of the world.

Naïve realism. A theory of perception that holds that there is no difference between a real object and the appearance of that object; what we perceive coincides exactly with what exists even though perceived objects exist independently of the perceiver.

Naturalism. A theory in which nature is accepted as the whole of reality but naturalists interpret "nature" in many different ways. This view holds that the universe is self-sufficient, without supernatural cause or control, and that in all probability the interpretation of the world given by the sciences is the only satisfactory explanation of reality. The theory implies that values and ideas are the product of evolution and, therefore, only an expression of the needs of the human species in the world of here and now. Critical naturalism regards strict materialism as too limited and stresses levels of reality, such as life and thought.

Naturalistic fallacy. The attempt to equate ethical terms and value judgments with factual terms and descriptive judgments.

Natural law. Abstract principles expressing relationships that are inherent in (part of) the universe (physical world). In ethical and political thought, institutional forms or rules of conduct that are held to be universal by virtue of being expressive of the basic nature of human beings and of human society. A violation would be a contradiction of human nature.

Natural theology. A term used to distinguish any theology based on the premise that human beings have the ability to construct a theory of God and the world out of the framework of their own experience and reasoning. Opposed to **revelation**.

Necessary cause. A condition that must exist for a given effect to occur.

Nihilism. Derived from the Latin word meaning "nothing"; the name of the doctrine that nothing exists or can be known or is valuable. As a social doctrine, it is the view that conditions are so evil that the present social order ought to be swept aside or destroyed to make room for something better.

Normative ethics. The attempt to formulate general ethical principles that can be rationally justified and then used for deciding issues of right and wrong, good and evil, in particular situations.

Norms (normative). That which constitutes (or relates to) a standard or regulative ideal. Thus, a normative judgment is one that expresses a preference or evaluation, in contrast to a cognitive or factual judgment. "The book is on the table" is not a normative judgment; "This is a good book" expresses such a judgment. *See* **Criterion**; **Axiology**.

Noumenon. A thing as it actually exists; a thing in itself, apart from how it may appear to us; to be distinguished from a phenomenon, or a thing as it appears to us.

Objective idealism. The metaphysical view that ultimate reality is ideas or spirit or Mind existing "out there," whether or not understood or perceived. Typically, the existence of a real world of ideas is confirmed by reason or intuition. Opposed to both **subjectivism** and **materialism**.

Objectivism. The doctrine that things or qualities or values exist in their own right independently of the knower and of the conditions of knowledge; the assertion of the universal validity of principles, values, and so on, as opposed to **relativism** and **subjectivism**. *See* **Absolutism**.

Occasionalism. The metaphysical theory relating the body and mind espoused by Nicolas de Malebranche. It argues that mental events parallel physical events due to the continuous interference of God.

Ontology. The subdivision of metaphysics that studies Being in its most abstract form: What is the nature of Being as such? Or, what does "to exist" mean? *See* **Metaphysics**.

Ordinary-language philosophy. A special emphasis in analytic philosophy and linguistic analysis in which study is focused on the forms and functions of language as it is typically used in everyday communication. *See* **Linguistic analysis**.

Panentheism. The view that God is immanent, interpenetrating everything (as in pantheism), but also transcendent, a conscious being (as in theism); God as the highest unity-in-multiplicity.

Pantheism. Literally, all God—God is all and all is God; the view that God is incorporated in and an essential quality of everything; the doctrine that God and the universe are identical. Opposed to the *transcendent* view of deity. *See* **Immanent**.

Perception. The act or process by which things are apprehended or brought into awareness; commonly applied to ordinary sense objects such as books, trees, and so forth.

Phenomenalism. The belief that we can know only appearances and not the ultimate nature of things; we merely know objects as they appear to our senses.

Phenomenology. A term originally associated with the philosophy of Edmond Husserl (1859–1938) who sought a completely objective and scientific philosophical method of investigating fundamental human activities such as religion and art. The aim was to determine the basic universal structure of consciousness and the conditions of types of human experience. To do this the researcher of any kind of experience must "bracket" his own beliefs and presuppositions and focus on the phenomena themselves as they appear in the experience being investigated.

Phenomenon. A thing as it is perceived or as it appears to us; to be distinguished from a noumenon, or a thing in itself.

Pluralism. The theory that there are not one or two but many ultimate realities. Pluralism stands in contrast to both **monism** and **dualism**.

Polytheism. The belief in many gods.

Positivism. The belief that knowledge is limited to observable facts and their interrelations and, hence, that the sciences provide the only reliable knowledge; on this basis it therefore asserts that speculations about the ultimate nature of things are meaningless. *See* **Logical empiricism**.

Postmodernism. A widely applied term that especially denotes the challenge to the modernist notion of the autonomous subject that is guided by a metanarrative that provides a universal and objective foundation for knowledge. It insists that the Self is the source of truth and meaning, and it emphasizes a pragmatic use of language and images without a transcendent center.

Pragmatism. The doctrine that asserts that the criterion of what is true or of value is to be found in the practical consequences of ideas, in how they work to solve problems and achieve human goals; concerned with action and practice rather than a priori principles. Ideas arose in the evolutionary process as guides to action; their truth and value are to be judged by their practical effectiveness. The function of thought is to serve as an instrument of adaptation and as a guide to action (Dewey).

Predestination. The doctrine that events in life have been decreed or determined beforehand by the sovereign will of a deity.

Preestablished harmony. The metaphysical theory relating the body and mind espoused by Gottfried Wilhelm Leibniz. It argues that mental events parallel physical events due to a preordained arrangement established by God.

Premise. A beginning statement or proposition from which an inference or conclusion is drawn; hence, a presupposition or something taken for granted or assumed. In logic, the first two propositions in a syllogism are called premises. *See* **Syllogism**.

Primary and secondary qualities. Every material object possesses five primary qualities: extension, shape, number, solidity, and motion or rest. Secondary qualities such as color, sound, taste, and smell are not inherent in objects but simply allow them to produce certain sensory effects.

Probability. The likelihood of something's occurring; the quality or state of being likely true or likely to happen. To be distinguished from "certainty."

Proposition. A declarative sentence that asserts or claims that some condition or relationship exists. Propositions express meaning and must be either true or false. Synonymous with **statement**. *See* **Premise**.

Psychological egoism. The theory that the determining motivation for every voluntary human action is the desire for one's own welfare. *See* **Hedonism**.

Radical empiricism. *See* **Sensationalism**.

Rational choice. An ethical stance that says that while values are relative to the individual, they can be validated only by careful reasoning. Decisions of right and wrong must be made in the recognition that feelings are trustworthy only to the degree that they are free, impartial, and informed—that they are rational.

Rationalism. The doctrine that knowledge and truth are ultimately to be tested by intellectual and deductive rather than sensory methods. Rationalists usually regard reason as a separate source of knowledge, in no way dependent on experience. Opposed to **empiricism**.

Reactionary. One who rejects current social trends and advocates return to some state of affairs that existed in the past.

Realism. The doctrine that the objects of our senses exist independently of their being known, perceived, or related to mind. It denies that the universe can be reduced to mind or thought and holds that the existence of the universe is independent of human consciousness. Opposed to **idealism**. *See* **Objectivism**.

Reason. The capacity for thinking reflectively and drawing inferences; the process of following relationships from one thought to another and thus discovering, when reasoning is performed correctly, what else must be true if the premises are true. *See* **Rationalism; Empiricism; Induction; Deduction**.

Reductionism. The idea that a whole can be completely understood by an analysis of its parts or that a developing process can be explained as nothing more than a resultant of its earlier and simpler stages. The reductionist believes that the explanation of every object and event can be *reduced* to a description in terms of mechanical processes.

Reflection. Consideration of some subject, idea, or purpose in the attempt to understand or accept it by viewing it in its true relations; introspective contemplation of the contents or qualities of one's own thoughts, feelings, or experiences.

Relativism. The doctrine that things are what they are only by virtue of relations to other things. The position that there is no objective, absolute, or final truth; truth is always relative to the locale, the time, the group, or the individual. Far more common is the doctrine of ethical relativism, which holds that rightness and goodness vary from age to age, group to group, and person to person. Opposed to **absolutism**. *See* **Cultural relativism**.

Reliability. The extent to which a test or measuring procedure yields the same result on repeated trials.

Religion. A pattern of beliefs, attitudes, and practices in which human beings exhibit a special concern for things supernatural, transcendent, or of ultimate meaning and value. There is great disagreement over the precise use of the term. *See* **Theology**.

Representative theory of perception. A dualistic theory of perception that claims that objects and ideas are separate. Objects stimulate the senses, which, in turn, copy, or "represent," the objects to the mind—much as a camera takes pictures of external objects. The mind processes, or "develops," the sensations to produce ideas. A form of epistemological dualism.

Revelation. The opening up of knowledge or meanings that are undiscoverable by the use of human powers alone. In religion, revelation is understood as one means by which divinity communicates with human beings.

Rhetoric. A form of communication designed to persuade or motivate people toward some particular opinion or action; the skillful use of language to elicit a particular response.

Romanticism. An assertion of the primacy of feeling and imagination over reason. As an artistic movement romanticism rejected traditional restraints and stressed that the world apprehended by our senses and reason, the world of space and time, is only an appearance or manifestation of a deeper spiritual reality that lies behind.

Science. *See* **Scientific method**.

Scientific method. A disciplined mode of inquiry based on reasoning by which empirical evidence is gathered, analyzed, and interpreted in order to discover the most probable general principle (theory) it suggests. Theories formulated from such evidence are regarded as tentative, or working, hypotheses, which then form the basis for further inquiry and experimentation under rigorous conditions of **verification**. The propositions (theories) must be either confirmed in all possible experiments or modified so as to account for all the evidence. This is the self-corrective process of the method; all scientific laws remain open to modification by additional evidence or may be challenged by alternative theoretical formulations.

Scientism. Adherence to or belief in the scientific method as the only reliable way of knowing anything. *See* **Positivism**.

Secularism. The view that emphasizes life in the immediate, practical, and concrete world of people and things. Opposed to sacred, spiritual, or otherworldly interpretations of meaning and action.

Self-determinism. A compromise position between the extremes of determinism and indeterminism. The advocates of self-determinism hold that our actions are indeed determined but not solely by external forces or conditions. It is the nature of the self (usually the psychological elements are stressed) that controls our choices, and this causality of the self is regarded as our essential freedom. "Self" is interpreted as the unique personality or as the process of insightful awareness.

Semantics. In linguistics, the study of meaning and changes of meaning of words and speech forms; in logic, the study of the relationship between signs (words, language) and what they denote (stand for).

Sensationalism. The epistemological view that insists that all knowledge is empirically derived and can be reduced to sense experience. Also called radical empiricism.

Situation ethics. Also called situationism. The view that what is good and right depends on particular circumstances and that it is an individual's obligation to decide in the light of what is the most loving, concerned, or human-helping thing to do. Love is absolute, but since love is not wholly knowable or understandable, a person's thoughtful and informed response must be made in the light of the unique circumstances present. Situation ethics is not legalistic or conventional, but neither is it totally relative or subjective. Often identified with the "new morality."

Skepticism. In its extreme form, the view that knowledge is impossible. Skepticism can take many forms, varying from the attitude of questioning all assumptions and conclusions until they are confirmed to the claim that the human mind cannot attain certain or absolute knowledge, or that, if the mind could, it would be unable to recognize that knowledge as certain. This denial can apply only to certain subjects or can extend into all fields. To be distinguished from **cynicism** but is loosely synonymous with **agnosticism**.

Social Darwinism. The view that society is an arena of social struggle in which the strongest are "selected" for survival. Any effort to soften the struggle or aid the weaker is rejected as an interference with the process of natural selection.

Social gospel. The view widely held in certain Christian denominations that there is a moral obligation to meet the basic needs of one's fellow human beings with regard to food, shelter, health, social justice, and so on. Work in the service of humankind becomes an important aspect of the religious life.

Socialization. The process by which the attitudes, values, and behavioral patterns of a group are inculcated in or built into the personalities of its members; social learning occurring typically during childhood.

Solipsism. The view that only I (that is, the solipsist) exist, that other persons and objects have no independent existence of their own but exist solely as creations of my consciousness when and insofar as I am conscious of them; the most extreme form of **subjective idealism**.

Speculative philosophy. The view that it is the legitimate task of philosophy to concern itself with the broadest questions such as the meaning of life, the nature of human beings and their values, and the characteristics of ultimate reality. Speculative philosophers try to sketch the "big picture" and to extend their vision in ways such that thoughts and experiences are integrated into some overall pattern of significance.

Statement. *See* **Proposition**.

Stoicism. An ethical system originating in ancient Greece and Rome in which virtue is the only good and is found through knowledge. Thus, virtuous individuals find happiness in themselves and are independent of the external world, which they have succeeded in overcoming by mastering themselves, their passions, and their emotions. The doctrine is pantheistic; living according to the all-pervading law is an individual's highest duty.

Subjective idealism. The theory of perception that maintains that what can be known is limited to a person's ideas; therefore, the ideas of a particular perceiver constitute reality. Also called mentalism. *See* **Solipsism**.

Subjectivism. The doctrine that all things that exist, exist only as the knowing and experiencing of conscious beings; that the world exists only in mind, and thus all existence is composed of minds and ideas; dependence on mind or on consciousness.

Sufficient cause. A condition in the presence of which a given event must occur.

Supernatural. That which is above, outside of, or somehow separate from nature or the physical universe. God and the spiritual realm are often conceived as being apart from the everyday natural world.

Syllogism. A logical form of deductive reasoning consisting of three propositions. The first two propositions are called the premises, and the third is called the conclusion. The first two propositions (the major and minor premises) are so related that they logically imply the third proposition (the conclusion). When the propositions are correctly stated and ordered, the conclusion is said to be valid. Example of a valid syllogism:

All firefighters are brave. (major premise)
Max is a firefighter. (minor premise)
Therefore, Max is brave. (conclusion)

See **Deduction**; **Validity**.

Symbol. Something that stands for, or represents, something else (for example, a word or a gesture). To be effective in communication, the meaning of a symbol must be agreed on by those who use it.

Symbolic logic. A special form of logic in which a system of precise and arbitrary symbols is used to clarify the principles of deductive reasoning.

Synergy. Working together; the cooperative action of two or more elements. A synergetic social order is one in which individuals by the same act and at the same time serve their own advantage and that of the group.

Taxonomy. Arrangement, classification; the study and application of the principles or rules by which things are grouped and classified; the department of science that deals with classification. Example: Mammals are classified into a number of orders, families, genuses, species, and varieties.

Teleological ethics. Any ethical theory that holds that certain actions are right or morally binding if their consequences are desirable.

Teleology. The theory that there is design, or purpose, operating through the structure of the universe; the interpretation of the universe in terms of tendencies, aims, or implicit purposes rather than in terms of antecedents (causes). Opposed to **mechanism**.

Theism. The theory that God exists transcendent to the world as the Creator who gives to the world its original existence and sustains it in existence; the view that God is the source and the ultimate end of existence.

Theology. Literally, the theory or study of God. In practice, the term is used to describe the beliefs or doctrines of some particular religious group or individual thinker. A God-centered philosophy.

Theory. An overall explanation that remains subject to verification or proof; organized knowledge of a relatively high degree of generality. Example: the theory of evolution. *See* **Hypothesis**.

Thomism. The systematically organized philosophical views of St. Thomas Aquinas; often identified with orthodox Roman Catholic theology.

Totalitarian. Pertaining to a centralized form of government that exercises control over *all* aspects of its citizens' lives.

Tradition. An inherited or established way of thinking, feeling, or doing; an aspect of culture such as an attitude, belief, practice, or institution preserved from the past.

Transcendent. That which is beyond. God is said to be transcendent in the following senses: God is (1) perfect, (2) unknowable, (3) remote from nature (*See* **Deism**), and (4) alienated from the natural person. Opposed to **immanent**.

Transcendental anthropology. A method of investigating the boundaries of human experience that seeks to apply religious symbols to dimensions of life that go beyond those boundaries.

Transcendentalism. The doctrine that human beings can attain or experience knowledge that goes beyond appearances, or phenomena. Any idealistic philosophy proposing that the ideal or spiritual (beyond nature) is somehow accessible to direct experience. In the Kantian sense the doctrine affirms the existence of a priori principles of cognition. Example: Our minds are so constructed that we "see" events as necessarily cause and effect, in space and time, and so forth.

Universal. Pertaining to or characteristic of the whole; what is general as opposed to what is specific or individual. In philosophy the term "universal" often describes those qualities or conditions believed to apply to everyone, everywhere, at all times.

Utilitarianism. An ethical theory that claims that what is good or useful is what produces the greatest satisfaction for the greatest number of people; thus, such utility or usefulness should be the aim and the standard for individuals and for social and political institutions. *See* **Hedonism**.

Utopia. A perfect society; any state, condition, or place of ideal perfection. The word is derived from the Greek word meaning "land of nowhere" and may thus imply a visionary or unrealistic scheme for social improvement. However, a utopia may simply be a projection of a social ideal by which the inadequacies of a present society can be judged.

Validity. The property of being legitimately derived from premises by logical inference. Thus, a valid conclusion is one that is inferred from antecedent premises. Validity should be distinguished from truth, since the question of the validity of an inference is independent of the truth of the premises from which it is derived. *See* **Syllogism**; **Reason**.

Value. That which has worth; that which satisfies a human need or desire.

Value judgment. An opinion or conclusion attributing the quality of worth or goodness (or, conversely, lack of worth or evil) to a person, thing, or condition.

Verification. Confirmation or authentication by means of some evidence; checking or testing to determine the truth of a statement or condition.

Virtue. Moral excellence. A virtue is a quality or character trait that one acquires through education and practice in order to perform one's function well. Thus, in the classical sense, wisdom is one trait that is necessary to live well as a rational human being.

Vitalism. The doctrine that living organisms possess unique characteristics that cannot be explained exclusively in physicochemical terms. Opposed to **mechanism**.

Weltanschauung. An all-inclusive worldview, or outlook; a somewhat poetic German term to indicate either an articulated system of philosophy or a more or less unconscious attitude toward life and the world. Examples: the beatnik *Weltanschauung* and the reactionary *Weltanschauung*.

Index

Note: * after page number denotes glossary term